THE TWENTIETH CENTURY

A WORLD TRANSFORMED

1900—95

Neil DeMarco & Richard Radway

Hodder & Stoughton

A MEMBER OF THE HODDER HEADLINE GROUP

Acknowledgements

The Publishers would like to thank the following for permission to reproduce material in this volume:

Appleton Century Crofts for extracts from *Documents of American History Vol. 2* edited by HS Commager; Arthur Barker/Pan Books for extracts from *World War 1939–1945* by P Young; Marion Boyars Ltd for extracts from *If I die in a Combat Zone* by T O'Brien; Aurum Press Ltd for extracts from *The World War Two Handbook* by J Ellis; Buchan and Enright for extracts from *The Middle Parts of Fortune* by F Manning; Jonathan Cape for extracts from *A Bright Shining Lie* by N Sheehan; Cassell for extracts from *The Second World War, Vol. 4 – the Hinge of Fate* by Winston Churchill; Cottage Publishing for extracts from *Growing up in the Thirties* by Horseman; Croom Helm Ltd for extracts from *Eye Deep in Hell* by J Ellis; Fourth Estate for extracts from *Doppelgangers* by Hugh Thomas; Grange Books for extracts from *The Experience of WW1* by JM Winter; R Hale Ltd for extracts from *The War Walk* by N Jones; Hamish Hamilton for extracts from *Inside Russia Today* by J Gunther; Heinemann for extracts from *Nazi Germany* by Stephen Lee; MacMillan for extracts from *Europe 1890–1990* by Traynor and *Aspects of the Third Reich* edited by Koch; McGraw Hill for extracts from *America, Russia and the Cold War* by W Lafeber; Nadre Deutsch/Pan for extracts from *The First Casualty* by P Knightley; Norton for extracts from *The Anxious Decades* by N Parrish; Oxford University Press for extracts from *English History 1914–45* by AJP Taylor and Oxford *Companion to the Second World War;* Paddington Press for extracts from *Weimar Chronicle* by de Jong; Papermac for extracts from *Somme 1916* by L Macdonald; Penguin for extracts from *First Day of the Somme* by N Middlebrook, *One Day in the Life of Ivan Denisovitch* by Alexander Solzhenitsyn, *Hitler, A Study in Tyranny* by Bullock, *The Road to Wigan Pier* by George Orwell, *Total War* by P Calvocoressi and *Khrushchev Remembers* by N Khrushchev; Penguin/Viking for extracts from *Hard Times* by S Terkel; Progress Publishing for extracts from *Illustrated History of the USSR* by K Tarnovsky; Putnam for extracts from *Virgin Soil Upturned* by Mikhail Sholokhov; Spartacus for extracts from *The Rise of Hitler* by Simpkin; The Daily Telegraph for extracts from *The Daily Telegraph* 6 December 1933 and 12 November 1938; The Listener for extracts from *The Listener* 26 October 1961; Victor Gollancz for extracts from *The New Legions*, quoted in *Sources and Documents of Modern World History* by P Speed; Weidenfeld and Nicolson for extracts from *Hitler* by Joachim Fest and *Khrushchev, The First Russian Spring* by F Burlatsky; Weidenfeld and Nicolson/Corgi for extracts from *Once a Warrior King* by D Donovan

The Publishers would also like to thank the following for permission to reproduce copyright illustrations in this volume:

Advertising Archives pp.94, 123r; AKG pp.67, 74, 77b, 82a, 86, 157; J.Appleton/Cartoon Collection, University of Kent pp.55, 75, 154b, 161; Associated Press p.224; Bilderdienst Suddeutscher Verlag pp.58, 61, 62a, 80b; Bodleian Library p.130; Bridgeman Art Library p.154a; Camera Press p.39a; Corbis-Bettman/UPI p.162; John Cornwell p.125; Mary Evans Picture Library p.135; Francis Frith Collection p.118; Hulton Getty pp.3, 23, 29, 34, 44, 65, 95, 97a, 99, 100, 102, 103, 109, 110, 112, 113, 124, 125, 129a, 132, 165, 167, 170, 171, 172, 176, 177, 180, 181, 183, 189, 191, 195, 197, 198, 199, 200; Hoover European Appliance Group p. 123l, IWM pp.7, 9, 10b, 12, 13, 15, 18, 24, 81, 178; Peter Kennard p.147; David King pp.30a, 32, 35, 38, 39b, 42, 43, 47, 50, 53, 69; Kobal Collection pp.225, 226; Labour History Museum p.129b; Neil de Marco pp.4, 10a; National Monuments Record p.141; Peter Newark pp.84, 93, 97b, 98, 114, 152; Robert Opie pp.132a, 133; Popperfoto pp.62b, 131, 138, 140, 153, 156, 158a, 211, 214, 215, 218, 221a; Punch pp.126, 136, 150, 189, 203, 221b, 222; Topham pp.16, 76a, 136a, 155, 158b, 175, 213, 229; Ullstein Bilderdienst pp.60, 85, 89; Wiener Library pp.80a, 82, 83, 87, 88;
   (**a** above; **b** below; **l** left; **r** right)

The authors would like to thank the librarians at
Chesham High School, Liz Osborne and Sheila Gardiner,
for their unstinting help in providing reference material
for this book.

British Library Cataloguing in Publication Data
A catalogue for this title is available from the British Library

ISBN 0 340 66412 6

First published 1997
Impression number   10   9   8   7   6   5   4   3   2   1
Year   1999   1998   1997

Typeset by Wearset, Boldon, Tyne and Wear.
Printed in Great Britain for Hodder & Stoughton Educational, a division of Hodder Headline Plc, 338 Euston Road, London NW1 3BH by Cambridge University Press, Cambridge.

Contents

1 The First World War

The chapter focuses on three key issues:

● *What was it like to fight on the Western Front?*

● *Why did the war last so long?*

● *How did the war change life in Britain?*

Try to bear these points in mind while you work through the chapter.

Outbreak of the First World War; Battle of the Marne halts German advance	**1914**
Allied landings at Gallipoli; Italy declares war on Austria	**1915**
German offensive at Verdun; Battle of Jutland; Battle of the Somme	**1916**
USA declares war on Germany; revolution in Russia; Russia agrees armistice with Germany	**1917**
Treaty of Brest-Litovsk; Germany agrees to armistice – the Great War is over	**1918**

'HELL'S LAST HORROR'

The British war poet, Siegfried Sassoon, described the First World War as 'Hell's last horror' and he became so opposed to the war that he risked death by firing squad for refusing to fight in it any further. A great many others shared his disillusionment and this chapter will try to explain why they turned against a war in which three million Britons volunteered to fight.

Shots in Sarajevo

The war was sparked off on 28 June 1914 by the assassination of Archduke Franz Ferdinand, the heir to the throne of the empire of Austria-Hungary. The murder took place in the Bosnian city of Sarajevo – a part of the empire. The assassins were Bosnian Serbs who came from within the Austrian Empire. They wanted Bosnia to be part of the independent state of neighbouring Serbia. The government of Austria-Hungary blamed the government of Serbia for the plot and declared war on 28 July.

A war between Austria-Hungary and Serbia would not have become a world war if it had not been for the system of alliances that tied the powers of Europe together. Countries made alliances with each other for protection. The alliance that linked Britain, France and Russia was called the 'Entente'. The alliance that linked Germany and Austria was the Central Powers alliance. Serbia was connected to the Entente because it was allied to Russia.

The Serbs called on their ally Russia to support them and Russia began to prepare (or mobilise) its army for war. The Austrians had an alliance with Germany and the Germans stepped in and declared war on Russia on 1 August. The French had an alliance with Russia and their army was also being mobilised, so Germany declared war on France as well and invaded Belgium. Britain had promised to defend Belgium and therefore declared war on Germany. All of this took place on 4 August.

These are the immediate causes of what became known at the time as the 'Great War'. But there were also other long-term causes. Among these was a bitter rivalry between Germany and Britain over trade, naval power and **colonies**. France also feared Germany and had quarrelled over colonies and wanted back territory that Germany had taken from it in 1870. Russia and Austria-Hungary had long been rivals in the region of south east Europe known as the Balkans. The tension between the great powers of Europe had been

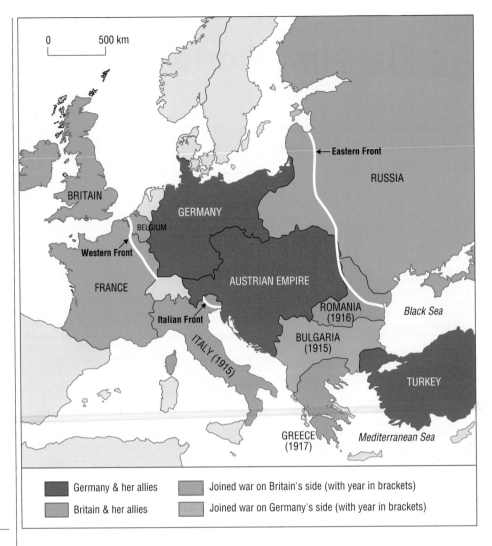

The alliance system in Europe in 1914.

Map legend:
- Germany & her allies
- Britain & her allies
- Joined war on Britain's side (with year in brackets)
- Joined war on Germany's side (with year in brackets)

getting worse for several decades before the war actually broke out. All that was missing was the incident that would push this tension into open conflict. This was provided on 28 June.

THE 1914–18 WAR

1914: 'Blow out, you bugles, over the rich Dead' Rupert Brooke

At first the war was what everybody had expected it to be – a war of movement with exciting cavalry and infantry charges. The German advance through Belgium into France was stopped in September, just 60 km from Paris, at the Battle of the Marne. This defeat meant that Germany would now have to fight on two fronts: against Britain and France on the Western Front and Russia on the Eastern Front. German efforts to reach the Channel ports were checked at the first Battle of Ypres (October–November). The Channel ports would have provided Germany with ideal bases for their U-boats (submarines). From here they could have sailed out to sink British shipping in the Channel.

Turkey joined the war on the side of the Central Powers (Germany and Austria-Hungary) in November. Both sides now dug trenches from the Belgian coast to the Swiss border (725 km) and settled into a war that was to last most of the next four years. It was a war of trenches, barbed wire, dug-outs and machine guns. On the Eastern Front early Russian gains were wiped out by a heavy defeat by the Germans at the Battle of Tannenberg.

1915: 'Who sent us forth? Who takes us home again?' Charles Sorley

The battles of 1915 made little impact on the war. Gas, a new German weapon, made a terrifying appearance in the second Battle of Ypres (April–May), but there was no breakthrough. The British, Australian and New Zealand Army Corps (ANZACs) tried to knock Turkey out of the war by landing at Gallipoli in Turkey (April 1915–January 1916), but the attack was a complete failure. Italy joined the war on the side of the Entente (Britain, France and Russia) and opened another front against the Austrians. It was called the Italian Front.

The Italian Front was probably the most difficult on which to fight. Both the Austrians and the Italians had to haul all their equipment up steep mountains. The snow and bitter cold were constant problems and every exploding shell showered jagged fragments of rock and metal over the troops. In this photograph Italian troops are moving guns to the frontier.

1916: 'The hell where youth and laughter go' Siegfried Sassoon

In 1916 two of the biggest battles of the war took place – the German attack on the French at Verdun (February–December) and the mostly British attack along the River Somme (July–November). The Germans failed to capture Verdun and the British managed no more than an eight-kilometre advance against the Germans. The battle is notable for the first use by the British of their own secret weapon: the tank. On the Eastern Front, the Russian General Brusilov had some success with his offensive against the Austrians and the Germans had to withdraw troops from the Western Front to assist the Austrians.

The most important battle of 1916 did not take place on land at all but at sea. In May the British and German fleets clashed at the Battle of Jutland. The smaller German fleet inflicted more British losses but it withdrew to their port at Kiel and stayed there until the war ended (see page 14). Britain now had control of the seas. This was a vital advantage which allowed the Royal Navy to blockade Germany.

Q

The Defence of Verdun, February–December 1916

Verdun was a city to the east of Paris that had little military value but the Germans knew the French would always defend it to the end. The Germans did not expect to capture Verdun and its 15 surrounding forts. Instead they planned to draw the French army to its defence and then destroy them in such numbers that the French would lose the will to fight. But the French did not give in and the city held. During the course of the eleven-month battle, the Germans fired 22 million shells on the forts around the city. The French lost 500 000 men killed or wounded but the Germans lost nearly 440 000. The battle for Verdun showed just how bloody-minded the First World War generals could be. They wanted to win the war by killing as many of the enemy as possible.

The two French forts that took the full force of the German attack in February 1916 were Douaumont and Vaux. The picture below shows how Fort Douaumont was constructed. It was protected by two layers of concrete 1.2 m thick and 5.4 m of earth on top of these. Anyone approaching the fort had to cross a bare slope called a 'glacis' –

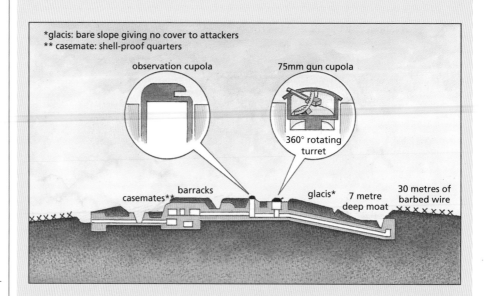

*glacis: bare slope giving no cover to attackers
** casemate: shell-proof quarters

observation cupola

75mm gun cupola

360° rotating turret

casemates**   barracks   glacis*   7 metre deep moat   30 metres of barbed wire

An artist's impression of Fort Douaumont. It was captured by the Germans on 25 February 1916 but then recaptured by the French on 24 October 1916.

The 75 mm gun turret of Fort Douaumont. Its observation cupola, or turret, is in the foreground.

after getting through 30 m of barbed wire and across a seven-metre deep moat. It was protected by two heavy guns, set in revolving steel turrets that could also be retracted or lowered, flush with the level of the concrete. But when the German attack began the fort had been run down by the French and had only a few defenders. It was captured in the first four days of the battle and it took the French eight months to get it back.

Despite this, the French belief in strong, fixed defensive fortifications was increased. After the war they built an even more impressive series of forts called the 'Maginot Line' along their frontier with Germany. They were confident that the Germans would never get past their Maginot Line just as they had never captured Verdun. In 1940 (in the Second World War) they sat back and let the Germans come at them again, but the Germans did not attack the forts; they simply went around them. The French had failed to learn a lesson from the Great War.

1 What was the German strategy at Verdun?
2 Why was the German strategy such a brutal one?
3 Why, in theory, was Fort Douaumont so difficult to capture?
4 Look at the photograph of the 75 mm gun turret and its observation cupola in the foreground. How does this photograph show the commanding position of the fort?
5 Why do you think the gun crew in the turret needed to have an observation position behind them?
6 Why was France's faith in the Maginot Line later to prove a mistake?

1917: 'What passing bells for these who die as cattle?' Wilfred Owen

1917 saw further British attempts to break through German lines with the third Battle of Ypres or Passchendaele (August–November). However, the entry of the USA in April on the side of the Entente Powers and the seizure of power by the Bolsheviks (**Communists**) in the Russian Revolution had more effect on the outcome of the war. The Bolsheviks promised to pull Russia out of the war and agreed to a cease-fire with Germany in December.

1918: 'Millions of the mouthless dead across your dreams in pale battalions go' Charles Sorley

Now with Russia out of the war, Germany was able to move troops from the Eastern to the Western Front for its massive spring offensive (the Hindenburg Offensive) in March. It was halted about 50 km from Paris and the Entente Powers, including the USA, launched their own counter-offensive in August. This involved 430 tanks. The exhausted German army was driven back and Germany's allies began to fall one by one: Bulgaria surrendered in September; Turkey in October; Austria-Hungary on 4 November and finally Germany also surrendered on 11 November.

The war on other fronts

In 1915 commanders on both sides realised that any battles on the Western Front would be very bloody affairs with little prospect of success. So instead they came up with 'the weak point strategy'. Both sides tried very hard to find allies in those countries that were not yet in the war. Germany persuaded Bulgaria to join them and attack Serbia. Italy joined the Allies and attacked Austria-Hungary. It was hoped that these new fronts would provide the much needed chance to break through the enemy lines.

Winston Churchill was in charge of the British navy in 1915. He wanted to attack Turkey through the Dardanelles (see the map below), seize Constantinople, knock Turkey out of the war, and link up with Russia. It was an ambitious plan that was botched from the start. The Turks had a month's

The Gallipoli campaign plan was ambitious. The British, Australian and New Zealand Army Corps (ANZACs) would land at Gallipoli and from there move on Constantinople, the capital of Turkey. With Turkey defeated, the Dardanelles Straits would be in Allied hands and badly-needed supplies could be brought to Russia across the Black Sea. The Allies got no further than five kilometres or so.

warning of the plan to land troops on the Gallipoli peninsula when a naval attack failed. So when the British and ANZAC forces landed on the beaches in April 1915 the Turks were ready for them. They were trapped on the beaches as the Turks fired down on them from the surrounding heights. During the next nine months 150 000 Allied troops were killed or wounded before the Gallipoli or Dardanelles offensive was abandoned. Churchill resigned as First Lord of the Admiralty. Gallipoli had proved to be anything but a 'weak point'.

In general, there were no breakthroughs at Gallipoli, the Balkans or the Middle East because these fronts were considered to be sideshows. Neither side would commit enough men and resources to stage a major offensive in these places. Basically, the high commands of both sides were convinced that the war would be won or lost on the Western Front. There was a real breakthrough on the Eastern Front in 1917 but it was a German one. Russia's government was overthrown in November 1917 by Lenin and the Bolsheviks and they pulled Russia out of the war within five weeks. The Germans were now able to move huge numbers of troops over to the Western Front.

Anzac Beach, on the Gallipoli peninsula. This is where the ANZAC forces landed in April 1915. The Turks controlled the surrounding high ground.

Q How does this photograph show the difficulties the ANZAC forces faced when landing at Gallipoli?

Q

1 What was the battle in 1914 that halted the German advance into France?
2 Why was this defeat a serious one for the Germans?
3 Why were the Germans so keen to reach the Channel coast?
4 Why was the Battle of Jutland such an important one?
5 Which two important events took place in 1917? Which one do you think was more important and why?
6 On pages 2, 3 and 5 you will have read extracts from poems written by soldiers who fought in the war. For example, the lines quoted for 1918 could be said to sum up the sadness at the loss of eight million dead who can no longer speak to us and are remembered only in dreams now that the war is over. Can you suggest why each of these extracts could be said to sum up attitudes to the war at the time?

WHY WASN'T THE WAR OVER BY CHRISTMAS?

If the German Schlieffen Plan had worked, the war could have been over by the end of 1914. General Schlieffen had drawn up his plan in 1905. It was designed to deal with a two-front war: the French in the west and the Russians in the east. Schlieffen knew that Germany could not win a two-front war and that one of the fronts would have to be closed quickly.

Schlieffen decided that the Germans should concentrate the larger part of their army against the French (about 90 per cent). In the meantime, the German forces would fight a defensive war against the Russians until France was defeated in about six weeks. Then the German army in the west could be transferred to the east before the Russians had fully mobilised their huge army. In practice, the German commander, von Moltke, lost his nerve. He weakened the strength of the forces in the west and sent them eastward to deal with a Russian army that had mobilised more quickly than expected. This meant that the German forces against France, Belgium and the small British Expeditionary Force, were not powerful enough to deliver the final blow by capturing Paris. Instead, the Germans were stopped at the Battle of the Marne – one of the most important battles of the war. Paris was saved and Germany now had to fight on two fronts. Eventually this would bring about Germany's defeat. Moltke knew the seriousness of the situation. He told Kaiser William: 'Your Majesty, we have lost the war'. The Kaiser sacked him. It would take another four years to prove that Moltke had been right.

General Schlieffen's plan to invade France demanded a very strong northern army and a much smaller southern army (see the map on the left). The idea was that the small southern army would be stopped easily by the French and driven back. French forces would be drawn from Paris to chase the retreating Germans. The much more powerful northern army would then swing down like a hammer, encircle Paris and attack the French from the rear. But the northern army was weakened just before the attack and the southern army was strengthened. The southern army did not fall back and the northern army was halted along the River Marne, 60 km from Paris (see the map on the right).

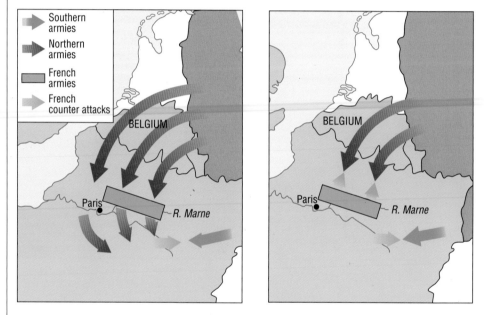

Why was there a military stalemate?

Both sides dug trenches during the winter of 1914–15 and waited for the weather to improve before launching new attacks in the spring. But the war would never become the one that both sides had expected. Cavalry played no useful part and infantry attacks offered only target practice for the defenders.

Trenches were very difficult to capture since a trench system consisted of at least three tiers of trenches. The frontline trench was backed up by the support trench and behind that was the reserve trench. These trenches were connected to each other by communication trenches. Each trench was protected by rows of barbed wire up to 30 m deep.

Every few dozen metres there would be a machine-gun position containing a machine gun capable of spitting out 450–600 rounds or bullets a minute. Such fire-power proved devastating against slow-moving infantry openly advancing across **No Mans Land** which stretched for 250 m on average. In some cases, though, the enemy lines could be as close as 100 metres. During enemy artillery bombardments the troops could take cover in underground bunkers. The German ones were especially deep and well-constructed because they chose to fight a defensive war once they were on enemy soil.

This is what the trench was supposed to look like. Here the trenches are propped up by wood and covered in protective barbed wire and sandbags. At 2.5 m deep the men were protected from sniper-fire and could stand on the firestep to shoot at any attackers. The duckboards kept their feet out of the mud and water at the bottom of the trench.

Trenches (especially Allied ones) were not always built according to the manual. This one, from 1917, shows Australians in a front-line trench at Ypres. It isn't zig-zagged, doesn't seem to have a fire-step and there is no barbed wire or sand bags.

Preparations for an offensive: no surprises

Before big attacks or offensives took place several preparations were necessary and each of them hinted to the enemy that an attack was being planned. Large numbers of extra troops had to be be moved to the front line. Extra ammunition and supplies were needed as well as coffins that had to be stacked along the roadside in full view of the advancing troops.

All of these preparations would be seen by the enemy. Flights by aircraft meant that nothing could go on behind the lines without the enemy finding out about it. However, even if all of this did not suggest to the enemy that a big attack was about to take place, then the heavy artillery barrages would have done.

This is what the trenches look like today at Beaumont Hamel on the Somme. Even after 80 years their zig-zagged layout is still clear, though they are not as deep now as they were.

Both sides used their artillery to shell the enemy trenches before a big offensive in an effort to kill troops and destroy barbed wire defences. Before the British Somme offensive in 1916 the British barrage lasted a week and over one and a half million shells were fired along a 30 km wide front. The barrage did little damage but the Germans had no doubt as to what was going to happen next. Most barrages stopped when the attackers were about to leave their trenches or 'go over the top'. This was to avoid shells dropping on your own men as they advanced across No Mans Land. The soldiers' task along the Somme was not made any easier by the order to walk towards the enemy. They did not have to run, the High Command told them, because all the Germans would be killed in the barrage! However, sometimes planners used what was called a 'creeping or rolling barrage' that continued, just ahead of your own men, as the attack advanced. In this way the enemy were kept in their dug-outs and could not fire at the attackers. Occasionally, however, the shells dropped short and killed your own men.

Before an attack could take place paths had to be cut in your own barbed wire so that your own men could get through. This would be done at night and the paths marked with tape. This not only provided further proof of an attack but allowed enemy machine gunners to direct their fire at the points where the troops would emerge. The practice of taping out the line of attack has given us the expression 'to have someone taped'.

Generals were convinced that a breakthrough would come if enough troops were concentrated along a small section of the front. In this way they would outnumber the enemy, break through, and then encircle them. After that, there would only be open countryside. But this overlooked the fact that the enemy could easily bring in reserves from another sector to plug any gaps in their front line. This was especially easy since only a small sector of the front was under attack.

These Australian troops are checking on enemy movements through the use of trench periscopes. The man on the right is using a 'sniperscope' (a rifle with a periscope attached to it). This allowed the soldier to fire at any careless Germans who showed themselves above the trench line.

Q Sniper shots tended to be almost always fatal. Can you think why?

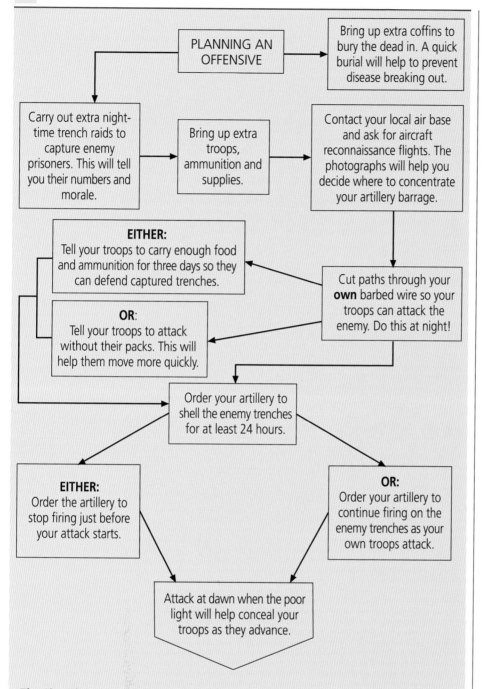

PLANNING AN OFFENSIVE

Bring up extra coffins to bury the dead in. A quick burial will help to prevent disease breaking out.

Carry out extra night-time trench raids to capture enemy prisoners. This will tell you their numbers and morale.

Bring up extra troops, ammunition and supplies.

Contact your local air base and ask for aircraft reconnaissance flights. The photographs will help you decide where to concentrate your artillery barrage.

EITHER: Tell your troops to carry enough food and ammunition for three days so they can defend captured trenches.

OR: Tell your troops to attack without their packs. This will help them move more quickly.

Cut paths through your **own** barbed wire so your troops can attack the enemy. Do this at night!

Order your artillery to shell the enemy trenches for at least 24 hours.

EITHER: Order the artillery to stop firing just before your attack starts.

OR: Order your artillery to continue firing on the enemy trenches as your own troops attack.

Attack at dawn when the poor light will help conceal your troops as they advance.

The Situation: You are a general planning your troops' next big offensive. This chart contains a number of preparations that you could make.

1 Follow the sequence of events in the 'Planning an Offensive' chart.

2 When you get to the box 'Cut paths through your own barbed wire' you have a choice as to what you would do next. Decide whether your troops should travel light or with full equipment. You must also decide whether to have a standard barrage or use the 'creeping' barrage method. Refer back to the text for help here.

3 Now copy out the chart with the choices that you have made included, and leave out the ones you have rejected.

4 Now you have to decide which of the boxes in your chart you would leave out if you were planning an offensive which will take the enemy by surprise and still be successful. Shade these boxes in one colour and the ones that you will carry out in another colour.

5 Give your plan a codename and write 150–200 words on why you think that your offensive will succeed and why you have left out some of the suggested preparations.

New weapons but no change

The First World War favoured defenders. Any new weapon technology tended to help those who defended trenches rather than those who attacked them. The machine gun was the supreme defensive weapon.

A brand new weapon like gas had little real impact on the war. It was first used by the Germans in April 1915. It was a terrifying surprise to the Allies. But soon they were able to use counter measures against its effects. The first of these counter measures, a cloth soaked in urine held over the face, lacked appeal. However, the gas mask meant that after 1916 only three per cent of gassed soldiers died and 93 per cent were able to return to duty. Changes in wind direction also made it a dangerous and unpredictable weapon because the wind could easily blow the gas back against its users.

Aircraft were useful, but not as offensive weapons. Planes were valuable for 'reconnaissance' or spying missions over enemy lines and provided a vital service as 'spotters'. Spotters told the artillery how accurate their fire was and what changes were needed to get the shells to hit their targets.

(below) This is an aerial photograph of a British and German trench system. We can tell from the amount of chalk in the picture that these trenches almost certainly belong to the Somme sector. This is a typical example of a section of the Western Front that stretched 725 km from the Belgian coast to the Swiss border. The numbers illustrate the following features:

1 German front-line trenches
2 British front-line trenches
3 British strongpoints. These were heavily defended positions to the rear of the lines, ringed by barbed wire and machine gun positions
4 Mine craters thrown up by German attempts to explode mines under the British trenches. The craters are surrounded by the chalk typical of the Somme region

5 No Man's Land
6 Here the lines were at their closest and this is where the most mines were exploded by both sides
7 German forward saps, probably containing listening posts to detect British underground-mining operations. Saps were trenches dug from the front-line trenches into No Man's Land
8 British support trenches.

> **Q** What do you think was the value of aerial reconnaissance photographs like these to the army commanders?

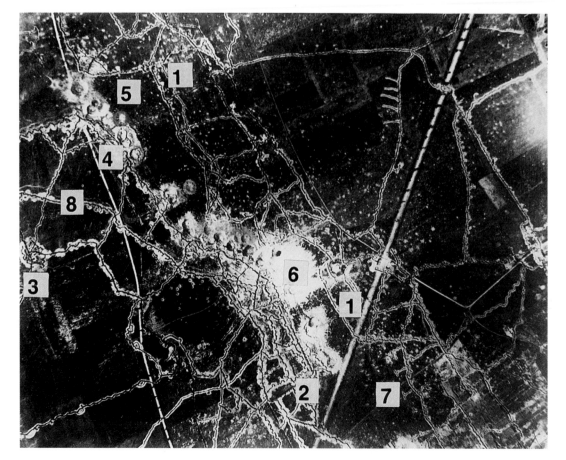

Submarines were another new weapon and the Germans made particularly good use of them. German submarines, called U-boats, sank many British merchant ships. Merchant ships were essential to Britain because it needed to import such a lot of food and supplies. At one stage in 1917 Britain had only two months' supply of wheat and flour. Despite this success, the Germans never sank enough merchant ships to bring Britain to the point of starvation. In April 1917 Britain introduced the convoy system of grouping merchant ships together and protecting them with anti-submarine warships called 'destroyers'. This defence proved to be very effective.

It could be argued that the German policy of 'unrestricted submarine warfare' helped to bring about Germany's own defeat. Unrestricted submarine warfare involved the sinking of all ships approaching British ports. This included the ships of countries that were not at war. Germany re-introduced this policy in February 1917 and immediately began sinking American merchant ships. Two months later the USA declared war on Germany.

Breakthrough on land

The stalemate on the Western Front was eventually broken in 1918 and another new weapon played a small part in this. The new weapon was the tank and it was introduced into the war by Britain. To keep it as secret as possible the machine was described as a 'water tank', but its official title was 'Trench Crossing Machine'. It was the word 'tank' that stuck. Its major purpose was to break through the enemy barbed wire, clear their trenches with machine guns and destroy their machine-gun posts. The infantry could then follow through. Unlike other weapons, this one had a clear role as a weapon of attack.

(below) The tank had some effect as a weapon but it did more to raise morale in Britain. Britons flocked to the cinema to see films of these steel monsters. The crew of eight men had to face many problems: they broke down, got stuck in mud and even rifle fire was a danger because bullets hitting the outside caused steel fragments to splinter on the inside. So the crews wore steel masks for protection. This British Mark I tank has a wire screen on its top to prevent grenades being thrown in. The wheels at the back are the steering gear.

The tank was not a great success when first used in September 1916 during the Battle of the Somme. Only 49 were used in the battle but of these 17 broke down before they even got to the British lines. Of the 32 left, 18 managed to attack the German lines and were successful enough to convince the army High Command that they must be used in greater numbers. They played an important role in the final Allied offensive of August 1918 when 430 were used but the losses were very high. There were only six left after just five days but the initial breakthrough had been achieved. The Germans began to retreat and they surrendered in November.

Breakthrough at sea

The final Allied offensive of 1918 devastated the Germans and shattered their will to continue fighting. The presence of 500 000 fresh American troops must have contributed to Germany's sudden collapse but it was the effect of the British naval blockade that was most significant.

In May 1916 the only big naval battle in the First World War took place off the coast of Jutland in the North Sea. Some 250 British and German ships clashed in a surprise engagement that the Germans claimed to have won. The British lost more ships than the Germans – 14 to 9, and more sailors. The British Admiral Jellicoe broke away from the battle to prevent further losses but the German fleet was much smaller than the British one and could not afford even small losses. The German Admiral Tirpitz kept his fleet in its well-protected base at Kiel until the war ended. This gave the Royal Navy control of the seas and it was able to prevent vital supplies reaching German ports. The German population went hungry and as many as 750 000 German civilians died as a result of diseases linked to their poor diet. This broke the morale of the 'Home Front' and led to food riots in 1918. Morale on the military front collapsed as a result.

Q

1 Why were the Germans content to fight a defensive war on the Western Front?
2 The stockpiling of coffins before an attack was necessary but what drawback did it have?
3 What were the problems with gas as a weapon?
4 How did Germany's policy of unrestricted submarine warfare backfire?
5 Which of the new weapons (gas, aircraft, submarine, tank) do you think had the biggest impact on the war? Explain your answer.
6 Why could the Royal Navy claim to have really won the war for Britain?

WHAT WAS IT LIKE TO FIGHT ON THE WESTERN FRONT?

It is worth pointing out that life in a First World War trench was one of boredom and routine and included duties such as replacing barbed wire, repairing and baling out flooded trenches, and digging and emptying latrines (toilets). Such duties were called 'fatigues'. In a 32-day period a typical soldier could spend eight days in the trench system. He might spend a further eight days there held in reserve in case of an enemy attack, and then 16 days away from the front in a town or village. Occasionally this would change when an offensive, launched by your side or the enemy, took place. Then the period in the trenches could last up to six weeks before relief came.

Trenches

In ideal circumstances a trench would be about two and a half metres deep with wooden duckboards along the bottom to keep feet out of the mud and water that always collected there. Feet immersed in water for long periods of time could swell inside boots so that the circulation was cut off causing the foot to rot. Circulation could also be cut off by frostbite. Toes were often lost in this way and sometimes even a whole foot. This was known as 'trench foot'.

Strict measures were taken to avoid trench foot. Men had to rub whale oil, a waterproofing agent, into their feet and soldiers would be punished if they did not do so. This was necessary because some men tried to get trench foot (even at the cost of losing toes or a foot) as a way of getting a 'blighty one'. 'Blighty' was the military slang for Britain and so a blighty one was a wound serious enough to get you sent home for treatment.

Each section of trench would have a firestep from which a soldier could fire or quickly observe the enemy trenches. Trenches were rarely dug in a straight line because the enemy would simply be able to fire straight down the length of the trench. This is called 'enfilading' fire. So trenches were zig-zagged and this shape also localised the impact of explosions inside the trenches.

Soldiers found humour where they could from the war's less grim aspects. One Canadian wrote in his diary in 1916:

'Then there is the trench cat, a strict neutral, we call him ''Wilson'' [the President of the neutral USA at the time] because we found him asleep on a haversack with a rat rifling the contents! . . . He walks across No Man's Land at will and knows the meal times on both sides.'

The Imperial War Museum Book of the First World War

This photograph shows a British soldier on sentry duty while three of his exhausted comrades sleep. The picture is a puzzling one since it clearly shows a firestep on the left while the soldier seems to be expecting the enemy from the right.

Q It may be that this is a photograph of a captured German trench. Can you suggest why?

The humour of the troops helped to keep them sane. Army food was a particular target for jokes. Sausages were known as 'barkers' because of the supposedly high dog-meat content in them. Cheese was called 'bung' because it caused constipation.

Why did the British attack on the Somme fail?

The first day of the Battle of the Somme in July 1916 was disastrous. 40 000 British troops were wounded and 20 000 killed. Most of these casualties happened in the first hour of the attack. There are many reasons for the failure of the five-month-long British offensive against the Germans between July and November in 1916. Explaining the causes of an event in the past, whether it is an unsuccessful battle, a revolution or the success of a political movement is an important part of the historian's role. Some factors are more important than others. 'Causal factors' (developments which help to bring about events) can be long or short term, economic, social or political, and they can be linked together like a spider's web.

Your task in this exercise is to decide what were the causal factors behind the failure of the first day of the Somme offensive. Study these sources:

SOURCE 1:

'The British often simplified the Germans' task. To allow the troops to get into No Mans Land it was necessary to cut gaps in the wire just before the attack. As one soldier who was there remarked: "The advertisement on our front was absurd. Paths were cut and marked . . . days before . . . Small wonder the German machine-gun fire was directed with such fatal precision."'

J Ellis: *Eye Deep in Hell* 1976

SOURCE 2:

'But all this immense shellfire had not fatally damaged the enemy as the Allied Commanders had fondly hoped; far from it . . . . Their defences consisted of a vast network of dug-outs, trenches dug to depths of forty feet [12 m] . . . This fundamental failure by the British Command to realise the strength of the enemy defences, coupled with the imperfectly cut wire and the rigid parade-ground manner in which the infantry attacked were the main reasons for the horrible failure of the attack.'

N Jones: *The War Walk* 1983

SOURCE 3:

'The explosion of the mine and the ending of the bombardment were the last signals the Germans needed that the attack was about to begin. The explosion of the mine happened, not at Zero hour when the attack was due, but ten minutes before the troops were to go "over the top". The Germans had plenty of time to rush from their dugouts, and plenty of time to set up their machine guns. They could aim their guns at the gaps in their own wire and also on the gaps in the British wire through which the British troops would have to pass.'

Adapted from Lyn Macdonald: *Somme* 1983

SOURCE 4:

Men going 'over the top' at the Battle of the Somme

SOURCE 5:

'After three or four days of continuous shelling, most of the targets should have been destroyed. Of these targets the wire, a vital one for the infantry, was the only one where the damage could easily be assessed . . . The reports were inconsistent: in some places the wire was well cut; in others there were a few gaps; but in several places the wire was still intact . . . The Germans spotted some of the gaps in the British wire and their machine-guns turned these narrow alleys into death-traps.'

M Middlebrook: *The First Day of the Somme* 1971

SOURCE 6:

'On the opening day the main problem would be the infantry holding the trenches captured from the Germans, in order to beat off the expected German counterattacks to get their trenches back. It was for this reason that when the British infantry went over the top early on 1 July 1916 they were weighed down with supplies and were ordered not to run forward.'

Adapted from JM Winter: *The Experience of World War 1* 1988

Historians make judgements based on the evidence. The six sources above provide quite a few reasons why the attack failed.

1 Your first task is to link the reasons in the top row of the table with the sources from which they come. In some cases this may be more than one source, as in the example that has been done for you.

Why did the British attack on the Somme fail?

Reason	The British had to cut and tape paths in their own wire before the attack. This tipped off the Germans.	Germans were able to fire into the gaps cut in the British barbed wire.	The British barrage inflicted little damage on the Germans or their trenches.	The barrage did not blast any gaps in the German wire to let the British through.	One of the British mines went off ten minutes early. This allowed the Germans to get back into their positions.	The troops were ordered to cross No Mans Land at walking pace, like on a 'parade ground', instead of charging.
Source where the evidence is found	Found in Source 1: '. . . paths were cut and marked days before . . .'; Source 3: '. . . to aim guns on the gaps in their own wire and also in the British wire . . .'					
How important is this reason?	This is important/ unimportant because . . .					

2 Now ask yourself this question: are any of these reasons more important than others in causing the failure of the attack? The way to approach this question is to decide whether removing any of these causes would have made any difference. For example, would the attack have been successful if the troops had been ordered to run across No Mans Land instead of walk? If the answer is 'yes' then being told to walk is clearly an important reason for the failure. Do this for each reason and write your views in the third row.

3 It is possible that several of the reasons are too closely linked together for any one of them to be the most important. Write a paragraph of 12–15 lines explaining how several of the causal factors in the top row link in with each other to contribute to the failure of the attack.

4 'The first day of the Battle of the Somme was a disaster because the generals cared little about the lives of their men.' Study Sources 1, 2, 3, 4, 5 and 6 and use them and your own knowledge to help explain whether you agree or disagree with this interpretation of the first day of the battle.

Why did men volunteer?

During August and September 1914 736 000 Britons volunteered for the British army. By 1916 over three million had done so. Their reasons varied. Most went to fight out of a sense of patriotism, honour and duty. They believed that it was their duty to fight for their country and that it was a matter of honour. Britain and its empire seemed to be threatened by the 'beastly Huns' as the Germans were often described in propaganda of that time.

Stories of the 'atrocities' committed by the Germans against 'gallant little Belgium' also led many to enlist. A report by Lord Bryce in May 1915 describing these 'atrocities' was translated into 30 languages. The report told of the public rape of 20 Belgian girls at Liege and of how eight soldiers had bayoneted a two-year-old child. Another German soldier had sliced off the breasts of a peasant girl. Bryce's committee had not interviewed a single witness to these events. The reports were supposedly based on 1200 statements taken from Belgian refugees in Britain but no trace of these interviews has ever been found. A Belgian investigation in 1922 could not find evidence to support these claims either. However, it is clear that some 5000 Belgian civilians did die during the German advance into Belgium. Some were shot as reprisals or simply killed during the fighting.

In December 1914 German ships shelled the town of Scarborough killing many of its inhabitants. The poster on the left, below, produced in 1915, was the response. The poster on the right is also a British poster aimed especially at Irishmen but its ideas would have been understood on the British mainland as well. There are some similarities and some differences in approach between these posters. (See next page)

Q

Use the following suggestions to compare the two posters on page 18:
1 How do the posters try to encourage feelings of
  a anger
  b shame among the men?
2 Which of the two posters makes the greater appeal to patriotism?
3 Which of the two posters do you think would have been the more effective in encouraging men to join up? Give reasons for your answer.

The Bryce Commission report had achieved its purpose in fuelling hatred for the Germans. But the British government did pay a price for using propaganda like this. Thirty years later, in the Second World War, there were stories of even more terrible crimes committed by the Germans against civilian populations. The British public was reluctant to believe this 'propaganda' even though, this time, the crimes were real.

Not all men enlisted out of honour or duty. To the unemployed the average wage of nine or ten shillings a week (about 50p) paid by the army encouraged some to join up. An unskilled worker in 1914, however, could expect to earn in the region of 27 shillings a week.

The glamour of a uniform and the chance for adventure attracted a good number of young men, especially as everybody expected the war to be over by the Christmas of 1914. In the meantime men who volunteered together were promised that they could fight together in what became known as the 'pals battalions'. Peer-group pressure was hard to resist. If all your workmates were joining up, it was easy to go along with the crowd. It took courage to resist this, especially when men out of uniform were handed white feathers by women as a sign of their 'cowardice'. If you were not in uniform you could find it hard to get served in pubs.

Sergeant Thomas Painting was taken prisoner in 1915 but escaped from a prison camp in Germany. He walked to the Danish frontier and from there he made his way back to England. On arriving in England in civilian clothes he was promptly handed a white feather! History does not record his reaction. For one reason or another, it seemed a lot simpler to sign up for a war which would be 'over by Christmas', anyway.

Q

The poster that never was

Government recruitment posters appealed to noble sentiments such as patriotism, honour, duty and defence of loved ones in an effort to get men to volunteer. However, some men enlisted to escape slums and poverty. Relations between employers and workers were very tense in 1914. Wages were not keeping up with prices and almost ten million days were lost in strikes as workers tried to improve their standard of living. But the government did not produce any posters using this theme. Your task in this activity is to design such a poster, urging men to volunteer to escape their slum conditions. When you have finished, suggest why the government would not have used it.

Why did some men refuse to fight?

Men clearly had many different reasons for supporting the war but there was also a tiny minority who opposed the war. In January 1916 the government introduced **conscription**. This meant that all single men aged between 18 and 41 now had to serve in one of the armed services. In March this was extended to married men. Conscription was necessary because not enough men were volunteering. In December 1915 only 55 000 volunteered, compared with 436 000 in September 1914.

The Military Service Act of January 1916 excused men in essential or 'reserved' occupations from service. This included men such as miners, shipyard workers and 'those who could show a conscientious objection'. Tribunals were set up to hear the cases of those men, called 'conscientious objectors' (COs), who would not fight on the grounds of conscience. 16 000 men were registered as COs for various reasons. Some objected to the war because of their religious views: they were pacifist Christians and opposed violence in all circumstances. Others were not pacifists but objected to this war in particular. These men were socialists and refused to kill their fellow workers, whether they were Germans or not. They believed that the war was being fought to make money for the wealthy factory owners.

The vast majority of COs agreed to do some kind of service that was helpful to the war effort but enabled them to avoid combat. Some of these became stretcher bearers or labourers on farms. A small minority, about 1500 men, refused to do even this. They were 'absolutists' and refused to do anything that would help the war. They argued that agreeing to do farmwork, for example, simply allowed another man to fight in their place. These absolutists were sentenced to hard labour in prison. When the war ended they were kept in prison for another six months so that the returning troops were the first to get jobs. They were also stopped from voting in elections until 1926.

▶ 'Joinin' up'

SOURCE 1:

Frederick Manning fought in the Great War and in 1929 published a novel in which one of the characters, Weeper Smart, is asked why he volunteered for the war.

'That's where you've got me beat, lad,' he admitted. 'When I saw all them as didn't know any better than we did joinin' up, and I went walkin' out wi' me girl on Sundays, as usual, I just felt ashamed . . . until in the end it got me down . . . and like a bloody fool, I went and joined up. But I tell thee now, that if I were once out of these togs and in civilian clothes again, I wouldn't mind all the shame in the world . . . Let them as made the war come and fight it, that's what I say.'

F Manning: *The Middle Parts of Fortune* 1929

SOURCE 2:

Lieutenant Carver came from a wealthy background. He wrote this to his brother to explain his reasons for fighting:

'The grand obstacle Hun hunt is now open. There is no charge for entry . . . However, if one does take a nasty toss [gets wounded or killed], there's always the satisfaction of knowing that one could not do it in a better cause. I always feel that I am fighting for England – English fields, lanes, trees, good days in England, all the things which stand for liberty.'

Adapted from Dennis Winter: *Death's Men* 1978

1 What basic reason does Weeper give for joining the army?
2 What do you think Weeper means by 'once out of these togs'?
3 Who do you think he has in mind by the last sentence, 'Let them as made the war come and fight it . . .'
4 In what ways are Lieutenant Carver's reasons for joining up different from Weeper's?

5 Can you suggest why Manning's book would not have been published during the war or immediately after it?
6 Using both sources above and your own knowledge comment on the view that 'Men joined up in 1914 out of patriotism and a sense of duty to their country.'

1 Some soldiers deliberately tried to get trench foot, even at the risk of losing a foot. What does this suggest about their enthusiasm for the war?

2 Was the government right to make use of the Bryce Commission report in its propaganda against the Germans, even if it knew the report was inaccurate?

3 Do you think peer-group pressure or patriotism was more effective in persuading men to enlist in the army? Explain your answer.

4 Do you think that men and women should have the right to refuse to help their country in a war which they oppose for political or moral reasons?

5 An American senator said in 1917 that 'The first casualty when war comes is the truth.' What do you suppose he meant by this and was he right?

Q

HOW DID THE WAR AFFECT THE POWER OF GOVERNMENT?

Before the Great War most politicians accepted the view that governments should interfere as little as possible in peoples' lives and in the running of the economy. This is one reason why conscription was delayed until 1916. The government believed it should be up to the individual to decide whether he would fight for his country or not. The Great War changed this attitude.

(DORA) Defence of the Realm Act

The government increased its control over peoples' lives through a series of measures passed through the Defence of the Realm Act (DORA). Through DORA the government was able to take over factories and make them produce munitions. It cut pub opening hours to limit drunkenness. This was a serious problem because pubs used to open at 5am and workers could stop off on their way to work. It also ordered beer to be watered down to make it less alcoholic. These measures were effective since convictions for drunkenness dropped to ten per cent of their 1914 numbers. The government also censored the press to make sure that it did not print stories that damaged morale or gave military information to the enemy.

State control

The government soon realised that vital industries such as munitions, railways, mines and shipbuilding all needed to be brought under **state control**. The public's attention was focused on this issue by the munitions scandal of 1915 when the Commander in Chief of the British army, Sir John French, blamed the failure of a British offensive on a shortage of shells. The scandal convinced the Liberal government of Herbert Asquith that the privately-run munitions industry was not providing enough shells for the war effort. If this was true for munitions then it was probably true for other industries too. It was accepted that the national interest in ensuring that these were run efficiently was more important than the private interests of their owners. After the war they were returned to their private owners but an important principle had been established. The Labour government (1945–51) used this same argument after the Second World War to justify its nationalisation (state-control) policies.

Industrial strength in 1914

The Great War was fought with ships, artillery, machine guns and rifles made from steel. Steel needed iron and coal. Industrial power was, therefore, a key factor for all sides. In 1914 the industrial might of the countries at war was as follows:

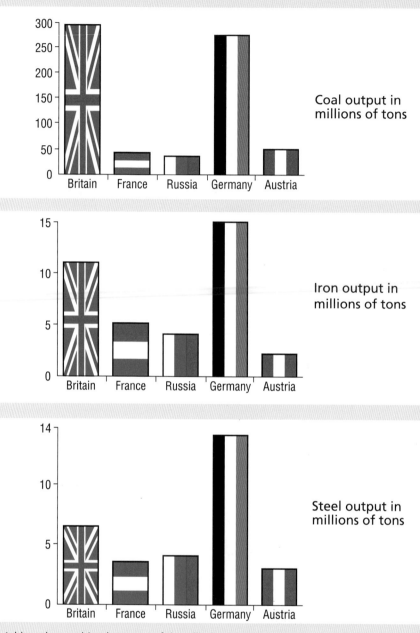

1 Add up the combined outputs of the Allied powers (Britain, France and Russia) and the Central Powers (Germany and Austria) for
   a coal;
   b iron;
   c steel.
2 Do these statistics suggest that the Central Powers were a long way behind the Allies in terms of industrial power? Explain your answer.
3 Do these statistics help to explain why the war was so evenly balanced until 1918? Give reasons for your answer.
4 In 1917 the USA joined the war. Its coal, iron and steel output for 1914 was: coal, 455 m tons; iron, 30 m tons; steel, 30 m tons. Why could it be said that the entry of the USA into the war against Germany meant that the Central Powers were bound to lose?

Rationing

In 1917 the government began to respond to the problem of food shortages caused by the effectiveness of the German U-boat attacks on merchant shipping. The price of a loaf of bread had more than doubled since 1914 and the government ordered a cut of 25 per cent in its price. Controlling prices was certainly new for a British government but in 1918 rationing was introduced for the first time. By mid 1918 meat, butter, sugar and margarine were all rationed. It seemed as though the government was exercising control over peoples' lives on a vast scale. However, the rations laid down were generous and caused little hardship. The queues disappeared and rationing was popular because people thought it was fairer.

WOMEN AND THE WAR: FLEEING THE CAGE?

Germaine Greer, a feminist writer of the 1970s, suggested that women in the First World War were a bit like captive birds whose cage is left open. They had looked outside but decided that life was better inside the cage. It is true that women seized the chance offered them by the war to show men (and themselves) what they were capable of doing. It is also true, however, that many of these changes were only temporary and life for women returned to its traditional pattern after the war.

Yet there were changes and these largely affected middle-class women. The war provided them with new career opportunities. In 1919 Oxford University allowed women to study for degrees for the first time. The Sex Disqualification (Removal) Act ended the ban on married women working as doctors, civil servants and solicitors. Women could stand for election to parliament and Lady Astor became the first woman to take her seat in 1919. These improvements, however, meant little to working-class women.

Women over the age of 30 gained the right to vote in 1918 but men could vote at the age of 21. Full equality did not come until 1928 when women were able to vote at the same age as men. Working-class women probably welcomed the right to vote but it was the work of courageous pioneers, like Marie Stopes, that actually improved their lives. In 1921 she opened Britain's first birth-control clinic – but only for married women. Perhaps it could be said that it was only because of the changes in attitude brought about by the war that birth control could be discussed openly for the first time.

Women! Stand by your lathes!

At first the government was reluctant to allow women to do the jobs left vacant by the men who had gone to fight. Emmeline Pankhurst, a leading **suffragette**, and one of her daughters, Christabel, campaigned vigorously to allow women more involvement in the war effort. The Pankhursts organised 'The Right to Serve' procession in 1915 in which 60 000 women took part. The government was soon forced to change its mind and allow women into industrial employment and other jobs. It was the only way to keep up the production of weapons and necessary resources.

The number of women involved in the munitions industry increased from 200 000 to 900 000 by 1918. Munitions work involved the manufacture of shells, weapons and the handling of chemicals. It was dangerous and unhealthy work. These women were nicknamed 'munitionettes' and, more seriously,

This type of work reflects the tremendous change in attitude to women as workers. The idea, before the war, that women should drive motor vehicles was remarkable enough. Here they are shown as engineers maintaining one.

A posed photograph no doubt, but the role of women in the munitions industry was real enough. There is a notice on the extreme left that sensibly bans smoking.

'canaries'. This was because the chemicals that they worked with turned their skin yellow. But the work, by women's standards, was well paid. A female industrial worker could expect to earn £3 to £5 a week which was a huge sum compared to the £2 a month paid to a domestic servant before the war.

Women filled all sorts of jobs, many of them dangerous and skilled. They worked in the shipyards and drove trams, buses and ambulances. 48 000 women worked as labourers on the land in the Women's Land Army. These jobs proved that women had the stamina and the skill to cope with tasks that people had thought only men could do.

Women at war

From the spring of 1917 there were many jobs in the armed services that women were able to do. 100 000 women served in the various sections of the armed services: the Women's Army Auxiliary Corps (WAAC); the Women's Royal Naval Service (WRNS) and the Women's Royal Air Force (WRAF). Here they took over the clerical and administrative jobs normally done by men. This allowed more men to go to the front.

23 000 women served as nurses close to the fighting and a further 15 000 volunteered to serve as assistants in the Volunteer Aid Detachments. Many upper- and middle-class women, dealing with the sick and wounded, the dying and the dead, came face to face with a side of life they had never experienced. The work was hard and unpleasant; as one nurse recalled: 'The leg I was holding came off with a jerk and I sat down still clasping the foot. I stuffed the leg into the dressing pail beside the other arms and legs.'

"I Summon you to Comradeship in the Red Cross"

Woodrow Wilson

Women were obviously expected to fulfil a more traditional role as nurses as well as doing other, less typical jobs. This American poster of 1918 is urging women to join the American Red Cross. The image of this open-mouthed, rather sexy nurse is surprising. It would not have been used in Britain.

Women in the 1920s

Women were forced to give up almost all of the jobs that they had done during the war. When the men returned they took back what few jobs there were and women accepted this. In 1921 the percentage of the female population with a job was 31 per cent which was one per cent less than in 1911. But although their jobs were taken from them, other benefits could not be taken back. Women in the 1920s were more confident and aware of their worth than they had ever been before. Many former domestic servants refused to go back to their old jobs: they wanted something better and more dignified.

Some young women, called 'flappers', took to wearing masculine clothes. They socialised with men on equal terms, smoked in public and drank in pubs. They went out with men without a chaperone (usually an elderly female relative) to keep an eye on them. Their behaviour shocked people but these women were determined to stay on the outside of the 'cage' once they had tasted 'freedom'. Their daring allowed other women to make less dramatic but important progress towards equality.

Q

1 Why did the 'munitions scandal' cause such anger in Britain in 1915?
2 Why was the idea of state control or nationalisation such a drastic change for Britain?
3 Was the government right to censor reports about the war that it did not want the public to know about?
4 Why could middle-class women claim to have benefited more from the war than working-class women?
5 Can you suggest several reasons why women were willing to do dangerous and difficult industrial work?
6 'The First World War was a decisive step in women's progress towards equality.' Do you agree? Explain your answer.

Extended writing
Answer one (or both) of the following questions in an essay of 250–300 words.

1 'There were no breakthroughs on the Western Front until 1918 because the generals used the wrong tactics.' What is your view of this claim? You could include in your answer the following points:
  ● problems involved in launching surprise attacks;
  ● the strength of the defenders' position;
  ● the industrial strength of each side;
  ● the reasons why there was a breakthrough in 1918.

2 How far did the First World War change the lives of people in Britain? Include in your answer:
  ● changes in the way the government controlled peoples' lives by conscription, rationing and censorship;
  ● changes in the status and role of women;
  ● changes in the way the government controlled the economy with state control of industries;
  ● in your conclusion comment on how important and how long-lasting these changes were.

Soldiers took what comforts they could – wherever they could find them.

Russia and the Soviet Union 1900–41

2

Part I: The fall of the Tsar and the rise of the world's first Communist state

This section focuses on three key issues:

- *Why did the Tsar lose power?*
- *Why was the Provisional Government unable to hold on to power?*
- *Why were the Bolsheviks able to hold on to power?*

War with Japan; revolution of 1905	1904–5
Outbreak of First World War	1914
Overthrow of the Tsar; Bolsheviks seize power	1917
Outbreak of Civil War	1918
Execution of Tsar and family	
End of Civil War	1920
Introduction of New Economic Policy	1921
Death of Lenin	1924
Trotsky exiled from Russia	1927
Stalin in control of USSR	
Introduction of first Five Year Plan	1928
Collectivisation begun	1929
Murder of Kirov	1934
Nazi-Soviet Pact	1939
Germans invade Russia	1941

THE RUSSIAN EMPIRE AT THE BEGINNING OF THE TWENTIETH CENTURY

In 1900 Russia was one of the **great powers** of the world. It was a huge country which spread across the continents of both Europe and Asia and it had a population of about 125 million. Just 55 million of these people were Russian. The rest were made up of 25 other nationalities. Many of these nationalities resented being part of the Russian Empire and wanted to be able to rule themselves.

Although it had a much larger population than the other major powers such as Britain and Germany, Russia was a very backward country. The majority of the population were peasants who farmed in very old-fashioned and inefficient ways. Russian peasants still used wooden ploughs, even though farmers in Britain and Germany had been using machinery for many years. It was only in 1861 that **serfdom** had been abolished in Russia. Until then peasants had been owned by the landowners. Even with the abolition of serfdom Russian peasants were still very poor because they had to pay redemption payments. These were payments made to the landowner in return for the little land they now owned. Village life was controlled by the commune or '*mir*'. This meeting, attended by the head of every household in the village, organized all aspects of village life including how much land each family held and which crops should be planted. It made sure that everyone in the village was treated fairly and had enough food and that everyone stuck to the old ways of farming.

Russia possessed huge amounts of raw materials such as coal and iron, but it had very little industry compared to the other powers and so the Tsar and his ministers wanted to develop industry. However, it would not be an easy task to turn Russia into an industrial nation because it cost a great deal to develop industries and there were few Russians with the money or desire to take the risk. Furthermore, **industrialisation** would require a work force. This would have to come from the countryside, which meant that the remaining peasants would need to grow far more food because the industrial workers would not be able to grow their own.

Between 1880 and 1905 there was an enormous drive to industrialise Russia and industrial production increased by over 300 per cent. Much of the money for this came from businessmen in western Europe. This created jobs in the cities and more and more peasants flocked to the towns. For instance, the population of the capital, St Petersburg, increased by over 50 per cent in the 20 years after 1880. By 1913 there were 2.3 million industrial workers in Russia and this created new problems. It was not simply that the Russian peasants were unable to grow enough food for the new city dwellers; there wasn't enough housing available for them and often the workers were crammed into huge rooms with very little space of their own. The factory owners cared little for the conditions of their workers because they could always replace them. The working day was usually 12 hours long and pay was very low. After 1900 there was a world trade slump and this led to unemployment which added to the misery in the Russian cities.

Q

Industrial progress. A comparison of Russian industry with that of the other European powers in 1900

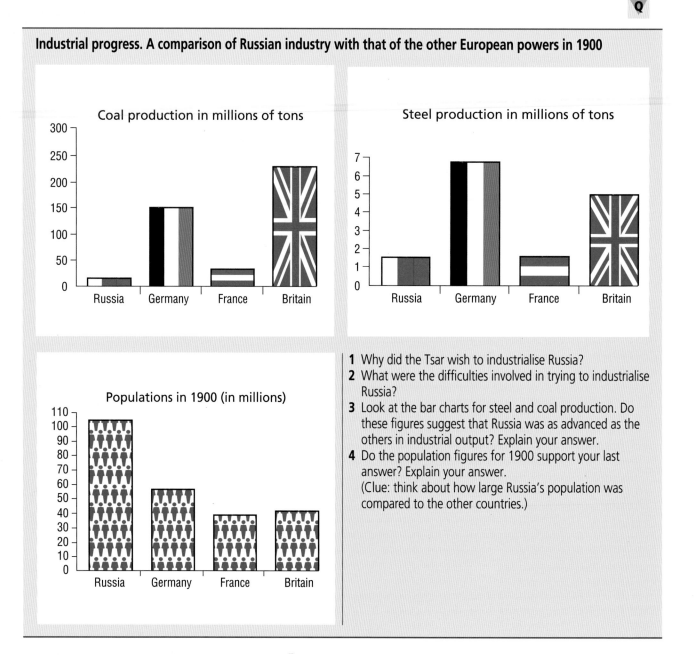

Coal production in millions of tons

Steel production in millions of tons

Populations in 1900 (in millions)

1 Why did the Tsar wish to industrialise Russia?
2 What were the difficulties involved in trying to industrialise Russia?
3 Look at the bar charts for steel and coal production. Do these figures suggest that Russia was as advanced as the others in industrial output? Explain your answer.
4 Do the population figures for 1900 support your last answer? Explain your answer.
  (Clue: think about how large Russia's population was compared to the other countries.)

To add to these problems, Russia under the tsars had no parliament and all political parties were banned. Not surprisingly those who opposed the tsar often felt they had no choice but to turn to terrorism. In 1881 a group called 'People's Will' had assassinated Tsar Alexander II, Nicholas's grandfather. In order to try and destroy these opposition groups the tsars had a secret police force, the Okhrana. Those opponents who were arrested were sent to appalling prison camps in the icy wastes of Siberia. To escape such a fate others fled the country to live as exiles in western Europe. The Okhrana spies followed them and attempted to infiltrate these exile groups by becoming members.

The revolution of 1905

In 1905 revolts took place in many areas of the Russian Empire. Shops were looted and workers went on strike. In the town of Kharkov the French consul reported that the educated middle classes, such as doctors, lawyers and teachers, were leading the disturbances. In the Black Sea port of Odessa sailors mutinied aboard the battleship *Potemkin* and refused to obey orders. The Tsar was in danger of losing control. Why did this happen?

Long-term causes

We have already come across the long-term causes of revolution in Russia in the previous section. Most peasants lived in poverty. They wanted more land of their own and they wanted to pay less taxes. Industrial workers lived in even worse conditions. They were crammed together and so they could easily organise strikes and protests. Unemployment now added to their problems. Other nationalities who were part of the Russian Empire were also angry that the Tsar showed no sign of allowing them more involvement in ruling their own areas. Factory owners, and even some of the landowners, looked at the Great Powers of Britain and Germany and saw that they were much more modern than Russia and that they had parliaments and political parties. The factory owners wanted political parties so that they would be able to influence the Tsar to rule Russia in the way that they wanted.

Yet these factors were true for most years in the early twentieth century. They explain why so many people inside the Russian Empire were discontented but they do not explain why a revolt broke out in 1905, as against any other year. To discover this we need to look at the short-term causes which triggered the revolt.

Short-term causes

• The war with Japan 1904–5

In 1904 Japan had declared war on Russia. Russia was a world power while Japan was a small country. The Russian people assumed that they would defeat the Japanese quickly. Instead they suffered a humiliating defeat. The Russian Pacific navy was attacked by the Japanese while the Russian officers were on shore attending a dance given by the admiral's wife. The Russian Baltic navy was then sent from St Petersburg, but it had to sail half way around the world to reach the Japanese. The Japanese had captured their target, Port Arthur, long before it reached the battle zone. When the navy finally arrived it was destroyed by the Japanese. The Russian people were horrified by this disaster. It suggested that Russia was not being ruled well and the people believed that the Tsar needed new advice.

The Tsar with the Tsarina and their son, Alexei, in the arms of a Cossack bodyguard.

Why was there a revolution in Russia in 1905?

SOURCE 1:

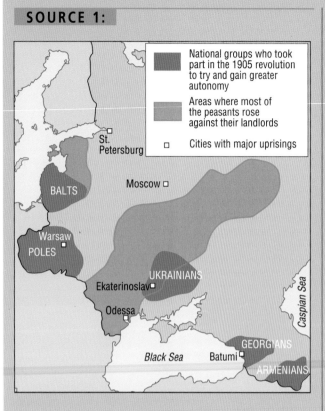

National groups who took part in the 1905 revolution to try and gain greater autonomy

Areas where most of the peasants rose against their landlords

☐   Cities with major uprisings

The extent of the 1905 revolution.

SOURCE 2:

Some of the protesters on 22 January 1905 in St Petersburg.

SOURCE 3:

A contemporary Japanese painting showing Japanese ships destroying the Russian navy in the Russo-Japanese war.

SOURCE 4:

'Employers paid little heed [attention] to standards of safety and provided few facilities for their workforces . . . Petrograd (St Petersburg) had the highest industrial accident rate of any region of Russia . . . At the Putilov works . . . there was an average of 15 accidents per month.'

S Smith: *Red Petrograd* 1983

SOURCE 5:

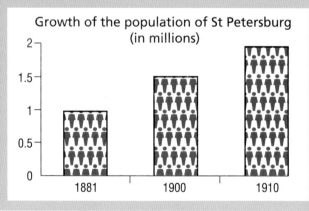

Growth of the population of St Petersburg (in millions)

1   What does Source 5 show about the population of St Petersburg?

2   What problems would this create?

3   How useful are Sources 3 and 4 in explaining why there was a revolution in 1905?

4   Why did a revolution break out in 1905?
To answer this question
   a   Draw up a list of the long-term causes which led to discontent with the Tsar's government. Then explain the effect of each.
   b   Explain how the short-term causes caused a revolution to break out in 1905 rather than in any other year.

5   How did the divisions among the revolutionaries and the role of the army help the Tsar to survive the revolution?

On 22 January 1905 a group of protesters gathered in St Petersburg, in the square outside the Tsar's Winter Palace. They wanted to present the Tsar with a petition asking him for reforms to improve their lives. In fact the Tsar was not in the Winter Palace. Nonetheless, troops guarding the palace opened fire on the protesters, possibly killing as many as 1000. The day became known as Bloody Sunday. In February the Tsar's uncle was assassinated and by October strikes and other protests had spread to many areas of the country.

On the advice of his Chief Minister Witte the Tsar survived by a mixture of concession and terror. He won the support of the middle classes with the October Manifesto that promised a parliament (or Duma). The Tsar also won the support of the peasants by cancelling the crippling redemption payments which they had been making since the abolition of serfdom. He then dealt with the workers. They were crushed by the troops returning from the war with Japan.

Years of reform 1906–13

The Tsar had survived the revolution of 1905 but unless he dealt with the problems that had caused this revolt he would face another revolution before long. His new Chief Minister was Stolypin who used a mixture of harsh treatment and concessions to prevent a new revolution. 21 000 people were sent to Siberia and a further 1000 were executed as punishment for the 1905 revolution. Stolypin also introduced reforms such as the abolition of redemption payments which satisfied the peasants in the short term. However, long-term improvements were still needed to keep them contented.

In 1906 and again in 1907 Stolypin introduced laws that allowed the peasants to leave the *mir*, the village council. Stolypin hoped that this would allow peasants who were more efficient to earn large profits. This would not only please enterprising peasants, it would also produce more food for the cities and make the industrial workers more content. Finally, the peasants would spend their profits on consumer goods produced in Russian factories, so stimulating industrial growth. Stolypin believed that after 20 years his reforms would have improved Russia and the Tsar would no longer need to fear revolt. But Stolypin was assassinated in 1911 and the outbreak of the First World War in 1914 halted all reform. By that time only 25 per cent of peasants had left the *mir*.

Many people had been won over by the promise of a parliament or Duma. However the Tsar had no desire to introduce a parliament in the western sense. He regarded the Duma as a body whose advice he could take or leave as he wanted. In 1907 the voting system was changed so that most peasants and industrial workers were unable to vote. The Duma had not made any changes in Russia. If people were unhappy with life in Russia they were still likely to turn to violence and revolt.

THE FIRST WORLD WAR AND THE FALL OF THE TSAR

When Russia entered the First World War the Tsar could hardly have seemed more popular. The Russians were carrying out their duty to protect the Serbs and crowds appeared in the streets of St Petersburg to cheer the Tsar and support the war. St Petersburg was soon renamed 'Petrograd' because St Petersburg sounded too German. This enthusiasm for the Tsar seemed so different to the feeling of 1905. Yet within three years the demonstrators would be on the streets for a different purpose. Over 300 years of Romanov rule ended when the Tsar was forced to **abdicate**. Why was it that the Tsar had been able to survive the revolution of 1905 and yet failed to survive in 1917 after a period of reform?

Military effects of the war

The war began well for the Russians as they invaded Germany. However, before the end of 1914 they had suffered two terrible defeats at Tannenburg and the Masurian Lakes which forced the Russian army to retreat. The Russian army relied on its superior numbers to defeat the enemy, but in the First World War numbers were no match for machine guns and artillery shells. Although the Russian army had six million men, they were poorly armed and equipped. The Germans inflicted terrible casualties and soon large numbers of Russians began to desert rather than face certain death. The Tsar decided to take control of the war in August 1915, making matters even worse. From that point onwards every military disaster would be blamed personally on the Tsar. The Tsar's future would now depend on the success of the Russian war effort. In 1916 the Tsar's best general, Brusilov, launched a series of attacks against both the Germans and their Austro-Hungarian allies. Although some advances were made the number of Russian soldiers killed was appalling. The land gained was also soon lost.

Casualties of the war. With its poor equipment and training the Russian army suffered appalling casualties in the First World War.

Economic effects of the war

Military disasters made the Tsar unpopular and the effects of the war were far-reaching. Before the war Russia had hardly been able to produce enough food to feed the people in the cities. The war made this situation far worse. With so many peasants called up to fight, there were fewer peasants actually growing food. This food had even less chance of reaching the cities because the railways were being used to move men and supplies to the front line. There were few trains available to take food from the countryside to the cities.

As the German army advanced into the Russian Empire it drove a flood of refugees before it. These refugees headed for the cities in the hope of finding food and safety and in this way the population of Moscow increased by 20 per cent during the war. Food shortages produced inflation and during the course of the war prices rose by almost 700 per cent. Wages did not increase as much as prices and so strikes and protests demanding food became more and more common.

Political effects of the war

In 1915 the Tsar called the Duma, yet he continued to ignore its advice. This would not have been serious if the war had been going well but, as disaster followed disaster, the Tsar became more and more unpopular with the politicians. To make matters worse, government in Petrograd was in the hands of the Tsarina because the Tsar was at the front commanding the army. The Tsarina's main concern was her son, the Tsarevich Alexei. He suffered from the incurable disease haemophilia. Haemophilia prevents the blood from clotting so that any injury might have caused Alexei to bleed to death.

Alexandra believed that the corrupt monk Rasputin could cure her son. Rasputin used his position to influence appointments in government and he regularly changed members of the cabinet, often appointing incapable people. This angered the Duma even more since many of them were far more able. Although Rasputin was murdered by a group of aristocrats in 1916 the damage had already been done. The Tsar would not listen to advice and the only way to change the way the war was being fought was to replace the Tsar.

▶ How did the war affect the Tsar?

SOURCE 1:

An English school history textbook, written in 1987:

'There is enough evidence to suggest that there would have been a revolution in Russia to overthrow the Tsar sooner or later. The First World War simply made it happen sooner.'

N DeMarco: *The World This Century*

SOURCE 2:

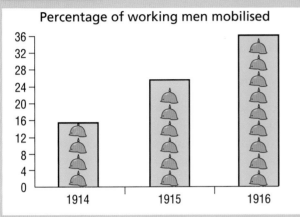

Percentage of working men mobilised

SOURCE 3:   Eastern Front in the First World

SOURCE 4:

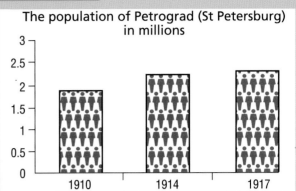

The population of Petrograd (St Petersburg) in millions

SOURCE 5:

Milyukov, a member of the Duma, made a speech to the Duma in November 1916:

'We have many different reasons for being discontented with the government. But all those reasons boil down to one general one: the incompetence and evil intentions of the present government. This is Russia's chief evil . . . And therefore in the name of the millions of victims and of their spilled blood, in the name of responsibility to those people who elected us, we shall fight until we get responsible government.'

Quoted in J Laver: *Russia 1914–41*

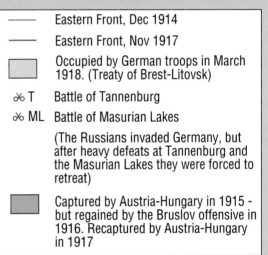

——	Eastern Front, Dec 1914
——	Eastern Front, Nov 1917
▨	Occupied by German troops in March 1918. (Treaty of Brest-Litovsk)
✂ T	Battle of Tannenburg
✂ ML	Battle of Masurian Lakes
	(The Russians invaded Germany, but after heavy defeats at Tannenburg and the Masurian Lakes they were forced to retreat)
▨	Captured by Austria-Hungary in 1915 - but regained by the Bruslov offensive in 1916. Recaptured by Austria-Hungary in 1917

1 Read Source 5. Who is Milyukov referring to in the term 'millions of victims'?

2 Milyukov says that 'We have many different reasons for being discontented with the government'. Which of these are referred to in Sources 2, 4 and 5?

3 To what extent was the fall of tsarism due to Nicholas II? Re-read the text on pages 31 and 32.
   a Make a list of the causes which were the fault of Nicholas II.
   b Make a list of the causes which were not his fault.
   c Decide which cause was the most important.

4 Do you agree with the statement made in Source 1?
   a What evidence can you find to suggest that the Tsar would have been overthrown without the war?
   b What evidence can you find to suggest that the war caused the overthrow of the Tsar?
   c What evidence in your answer to **b** actually added to the problems which you had identified in your answer to **a**?
   Now answer the question using the material you have gathered in answer to parts **a**, **b** and **c**.

* The revolution is known as either the February or the March revolution. This is because Russia used the Julian calendar while western Europe used the Gregorian calendar which was 13 days ahead. Therefore the revolution took place in February in Russia but in March in the west!

The March* Revolution 1917

The strikes that had been building up during the war came to a head in early March. There was a huge demonstration on International Women's Day, 8 March. Women from Petrograd joined workers from the vast Putilov factory. There were as many as 200 000 protesters on the streets of the capital. In the days that followed, the protests turned into a general strike with more and more people joining it. They were not only demanding more food but also an end to the war and the removal of the Tsar. In 1905 the Tsar had been able to call on the troops to put down the revolt. This was not the case in 1917. Many of the troops were sick of the war and so they joined in the protests rather than put them down. On 15 March Tsar Nicholas was forced to abdicate. He handed over power to his brother, Grand Duke Mikhail. However, Mikhail realised that very few people wanted an all-powerful ruler and so he stood down as well. Three hundred years of Romanov rule was over.

The Provisional Government

The government that took over from the Tsar was made up of leading members of the Duma. They were called the Provisional (or temporary) Government, because they were only to rule until a new form of government was chosen. The plan was to hold elections for a Constituent Assembly. This would draw up a constitution, or set of laws, laying down how the new Russia would be governed. Then further elections would be held to choose a new government. However, in less than eight months the Provisional Government was itself overthrown, having not held any of the promised elections. Why was this? There were three main reasons: the continuing war; the land question and the lack of an elected government.

The problems associated with the war had played a major part in bringing down the Tsar. The war was extremely unpopular and it was difficult to see how the government could get enough food to the cities while it continued. The tsarist government had found this difficult enough in times of peace. However, the Provisional Government felt that it could not afford to stop fighting the war. Large areas of Russia were under German control and to allow the Germans to keep this land would be a national humiliation.

The war had also bankrupted the Russian government. The Provisional Government needed money. The western Allies were willing to give them money but only if the Russians stayed in the war. If Russia pulled out of the war the Germans would be able to transfer their troops to the Western Front. Yet because so many Russians wanted peace the Provisional Government did make one concession. It changed the reason it was fighting the war: the government now only wanted to drive the Germans from Russian soil.

The mass surrender of Russian troops in 1917.

Q Why did the Provisional Government continue to fight the war?

In May the Foreign Minister, Milyukov, and the War Minister, Guchkov, were both forced to resign because they wanted to fight the war until Germany had been defeated. The Provisional Government hoped that the people would support a war with the more limited aim of keeping Russia free from foreign occupation. However, they misjudged the situation. Far too many people had suffered from the war and so they just wanted it to end quickly. The Provisional Government was committed to fighting a war that was extremely unpopular with the people and yet it was no more successful in running the war than the Tsar had been. An attack, launched in June 1917, was a disaster. Deserters fled the army in huge numbers.

Under the Tsar the peasants had owned very little land. With the March Revolution the peasants hoped that all this would change. They were disappointed. The Provisional Government represented the landowners who did not want to hand over their land to the peasants. As a result, peasants began to take the law into their own hands and seize land for themselves all over the country. This increased desertions from the army as soldiers feared that there would not be any land left for them if they waited until the end of the war.

Members of the Provisional Government also had to deal with a problem that the Tsar had not faced. They had little claim to be the legitimate government of the country. Why should people obey them? No one had elected them to government. Even the system that had elected them to the Duma excluded most peasants and industrial workers. In the weeks after the March Revolution, 'soviets' (or councils) sprung up in towns and cities throughout Russia. These soviets were elected councils that decided policies for the workers and peasants. The most important of these was the Petrograd Soviet in the nation's capital. In March it issued its 'Order No. 1' which stated that all soldiers should obey only those orders approved by the Soviet. The Provisional Government no longer controlled the army.

Kerensky (standing on the right) visiting troops at the front. The original leader of the Provisional Government was the aristocratic landowner Prince Lvov. In July 1917 Alexander Kerensky, the War Minister, took over as Prime Minister. He was a member of the Petrograd Soviet and very popular with the workers and peasants. However, his own personal popularity could not save a government following such unpopular policies.

Q What advantage was there in Kerensky being a member of the Petrograd Soviet as well as Prime Minister?

The Provisional Government would have had more support if it had organised elections. However, this could not be done quickly as the Constituent Assembly would have to be elected first. Also, as the Provisional Government was becoming more and more unpopular, any election was likely to see its members defeated. So why should they carry out a policy that would make them lose control of the country?

How did inflation affect support for the Provisional Government?

SOURCE 1:

Inflation

Year	Value
1913	100
1915	130
1916	155
Jan 1917	300
Oct 1917	755

This table shows the movement of prices. 100 is the figure for prices in 1913. So 200 means a doubling of prices. Prices rose as areas such as Poland, which contained factories, fell into German hands. Also more and more of the remaining production was used in the war effort.

SOURCE 2:

General Baluev reporting on the food problem on 13 October 1917:

'The front, already in a serious condition, is confronted by a great new danger from a starving population. A total breakdown in supply is possible. It is now 13 days since the ration was fixed at 1 poud of bread and 7/8 of a poud of hardtack (dried meat). [A poud is a measurement of weight.] During that time there has been a 68% shortfall in deliveries of flour. The hardtack is almost gone.'

quoted in McCauley: *Russian Revolution and the Soviet State*

SOURCE 3:

Resolution of the All Russian Conference of Soviets. After the fall of the Tsar soviets sprang up all over Russia, though the Petrograd Soviet remained the most important. In April representatives of these soviets met.

'The conference appeals to the people to support the Provisional Government, as long as the government expands the gains of the revolution and so long as its foreign policy is not based on conquering foreign territory.'

quoted in J Laver: *Russia 1914–41*

SOURCE 4:

Soviet Order No. 1:

'The orders of the Military Committee of the State Duma [Provisional Government] are to be obeyed, with the exception of those instances in which they contradict [disagree with] the orders and decrees of the Soviet of Workers and Soldiers Deputies.'

1 What do you notice about inflation in Source 1 in 1917 compared to earlier?
2 Why do you think the shortage of flour mentioned in Source 2 was so serious?
3 Why was inflation likely to be such a serious problem, in view of what you know about wages at this time?
4 What do these sources suggest about how far the Soviet was prepared to support the Provisional Government?

The success of the Bolsheviks

Since the government failed to deal with the three major problems of the continuing war, land and the right to govern, it is perhaps hardly surprising that its rule was so brief. What is much more surprising is that it was overthrown by the Bolshevik Party. The Bolsheviks were a **Communist** party.

They concentrated on building support among the workers and so they were quite a small party, since the Russian working class was still a small percentage of the population. The peasants, who made up over 80 per cent of the population, supported the Social Revolutionaries. It was the SRs, therefore, who would have won the most support in an election. But Bolshevik success was equally surprising given that in March 1917 they had been caught completely off guard by the revolution. Most of their leaders were still in western Europe, hiding from the Okhrana, the Tsar's secret police. So how was it that this small Communist party became the next government of Russia, rather than the Social Revolutionaries? There were a number of reasons for this, but the most significant was probably the role of its leader, Vladimir Ilyich Lenin.

Lenin's role in the revolution

Lenin was vital to the Bolshevik success because he was willing to adapt Communist theories taking the situation in Russia into account. Many Bolsheviks, like other **socialists**, believed that there could not be a socialist revolution until a large working class had been established. So they supported the Provisional Government because it would encourage the growth of factories. With these factories would come workers. A revolution by the working class was seen as being a long way off in the future.

When Lenin arrived in Russia in April 1917 he changed all of that. Lenin decided that the Bolsheviks should seize power straight away. Once in power the Bolsheviks would introduce policies to move Russia towards socialism. The importance of this policy was that it meant that the Bolshevik Party was the only party in Russia to oppose the Provisional Government. As the Provisional Government became less and less popular the Bolsheviks were likely to pick up more and more support. Lenin also changed a number of other policies to adapt to the situation in 1917.

Karl Marx, a German, originally developed the theory of Communism in the nineteenth century. In his theory the peasants had no part to play in bringing about socialism. Yet in Russia they were the largest class and Lenin realised that they could not possibly be ignored. So he simply adopted the SRs' agricultural policy by promising land to the peasants. This won some peasant support for the Bolsheviks and at least ensured that the peasants would not be against them.

Lenin had always been opposed to the war. He felt that the peasants and workers were being slaughtered in a war which was being fought for the benefit of the rich factory owners and landowners. As the Provisional Government continued to fight the war, the Bolsheviks offered the only alternative to those people who wanted to end the war. Therefore, between March and November, support for the Bolsheviks grew, especially in the soviets. By October they were the largest group in the Petrograd Soviet.

How did Lenin change the Bolsheviks' success?

Lenin arrived in Russia in April 1917. He came secretly in a train provided by the German government, who hoped he would succeed in pulling Russia out of the war.

Like most of the leaders of the Bolshevik Party, Lenin was a member of the middle class. He came from a relatively wealthy background. His brother had been executed for plotting to assassinate Tsar Alexander III. Lenin did not believe that assassinating a single tsar was the solution to Russia's problems. Instead he turned to the theories of Karl Marx. Lenin's real name was Vladimir Ilyich Ulanov. Most revolutionaries chose false names to try and prevent their identification. Even though they were forced to live abroad they all still had

A contemporary socialist, Victor Serge, recalls the arrival of Lenin in Russia in April 1917:

'Hardly off the train, he [Lenin] asked the party comrades "Why didn't you seize power?" At once he comes out with his April theses . . . He is called mad . . . The experienced Bolsheviks criticise him . . . But suddenly it becomes clear that he has the support of the man in the street and of the man in the factory and barracks. His whole genius consists only in his ability to say what these people want to say, but do not know how to say.'

(above) A Bolshevik painting of Lenin's arrival in Petrograd in April 1917.

Q What impression of Lenin does this give?

families in Russia who could be punished. Lenin had a forceful personality. He was determined to bring about a revolution in Russia and would use any methods necessary – even accepting the help of the German government. But he was flexible and willing to change his ideas if necessary. For example, he won peasant support by allowing them to own their land, even though this went against Communist theory.

Q

1 Which problem – the war, land, or legitimacy – do you think was the most serious for the Provisional Government? Explain your answer.
2 Why was Lenin's opposition to the war so important in increasing Bolshevik support?
3 Why did Lenin feel that the support of the peasants was necessary?
4 Was the success of the Bolsheviks in November 1917 due to the abilities of Lenin or the failures of the Provisional Government? Decide:
   a What were Lenin's abilities and how did they influence events?
   b What were the important failures of the Provisional Government?
   c What other factors played a part?

Trotsky

Trotsky's real name was Leon Bronstein. He had not originally been a supporter of Lenin. In 1905 he had been chosen as the leader of the Petrograd Soviet in the failed revolution. He was also a prominent figure in the events of 1917. In the summer of 1917 he decided to join Lenin and the Bolsheviks and in September he was elected leader of the Petrograd Soviet again. His speeches were very inspiring and made him a popular figure.

Trotsky.

The November Revolution

In October 1917 the Bolsheviks decided to support Lenin's plan to seize power in Russia. Lenin was lucky to be in a position to do so. In July, during a time that became known as the 'July Days', the Bolsheviks had supported massive anti-government demonstrations. Kerensky had found enough loyal troops to put down the revolt and 400 demonstrators were killed. Lenin had opposed support for the revolt on the grounds that the Bolsheviks were not yet ready, but most of the Bolsheviks had decided to try to overthrow Kerensky.

The Bolsheviks were now enemies of the State. Lenin was forced to flee Petrograd. However, the Bolsheviks were saved by the actions of the commander of the army, General Kornilov. In August he attempted to overthrow the Provisional Government and Kerensky was forced to call on Bolshevik support to help him defeat Kornilov. The Bolsheviks were now the heroes and Trotsky was soon elected leader of the Petrograd Soviet. He was also head of the Soviet's newly-created Military Revolutionary Committee (MRC). This was responsible for gathering weapons to enable the Soviet to defend itself but Trotsky used it as a front for the Bolsheviks to organise their armed seizure of power.

(above) Lenin in disguise. In July 1917 there was a failed attempt to get rid of the Provisional Government. The Bolsheviks were involved and so when the rising failed many Bolsheviks were imprisoned. Lenin managed to escape by using this disguise.

(left) General Kornilov. In August General Kornilov, the Commander-in-Chief of the army, marched on Petrograd to get rid of the Provisional Government and the Soviet. Kerensky was forced to release the imprisoned Bolsheviks to defend the capital city. The Bolsheviks' popularity soared as Kornilov was defeated.

> ❓ **Why do you think that Kornilov's revolt was an important event in 1917?**

On the night of 5 November Kerensky discovered that the Bolsheviks were planning a takeover and he sent troops to close down two Bolshevik-controlled newspapers, *Izvestia* and *Pravda*. Kerensky's troops were prevented from doing this by troops belonging to the MRC. Trotsky had already checked on the loyalty of the 18 armed units that defended Petrograd through the MRC and found that 15 of them supported the Bolsheviks. When the Bolsheviks launched their takeover on the night of 6 November there were hardly any troops willing to defend the Provisional Government. Kerensky managed to escape but the Bolsheviks had taken control of Petrograd with very little force. Only five people were killed. However, it took a week of fighting before the Bolsheviks in Moscow had a similar success and only after the deaths of 200 Russians.

Q

> **1** Trotsky said that 'War is the locomotive of history.' By this he meant that war makes things change more quickly. Do the events of 1917 support his view?
> Look at the effects of the war on:
> **a** the economy;
> **b** the political situation.
> Was war the main cause of change in 1917?

RUSSIA UNDER COMMUNISM: THE AFTERMATH OF VICTORY

Lenin had seized power but he faced exactly the same problems as the Provisional Government: legitimacy (the right to rule); land and the war. Unless he was able to deal with these problems more effectively than Kerensky, Lenin would not remain in power any longer than Kerensky.

Legitimacy

This did not pose exactly the same problem for Lenin as it had for Kerensky. As far as Lenin was concerned his government's right to rule came from the fact that they were seizing power on behalf of the workers. This would create a socialist government which would benefit all working people. The Constituent Assembly did actually meet but Lenin used armed soldiers to close the meeting down after just one day. Lenin had not seized power in order to establish a western parliamentary democracy that might vote the Bolsheviks out of office and establish a non-socialist government. This caused the enemies of the Bolsheviks to join together and launch a civil war against the Bolsheviks (see pages 42–3).

Land

According to Marx no individual would own factories or land in a socialist state. The Bolshevik government's decree (law) on land appeared to follow this line but in reality Lenin allowed the peasants to keep all the land they had seized from the landlords. He had no way of taking it back from them and he needed peasant support for the new government.

War

This was the most difficult problem for Lenin. The pressures of the war had defeated both the Tsar and the Provisional Government. Lenin was in no doubt that Russia would have to end the war if the Bolshevik government were to survive. The front line was now so close to Petrograd that the Bolsheviks moved the capital to Moscow. Trotsky went to Brest-Litovsk, a Russian town now in German hands, to negotiate with the Germans. The Germans forced the Bolsheviks to sign a humiliating treaty (called the Brest-Litovsk Treaty), handing over huge areas of land to the Germans. Most Bolsheviks were horrified and opposed the treaty.

Trotsky and Lenin were well aware that the Russian army was too weak to defend these lands and so the Germans would capture them anyway. Lenin gambled that the Allies would eventually defeat the Germans and so allow the Russians to recapture the land lost at Brest-Litovsk. It was a gamble that appeared to work when the Germans surrendered to the Allies only eight months after signing the Treaty of Brest-Litovsk. However, taking back the

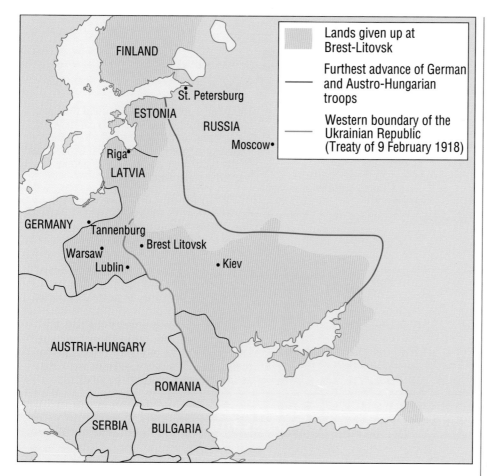

Map of the Treaty of Brest-Litovsk, March 1918.

territories proved much more difficult than Lenin may have imagined. By then the Bolsheviks were engaged in a civil war against the Whites, or anti-Bolshevik forces. Also the people of the areas handed over to Germany were not Russian; they were Poles, Ukrainians, Letts and many other nationalities. They wanted independence rather than the re-establishment of Russian rule. Much of the land was not regained for this reason.

THE CIVIL WAR

Who was fighting against the Bolsheviks?

Many people in Russia did not want the Bolsheviks to stay in power and so, in 1918, civil war broke out. The Bolsheviks were known as the Reds and their enemies were known as the Whites. As the map on page 42 shows, the Reds were surrounded and lost control of large areas of the Russian Empire. The White forces were very varied. They included:

- A number of former tsarist generals such as Denikin and Yudenich. They led armies to overthrow the Bolsheviks. They received weapons and money from the western Allies because they promised to rejoin the war if they were in control of Russia.
- Nationalist groups such as the Ukrainians and Baltic peoples who wanted to establish their own countries free of Russian control.
- Troops sent by the western Allies to keep Russia in the war against Germany. The British sent troops to Murmansk, for example.
- The Poles. They tried to use the chaos of the Civil War to attack the Reds and seize more land for their own country recently set up by the Paris Peace Conference.

Map of the Russian Civil War.

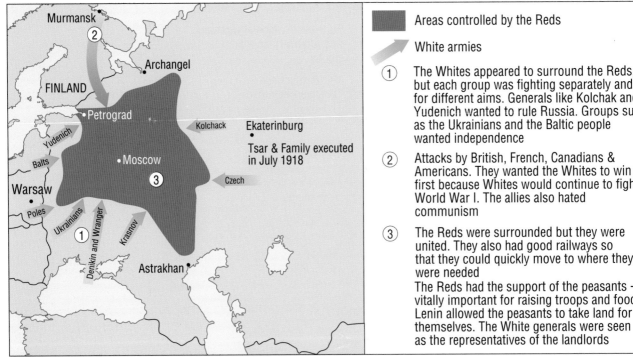

Areas controlled by the Reds

White armies

① The Whites appeared to surround the Reds, but each group was fighting separately and for different aims. Generals like Kolchak and Yudenich wanted to rule Russia. Groups such as the Ukrainians and the Baltic people wanted independence

② Attacks by British, French, Canadians & Americans. They wanted the Whites to win at first because Whites would continue to fight World War I. The allies also hated communism

③ The Reds were surrounded but they were united. They also had good railways so that they could quickly move to where they were needed
The Reds had the support of the peasants - vitally important for raising troops and food. Lenin allowed the peasants to take land for themselves. The White generals were seen as the representatives of the landlords

► How did the Bolsheviks put their message across?

SOURCE 1:

'Wrangel is still alive. Finish him.' A Bolshevik poster from 1920. The severed heads of the defeated generals such as Kolchak and Denikin are shown on the ground.

SOURCE 2:

'And now for Wrangel.' A Bolshevik poster from 1920. Other White generals such as Kolchak are shown already defeated on the lance of the Red Army.

1 The majority of the people of Russia were illiterate. They could not read or write. How do Sources 1 and 2 get their message across?
2 What is the message being put across by Sources 1 and 2?
3 Draw your own poster. Use similar techniques to put across the Bolshevik message using as few words as possible because most of the population could not read.

Despite being surrounded, the Reds had defeated the Whites by 1920. How were they able to achieve this? The Bolsheviks had two main strengths. Firstly, although they were surrounded, they controlled the railways and could quickly move men and supplies to wherever they were needed. Secondly, Trotsky reorganised the Red Army. Under the Provisional Government men had elected their own officers and capital punishment had been banned. This meant that the army had become ineffective. Trotsky reintroduced capital punishment and recalled the best former tsarist officers. He ensured that they were loyal by holding their families as hostages.

In contrast the White forces were divided and did not work together. This meant that the Red Army was able to deal with each White force individually. Morale among White troops was generally much poorer than among the Reds. Generals such as Kolchak restored lands to the landlords and lost the support of the peasants. The fact that the generals relied on foreign support also meant that the Bolsheviks could claim that they were defending Russia against foreign invaders.

Q

1 Was the Red victory in the Civil War due to the weakness of their enemies or their own strengths?
To answer this question you will need to decide:
a What were the weaknesses of the Whites?
b What were the strengths of the Reds?
c Which were the more important?

(above) The Tsar under arrest during the Civil War. The Tsar and his family had been moved out of Petrograd to avoid the anger of the local people. However, the Bolsheviks found that they were just as likely to be captured in Siberia once the White forces advanced along the Trans-Siberian railway. Therefore in July 1918 the Tsar and his family were executed by the retreating Bolsheviks at Ekaterinburg.

Q Why do you think that the Bolsheviks did not want the royal family to be captured by the Whites?

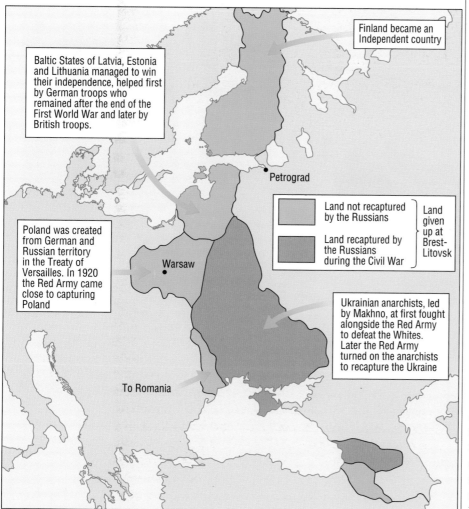

Finland became an Independent country

Baltic States of Latvia, Estonia and Lithuania managed to win their independence, helped first by German troops who remained after the end of the First World War and later by British troops.

Petrograd

Land not recaptured by the Russians

Land recaptured by the Russians during the Civil War

Land given up at Brest-Litovsk

Poland was created from German and Russian territory in the Treaty of Versailles. In 1920 the Red Army came close to capturing Poland

Warsaw

Ukrainian anarchists, led by Makhno, at first fought alongside the Red Army to defeat the Whites. Later the Red Army turned on the anarchists to recapture the Ukraine

To Romania

Map showing areas under Russian control at the end of the Civil War. By the end of the 1920s the Reds had defeated their White enemies. However, they had not recovered all of the lands that they had given up at Brest-Litovsk.

Lenin's economic policies: War Communism

While Trotsky's reforms of the Red Army may have indeed played a vital part in the Bolshevik victory in the Civil War, so too did the economic policy that Lenin had adopted. This was known as 'War Communism'. The government took control of all industries with more than ten workers. All private trade was banned. It was illegal to go on strike and strikers could be executed. Peasants were only allowed to keep enough of their crops to feed themselves. The Bolshevik secret police, the *Cheka*, forced the peasants to hand over everything else. The whole point of War Communism was to ensure that the Red Army had enough food and supplies. If the Civil War was lost then it would be the end of Communism in Russia and so no sacrifice was too great to achieve victory.

However, War Communism made the rule of the Tsar seem mild. There was terrible famine as the peasants grew just enough food to feed themselves. There was no benefit in growing any more as the *Cheka* would seize it without payment. Then a drought in 1920 caused the crop to fail. The result was another famine and millions died. Starving workers left the cities to search for food and so industrial production collapsed as well. Even previous supporters of the Bolsheviks were horrified. In March 1921 the sailors at the Kronstadt naval base near Petrograd rebelled demanding 'Soviets without Bolsheviks'. The Red Army stormed the base and destroyed the rebellion. Lenin and Trotsky had showed how ruthless they could be.

▶ What were the effects of War Communism?

SOURCE 1:

Russian children starving in 1920.

SOURCE 2:

Three bar charts showing the Russian economy.

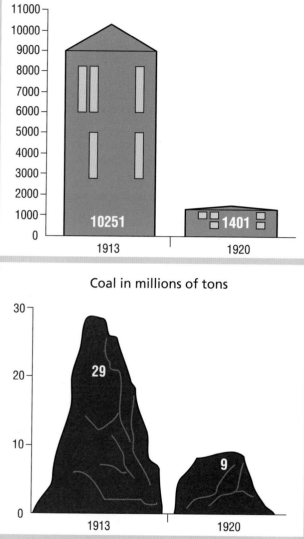

Factory production in millions of roubles

10251   1401

1913   1920

Coal in millions of tons

29   9

1913   1920

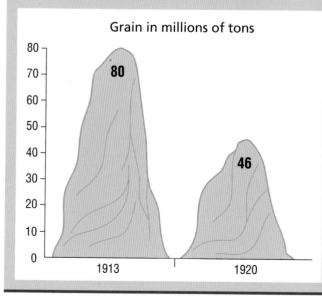

Grain in millions of tons

80   46

1913   1920

SOURCE 3:

Lenin to Trotsky, February 1920:

'The situation concerning railway transport is really catastrophic. Grain supplies are no longer getting through. . . . The individual bread ration is to be reduced for those who do not work in transport, and increased for those who do. Thousands more may perish but the country will be saved.'

Quoted in McCauley: *The Russian Revolution and the Soviet State*

SOURCE 4:

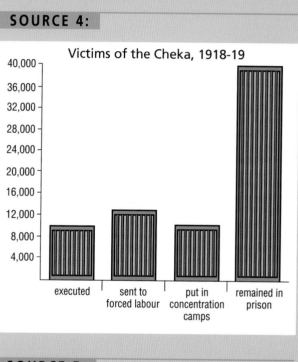

Victims of the Cheka, 1918-19

executed   sent to forced labour   put in concentration camps   remained in prison

SOURCE 5:

An English school textbook, written in 1987:

'Lenin had governed Russia firmly but without cruelty. He was a modest man who shunned public attention and had always been concerned with the welfare of ordinary Russians.'

N DeMarco: *The World This Century*

1 What were the causes of such scenes shown in Source 1?
2 What were the causes of the figures shown in Source 2?
3 What were the effects on the people of the figures shown in Source 2?
4 Look at Source 5.
   a What evidence can you find that disagrees with this statement about Lenin?
   b What evidence can you find that supports the statement?

The New Economic Policy

The lessons of Kronstadt and the famine were not lost on Lenin. Since 1914 Russia had suffered six years of continuous brutal warfare. Grain production was just 50 per cent of the 1913 figure while industrial production in 1920 was a mere 18 per cent of production in 1913. Desperate measures were needed and Lenin introduced the 'New Economic Policy' (NEP). This allowed peasants to sell any grain they had left after the government had taken its share. This would encourage them to grow more grain. However, they would only do this if there were goods to buy with the money they earned. Therefore factories with fewer than 20 workers were returned to their owners. Many Bolsheviks were opposed to the NEP but once again Lenin was displaying his ability to adopt a realistic approach. As he himself commented 'Let the peasants have their little bit of profit as long as we keep power.'

Gradually the economy began to recover under the NEP. In 1913 grain production of 80 million tonnes had been just enough to feed the population. Grain production collapsed to 36 million tonnes in 1921 but recovered to 73 million tonnes by 1925. This was still not enough but at least it encouraged the workers to return to the towns.

Q

Production figures 1913–28

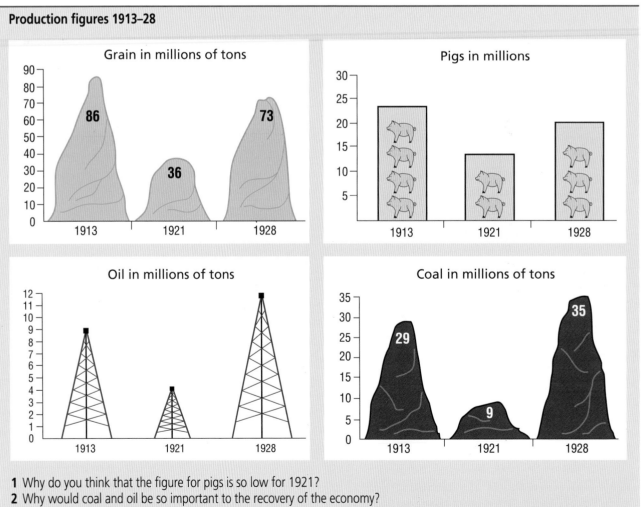

1 Why do you think that the figure for pigs is so low for 1921?
2 Why would coal and oil be so important to the recovery of the economy?
3 Why do you think the increased output of grain encouraged the workers to return to the towns?
4 What impact might this have had on industrial output?
5 According to these figures, how successful was the New Economic Policy by 1928?

Part II: Russia under Stalin 1928–41

This section focuses on three key issues:

- *Why did Stalin become the ruler of Russia?*
- *How successful were Stalin's economic changes?*
- *What was life like in Stalin's Russia?*

Lenin died on 21 January 1924. For the last two years of his life he had found it increasingly difficult to play a leading political role as his health got worse after a series of strokes. Who would succeed Lenin as the ruler of the newly-named USSR? (In 1922 the name of the country had been officially changed to the USSR, the Union of Soviet Socialist Republics.)

There were two main candidates, Stalin and Trotsky. Trotsky was Lenin's favoured choice but Lenin did not force his views on his colleagues. He wrote a testament (or will) in which he stated that Trotsky was the most capable of the leaders. He also added that Stalin was not to be trusted with power. However, after Lenin's death the leaders decided not to publish his views and so these criticisms of Stalin did not become known to the party members. If they had been made public they would probably have prevented Stalin from succeeding Lenin.

Lenin's embalmed body. Lenin was preserved and buried in a glass case, just like a Russian holy man. The body was then placed in a tomb in Red Square. Stalin helped to carry the coffin at the funeral. Trotsky was not even present and it seemed as if he was insulting Lenin. Trotsky claimed that Stalin misled him by telling him the wrong date of the funeral. This photograph shows the head of the Cheka, Dzerzhinsky (left), paying his respects to Lenin.

STALIN TAKES OVER

At first Stalin joined with two important Communists, Kamenev and Zinoviev, and used their support for the policy of 'Socialism in One Country' to defeat Trotsky's policy of 'World Revolution' at the 1924 Party Congress. In the following year Trotsky resigned as Commissar (minister) for War. However, Stalin then turned against Kamenev and Zinoviev. He took over the defeated Trotsky's policy of rapid industrialisation while Kamenev and Zinoviev still supported the NEP. Trotsky had argued that Russia needed to concentrate on heavy industry such as coal, steel and iron. This meant that fewer goods would be available for people to buy in shops.

Stalin made sure that most of the delegates at the 1925 Party Congress were loyal to him by using his position as Party Secretary. Kamenev and Zinoviev were defeated and the next year they were dropped from the government. In 1927 Trotsky was expelled from the Communist Party and exiled from the USSR. Stalin was now in control.

Q

The Struggle for Power

Trotsky	Stalin
A Jew. There was still a great deal of anti-Semitism in Russia, even among Communists.	A Georgian. Most party leaders were Russian, yet the USSR was supposedly a union of equals, not a Russian Empire.
A member of the bourgeoisie (middle class). Although most leaders of the party were middle class the party was supposed to be a workers' party, and some people felt that he was too intelligent.	The son of a peasant. Stalin portrayed himself as an ordinary person; a man of the people.
Trotsky had been a Menshevik. He had only joined the Bolsheviks in August 1917. Some people felt that he was an opportunist and they did not trust him.	Stalin had supported Lenin since 1903, when the Bolsheviks had split from the Mensheviks.
The hero of the October revolution and the Civil War when he had reorganised the Red Army.	A junior member of the leadership in the October Revolution.
Regarded by Lenin as the most able member of the party leadership.	Regarded by Lenin as rude and not to be trusted with power. Lenin recommended that he should be removed from his position as General Secretary of the party.
Commissar for War. He made no attempt to win support from party members.	General Secretary of the Communist Party. This meant he could reward followers with good jobs in the party. It paid to be loyal to Stalin.
Trotsky supported the policy of 'World Revolution'. The Russian revolution was only the beginning. The main aim of Russian Communists should be to encourage revolutions in other countries. This was unpopular with many Communists.	Stalin supported the policy of 'Socialism in One Country'. Stalin believed that Bolsheviks should concentrate on building socialism in Russia and not worry about revolutions in other countries.

Do you think that Trotsky failed to gain power because of his own failings or because of the strength of Stalin? To answer this question you should first list all the weaknesses of Trotsky. Then look at Stalin to see if he takes advantage of these weaknesses. Also decide whether Stalin's position had strengths which are nothing to do with Trotsky's weaknesses.

Industrialisation

Stalin was convinced that the rich countries in the West wanted to destroy the Communist **Soviet Union**. These countries were far more industrially advanced. So Stalin believed that the USSR must industrialise as quickly as possible to discourage an invasion. In 1931 he declared that 'We are 50 or 100 years behind the advanced countries. We must make good this distance in ten years. Either we do it or we shall be crushed.' The drive to industrialise was to be a national crusade to save the world's only Communist state. No sacrifice would be too great.

A 1930 poster. Workers were expected to write the names of any colleagues who did not work hard enough on the poster. Industrialisation was a crusade for the Soviet Union's very survival. Failure to work hard was seen by Stalin as a crime against the State.

The Dniepr dam. When it was completed in 1932 it was the largest power station in the world.

The pace of industrialisation was to be achieved through a series of Five Year Plans. Every five years the government would set targets that industries would have to meet. The key to industrialisation was heavy industry. New factories were built, especially to the east of the Ural mountains. This was because Stalin was certain that invasion would come from the west as it had done in 1914. The German invasion in the First World War had crippled Russia because so much industry had been captured. By placing so much of the new industry to the east of the Urals Stalin was making sure that the USSR would be able to continue to fight even if it suffered another invasion.

Construction work at Magnitogorsk. This was one of the industrial centres built to the east of the Urals. Huge numbers of workers made up for the lack of modern equipment. Large numbers of the workers died in the terrible conditions. The American, John Scott, visited Magnitogorsk. He estimated that 75 per cent of the workers came to Magnitogorsk through choice because they were desperate for a job.

Q What does this tell you about the Soviet Union under Stalin?

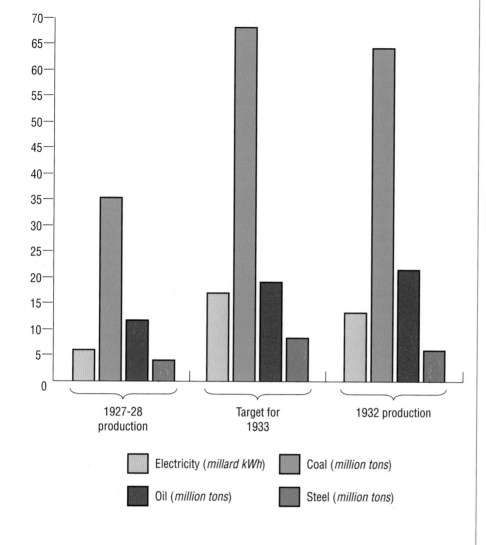

Production targets and achievements for the first Five Year Plan. In 1932 Stalin declared that targets had been met a year early and so a second Five Year Plan with new targets was launched.

○ **Which industries did not meet their production targets for the first Five Year Plan? Does this mean the plan was a failure? Explain your answer with reference to evidence from the text and the other sources.**

Electricity (*millard kWh*)   Coal (*million tons*)

Oil (*million tons*)   Steel (*million tons*)

Collectivisation

In 1929 Stalin announced that individual ownership of land, which Lenin had allowed, was now to be abandoned. Peasants would have to give up their land and be forced to live on collective farms. Those richer peasants, the kulaks, who owned some land of their own, would desperately oppose this policy. Stalin would have to destroy the kulaks to stop them standing in his way.

Stalin had two reasons to carry out collectivisation:

- Collectivisation fitted in with Communist theory. Lenin had allowed private ownership of land because he did not have any choice. The peasants had already seized the land and the Bolsheviks could not stop them.
- Stalin had decided to industrialise at top speed. This would require investment, but the capitalist countries of the West would not invest in a Communist country. So the peasants would have to produce more grain that could be sold abroad. The money earned from this could be used to buy the advanced machinery needed. Industrialisation would also mean more factory workers who needed to be fed. However, the 25 million peasant farms which were spread across the Soviet Union could not produce this surplus food. Most peasants still farmed in the old, inefficient ways. Collectivisation would get rid of small fields and introduce machinery and fertiliser so that crop yields would be much higher.

How was collectivisation carried out?

When Stalin had originally proposed to collectivise agriculture in 1927 he had said it would be a peaceful process. Peasants would have to be convinced that collectivisation was right for them. Undoubtedly many of the 100 million landless peasants were indeed very pleased to be joining a *Kolkhoz* (collective farm). They had nothing to lose, but the richer peasants could see no benefit in giving up their land and animals. Many families killed and ate their animals rather than hand them over to the collectives. In 1929 all peasants were forced to join the collectives. Stalin announced that all opposition from the kulaks, or rich peasants, was to be destroyed. Kulak families were deported and sent to areas far away from their homes. As many as ten million kulaks may have suffered this fate.

▶ Was collectivisation a success?

SOURCE 1:

Stalin's views on collectivisation in 1943, as reported by the British Prime Minister, Winston Churchill:

'It was absolutely necessary for Russia, if we were to avoid famine, to plough the land with tractors. We must mechanise our agriculture . . . We took the greatest trouble to explain it to the peasants. It was no use arguing with them . . . They always answer they do not want the collective farm.'

W Churchill: *The Hinge of Fate*

SOURCE 2:

Stalin addressing the party in 1929:

'We must break down the resistance of the kulaks and deprive this class of its existence. We must eliminate the kulaks as a class. We must smash the kulaks.'

Quoted in Downey: *The USSR*

SOURCE 3:

A Russian view of collectivisation in 1982 (when Russia was still a Communist country):

'Immediately after the end of the Civil War poor peasants showed a desire to work collectively. In the late twenties, when the first tractor plants were built, it became possible for the state to give more funds and machinery to the development of agriculture. After that not only poor but also middle peasants joined the collectives.'

K Tarnovsky: *Illustrated History of the USSR*

SOURCE 4:

The Russian author, Mikhail Sholokov, describes the reactions of peasants to the news that their village was to be collectivised. This is an extract from a novel, but Sholokov did live in the Soviet Union throughout these events:

'Men began slaughtering their cattle every night at Gremyachy . . . They slaughtered oxen, sheep, pigs . . . "Kill, it's not ours now! Kill, the state butchers will do it if you don't. Kill, they won't give you meat in a collective farm." And the villagers killed. They ate until they could eat no more. Young and old had bellyache.'

M Sholokov: *Virgin Soil Upturned*

1 What reason for the collectivisation of agriculture is given in Source 1?
2 Is Stalin's attitude to the peasantry different in Sources 1 and 2? Explain your answer.
3 Do you believe that Source 1 is more or less reliable than Source 2? Explain your answer.
4 What impression does Source 3 give about collectivisation?

5 In what ways is this a different impression to Source 1?
6 According to Source 4, why are the villagers killing their animals?
7 'Source 4 is from a novel. Source 3 is from a history book. Therefore Source 3 must be more reliable than Source 4.' Using the evidence from this chapter show whether you agree or disagree with this statement.

SOURCE 5:

A government photograph from 1931 called 'We will work together'.

SOURCE 6:

A feast on the *Kolkhoz* (collective farm) painted by Gerasimov in 1937.

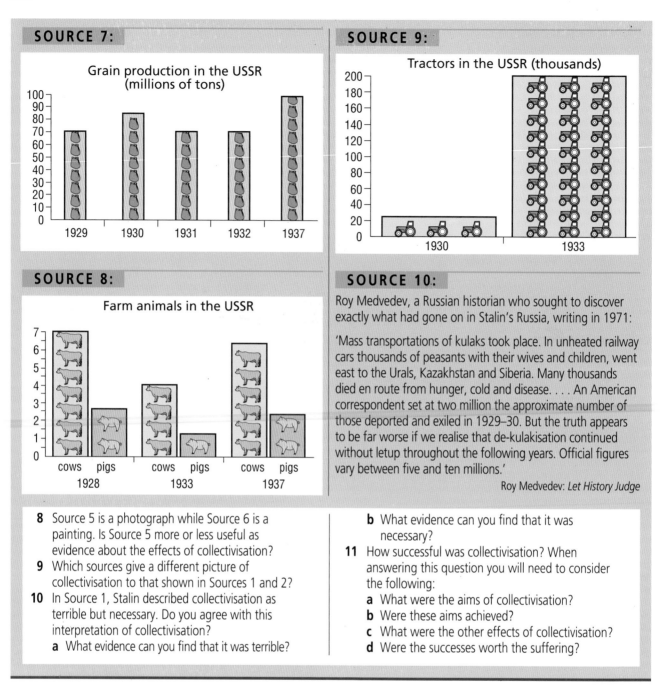

SOURCE 7:

Grain production in the USSR (millions of tons)

1929 / 1930 / 1931 / 1932 / 1937

SOURCE 8:

Farm animals in the USSR

cows pigs 1928 / cows pigs 1933 / cows pigs 1937

SOURCE 9:

Tractors in the USSR (thousands)

1930 / 1933

SOURCE 10:

Roy Medvedev, a Russian historian who sought to discover exactly what had gone on in Stalin's Russia, writing in 1971:

'Mass transportations of kulaks took place. In unheated railway cars thousands of peasants with their wives and children, went east to the Urals, Kazakhstan and Siberia. Many thousands died en route from hunger, cold and disease. . . . An American correspondent set at two million the approximate number of those deported and exiled in 1929–30. But the truth appears to be far worse if we realise that de-kulakisation continued without letup throughout the following years. Official figures vary between five and ten millions.'

Roy Medvedev: *Let History Judge*

8 Source 5 is a photograph while Source 6 is a painting. Is Source 5 more or less useful as evidence about the effects of collectivisation?

9 Which sources give a different picture of collectivisation to that shown in Sources 1 and 2?

10 In Source 1, Stalin described collectivisation as terrible but necessary. Do you agree with this interpretation of collectivisation?
   a What evidence can you find that it was terrible?

   b What evidence can you find that it was necessary?

11 How successful was collectivisation? When answering this question you will need to consider the following:
   a What were the aims of collectivisation?
   b Were these aims achieved?
   c What were the other effects of collectivisation?
   d Were the successes worth the suffering?

The immediate result of the disruption caused by collectivisation was a fall in the grain harvest. This did not cause Stalin to change his policy of exporting grain and building more industry. Communists were sent into the countryside to seize the grain needed, even though this meant that there was not enough left for the peasants. The result was famine in which as many as five million people may have died during 1932 and 1933.

The Purges

At the 1934 Party Conference Kirov, the head of the party in the capital Leningrad,* got as much applause as Stalin. In December 1934 Kirov was shot dead. At the time Stalin ordered that the assassins be discovered and shot. Khrushchev, who succeeded Stalin as leader of Russia, blamed Stalin for ordering the murder of his rival. Over the next four years most of the leaders of

After Lenin's death the old capital of Petrograd had been renamed Leningrad in his honour.

COMRADE STALIN, HAVING RUN OUT OF PLOTTERS, EXECUTES HIMSELF FOR TALKING IN HIS SLEEP.

A cartoon from the Evening Standard.

Q On the floor lie the bodies of Litvinoff and Krilenko. What sort of people do you think they were?
Why do you think that the cartoonist has placed a bust of Marx on the chair?
What is the attitude of the cartoonist towards Stalin? Explain your answer.

the Communist Party who had taken part in the revolution of 1917 were also killed. However, they were not murdered. Instead they were tried for treason in what were known as show trials. Kamenev, Zinoviev, Bukharin and others were sentenced to death for crimes they could not have committed. Yet out of loyalty to the party they accepted their fate. Stalin felt that he could trust very few people. An unknown number of Communists were sent to their deaths in the name of Lenin and Communism.

It was not only the party leaders who were removed. Ordinary Russians were also subjected to Stalin's terror. Hundreds of thousands were executed and millions more were sent to labour camps, the *gulags*, in the frozen wastes of Siberia.

The coming of war

As you will remember, Stalin believed that sooner or later the West would try to destroy the Soviet Union. This did not stop him from extending the purges to the armed forces. Marshal Tukhachevsky was the Commander in Chief of the Red Army. He was a man who had proved his undoubted loyalty to the party when he had destroyed the Kronstadt rebellion in 1921. In 1937 Stalin had him executed without a trial. Over the next four years, two-thirds of all the officers in the Red Army were either executed or sent to the prison camps. This meant that Stalin had decisively weakened the ability of Russia to defend itself at exactly the time that Hitler was building up his armed forces. Stalin also felt that the British and French attitude to Czechoslovakia (see Chapter 6) meant that he could not rely on their support if Hitler chose to attack Russia.

As a result, Stalin stunned the world in August 1939 when he signed a **non-aggression pact** with Nazi Germany. In this the Soviet Union and Germany agreed not to go to war against each other. The pact also contained a secret agreement to divide Poland between the two countries. With this treaty Stalin bought himself almost two years of time in which to build up his armed forces after the terrible effects of the purges. However, on 22 June 1941, Germany did invade the USSR and 20 million of its citizens were to die in the war that followed.

Suren Gazarian describes his experience of being arrested by the NKVD, the secret police who were responsible for the purges:

'Five men beat me viciously. They beat me with fists, feet, birch rods, tightly twisted towel; they beat me with anything anywhere . . . How long they beat me I do not know . . . My shirt had turned to bloody shreds. I lay on the floor in a pool of blood.'

Alexander Solzhenitsyn spent eight years in prison camps for criticising Stalin. This account comes from his novel One Day in the Life of Ivan Denisovich:

'The cold stung. A murky fog wrapped itself around them and made them cough. The temperature out there was 27° below zero. The prisoners, now clad in all their rags, a cord round their wrists, their faces bound from chin to eyes with bits of cloth against the cold, waiting with heavy hearts for the order, "Out you get."'

Germany 1918–39

Part I: Weimar Germany 1918–33

This section focuses on three key issues:

● *Why did democratic government last for such a short time in Germany?*

● *How did democracy survive at all?*

● *Was it inevitable that Hitler became the ruler of Germany?*

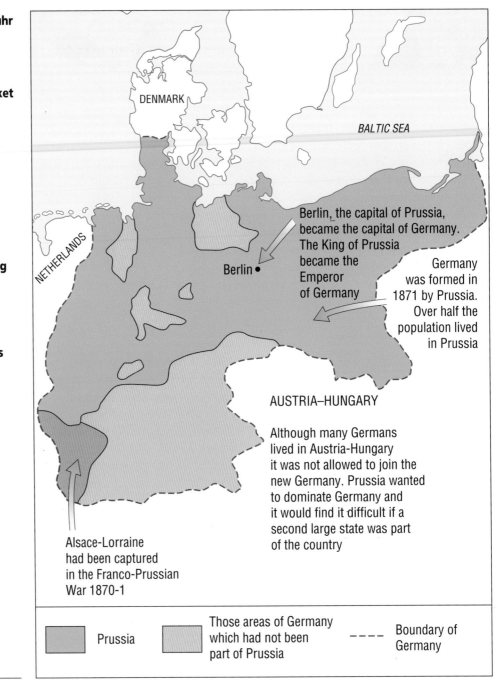

Berlin, the capital of Prussia, became the capital of Germany. The King of Prussia became the Emperor of Germany

Germany was formed in 1871 by Prussia. Over half the population lived in Prussia

AUSTRIA–HUNGARY

Although many Germans lived in Austria-Hungary it was not allowed to join the new Germany. Prussia wanted to dominate Germany and it would find it difficult if a second large state was part of the country

Alsace-Lorraine had been captured in the Franco-Prussian War 1870-1

| | Prussia | | Those areas of Germany which had not been part of Prussia | - - - - | Boundary of Germany |

The birth of Germany.

The Second Reich
Reich *is German for empire. Hundreds of years before, a German empire had controlled central Europe. This was the First Reich, known as the 'Holy Roman Empire'. The term 'the Second Reich' promised that Germany would once again dominate central Europe. When Hitler gained power in Germany in 1933 he called his new Germany the Third Reich.*

THE SECOND REICH

Germany was a new country and had only come into existence in 1871. It was created in Prussia by the Prussian **Chancellor** Otto von Bismarck. However, as the map shows, the new Germany did not contain every German who lived in Europe. In particular, Bismarck made sure that Austria-Hungary was not in his new Germany. This was to have important results. Many Germans who did not live in the new Germany wanted to create a Greater Germany that would include all the areas where Germans lived.

Great Britain, as the first country to industrialise, had become the most powerful country in the nineteenth century with an empire that stretched across the world. However, by the outbreak of the First World War Germany was rivalling Britain's industries and had begun to acquire an empire of its own.

The end of the Second Reich

On 29 September 1918 the Allied troops broke through the German defensive line, the Hindenburg Line. Germany's defeat was now inevitable. The blockade of German ports by the British navy meant that the people were starving and German soldiers and sailors were rebelling against their officers. On 30 October sailors from the German High Seas Fleet refused to take part in a final attack on the British navy. The Germans were faced with defeat and so signed an **armistice** that ended the fighting on 11 November. However, the American President Wilson had insisted that successful peace talks would only occur if Germany became a **democracy**. The German Kaiser (king) William II abdicated the throne and was not replaced.

GERMANY'S PROBLEMS 1919–28

A government in Weimar

Because there was an attempted Communist revolution in Berlin the new government first met in the small town of Weimar. Its first job was to draw up a **constitution** for the new Germany. Therefore, this period, when Germany was ruled by a democratic government, is known as 'Weimar Germany' even though the government soon moved back to Berlin. Elections were held and

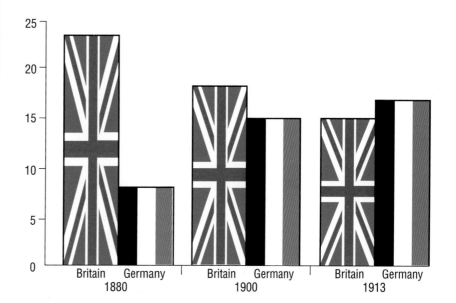

Percentage share of world industrial production.

The German navy mutinies. The sailors use their ammunition to create a gigantic 'firework' display rather than launch a final assault against the British.

the **socialist** Ebert became the first ever President of Germany with his fellow socialist Scheidemann as Chancellor.

Weimar Germany lasted only 15 years. Why did democratic government last for such a short time in Germany? The usual answer is that a huge number of problems gradually crushed the government. Many of these problems happened in the first few years. There appears to have been more problems in 1923 than at any other time. It is not simply a question of why Weimar Germany lasted for such a short time, but why it actually survived for as long as it did. Why did it finally end in 1933 rather than ten years earlier?

The Treaty of Versailles

The armistice that had been signed meant that Germany had surrendered. However, Ebert and the Germans did not expect the harsh terms outlined in the Treaty of Versailles that were presented to the Germans in June 1919. Germany lost 13 per cent of its territory containing 48 per cent of its iron production, 15 per cent of its agricultural production and almost six million of its people. Look at the map on page 59. There were so many punishments. Germany was only allowed to have a small army of 100 000 men. None of them could be kept in the Rhineland, the area next to France. Germany could not have an airforce and the navy could not have any battleships. Worst of all was the War Guilt Clause, which blamed the war entirely on Germany. Germany was also given a bill of £6600 million to repair the damage done by both sides in the war. Scheidemann resigned as Chancellor rather than accept the terms but Germany still had to sign. If they refused the Allies would simply invade their country.

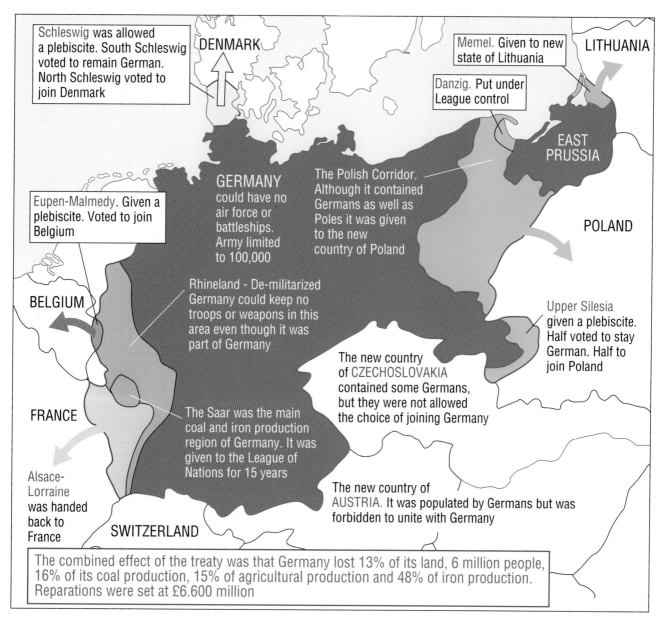

The map contains the following labels:

Schleswig was allowed a plebiscite. South Schleswig voted to remain German. North Schleswig voted to join Denmark

DENMARK

Memel. Given to new state of Lithuania

LITHUANIA

Danzig. Put under League control

EAST PRUSSIA

Eupen-Malmedy. Given a plebiscite. Voted to join Belgium

GERMANY could have no air force or battleships. Army limited to 100,000

The Polish Corridor. Although it contained Germans as well as Poles it was given to the new country of Poland

POLAND

BELGIUM

Rhineland - De-militarized Germany could keep no troops or weapons in this area even though it was part of Germany

Upper Silesia given a plebiscite. Half voted to stay German. Half to join Poland

FRANCE

The new country of CZECHOSLOVAKIA contained some Germans, but they were not allowed the choice of joining Germany

The Saar was the main coal and iron production region of Germany. It was given to the League of Nations for 15 years

Alsace-Lorraine was handed back to France

SWITZERLAND

The new country of AUSTRIA. It was populated by Germans but was forbidden to unite with Germany

The combined effect of the treaty was that Germany lost 13% of its land, 6 million people, 16% of its coal production, 15% of agricultural production and 48% of iron production. Reparations were set at £6.600 million

The effect of the Treaty of Versailles on Germany.

The treaty left many German people feeling humiliated and wanting revenge for the way that the Allies had treated their country. The cost of the **reparations** threatened to affect everyone in Germany. Many Germans blamed the new government for signing the armistice that had led to the treaty. They referred to the government as the 'November Criminals' because of the fact that the armistice had been signed in November. The government was accused of stabbing the German army in the back because the army would have won the war if the armistice had not been signed. This, of course, was not true. However, the fact that many Germans came to believe this 'stab in the back' theory meant that the new democratic government was blamed for the humiliation caused by the Treaty of Versailles. It might have been more accurate to blame the Kaiser for leading Germany into the war, or the army leaders for recommending an armistice. Nonetheless, it was the government that was blamed.

1 Why were so many Germans likely to believe the 'stab in the back' theory?

2 Look at the map showing the effect of the Treaty of Versailles on Germany. Make a list of all the punishments that the German people would have thought were unfair.

Q

Germans protest against the Treaty of Versailles.

Do you think that this was surprising?

The Weimar constitution

A constitution is a set of rules for governing a country. The new German constitution established democracy in Germany. It stated that the leaders of Germany would be elected. The day-to-day government of the country would be carried out by a **chancellor** and he would have to have the support of the majority of MPs in the parliament, the **Reichstag**. However, the chosen voting system was **proportional representation.** This meant that if a party won only one per cent of the votes cast, it got one per cent of the MPs in the Reichstag. This encouraged the formation of a large number of parties since they were almost guaranteed to get at least one MP into the Reichstag. With so many parties standing in elections it was impossible for any one party to get more than 50 per cent of the MPs required to form a government. Therefore governments had to consist of groups of parties joining together to form a **coalition** government. Since these parties had different aims it sometimes made it difficult for the government to agree on policies. The constitution allowed the chancellor to temporarily abandon democracy and rule by Presidential Decree when the parties couldn't agree. This meant that if the Reichstag refused to pass a law the president could overrule it.

Although a democratic government was being set up in Germany, many Germans did not want democracy. Groups of these people tried to take over the government of Germany.

The Spartacists

The Spartacists were a group of **Communists** led by Karl Liebknecht and Rosa Luxembourg. They took their name from the Roman slave Spartacus who had led a slave revolt 2000 years earlier. They were also trying to follow the example of the Bolsheviks who had taken control of Russia in 1917. In January 1919 they attempted to take control of Berlin. After two weeks the revolution was defeated. It had been crushed by the *Freikorps*. These were ex-soldiers who formed themselves into unofficial armed groups at the end of the war. They hated Communism and they were helped by the regular army, the *Reichswehr*, who gave them weapons.

The Kapp Putsch

The *Freikorps* not only hated Communism, they also hated the humiliation of the Treaty of Versailles and the new German government that had signed it. In 1920 a group of *Freikorps*, led by Dr Kapp, attempted to take power in Berlin. The army refused to stop them. However, the workers of Berlin did not support the *Freikorps* and so they went on strike. Kapp and the *Freikorps* found that they could not govern Berlin and so the revolt ended.

The Munich Putsch

Between 1921 and 1923 there were many attempts by extreme groups to seize control of various German cities. They all failed. The most famous example came in November 1923 when Adolf Hitler tried to take control in Munich, the capital of the huge south German state of Bavaria (see page 64). The Munich Putsch failed because the police fired on Hitler and his supporters.

A worker in Berlin is held captive by Freikorps *supporters of Kapp.*

> **Q** **What does this photograph tell you about the *Freikorps*?**

Hyper-inflation

Germany had to send large quantities of goods to France and Belgium as war reparations. This meant that there was a shortage of goods in Germany and so prices rose. The German government also printed more money to pay reparations and to pay workers. This just made the inflation worse. In 1923 inflation suddenly shot out of control. In 1918 a loaf of bread had cost 60 pfennigs, that is 0.6 marks. By January 1923 it cost 230 marks and by September the price had rocketed to an unbelievable one and a half million marks. Workers had to be paid twice a day and they brought wheelbarrows and suitcases to carry home their wages.

German money had become almost worthless. Many people suffered. It was particularly bad if you were on a fixed income and there was no way you could increase your pay. (An example would be a pensioner.) If you had money in the bank then your life savings were wiped out. Not everyone suffered, however. Many businessmen did well; high inflation could lead to big profits especially as the increase in wages did not keep pace with the increase in prices. Many

A huge pile of worthless German bank notes.

businessmen had also borrowed money from the banks and these debts were wiped out. The rise in prices was also good for farmers. In a period of serious inflation food prices will always rise highest. People will give up buying less essential goods before they stop buying food!

Invasion of the Ruhr 1923

By January 1923 Germany had fallen behind with reparation payments to Belgium and France. As a result, French and Belgian troops were sent into the Ruhr, the industrial centre of Germany. The Ruhr is sited in the Rhineland so there were no German soldiers to stop the invading troops. The French and Belgians had decided to take the goods that they needed, rather than wait for the Germans to send them. However, the German workers in the Ruhr went on strike as a protest against the invasion. This meant that even fewer goods were being produced in Germany and so this made the inflation even worse. The strikers became heroes amongst the German people. They were opposing the humiliating Treaty of Versailles and showing that Germany refused to be crushed. The German government also printed more money to pay the strikers. Combined with the collapse in production this helped to turn inflation into hyper-inflation.

Why did democracy survive in 1923?

In 1923 the Germans suffered an invasion by foreign troops that they were powerless to stop. Hyper-inflation had also destroyed the savings of millions of people. It seemed an ideal time for desperate people to turn their backs on democracy and support one of the extremist groups that were trying to seize power. Yet this did not happen.

Gustav Stresemann became the new Chancellor in August. Although he was the head of a coalition government he was not prevented from taking decisive action. He introduced a new currency, the Rentenmark, to replace the old worthless mark. He ordered the striking workers of the Ruhr back to work, and agreed that Germany would start to pay reparations again. Germany was rewarded with the introduction of the Dawes Plan in 1924. America agreed to loan Germany 800 million marks. The Germans could use this to build new factories which would produce jobs and goods that would raise the standard of living for German people. In 1925 the French and Belgian troops left the Ruhr. Democratic government was being successful and so the people were willing to give democracy a chance.

French soldiers in the Ruhr in 1923.

> **❓ How do you think you would feel if your country was occupied by foreign troops?**

The successes continued. The German economy recovered and soon many Germans were enjoying a higher standard of living. Other countries began to treat Germany as an equal. In 1925 Germany and France signed the Treaty of Locarno in which they agreed never to try and change the border between them. In 1926 Germany was allowed to join the League of Nations. Finally the Young Plan was introduced in 1929 and it reduced reparations by over 67 per cent. Stresemann died in October 1929, having apparently led Germany to a complete recovery from the disaster of the First World War.

One of the most important questions that a historian has to answer is 'Why?'; in this case 'Why did democracy survive in 1923?' It is never easy. There is no simple explanation and that is not just because there are several reasons. The reasons interact with one another and they are not always as equally important as each other. To show how this works we will look at the example of German hyper-inflation.

1 The table below gives three reasons for this inflation. Draw the table in your book and then explain how each of the reasons led to hyper-inflation.

Reason	Effect
1. Reparations.	
2. The invasion of the French and Belgian troops.	
3. The German government's support for the strikers.	

2 Pick any one of the causes and pretend that it did not happen. Write down how you think the other two causes would have been affected. Would inflation have been as bad, or would it have happened at all?

3 Which cause do you think would have had the greatest effect on hyper-inflation? Which of the three causes has the greatest effect when you remove it?

4 Why did foreign invasion and hyper-inflation not cause the German people to abandon democracy? Below is a table of reasons. Again explain how each of them led to support for the government.

Reason	Effect
1. Some people benefited from hyper-inflation.	
2. The army was loyal to democracy.	
3. The German army was not strong enough to drive out the invading army.	
4. The government took decisive action.	
5. The USA was willing to help a democratic Germany.	

5 By leaving out each reason in turn decide which is the most important. Explain your answer.

Q **Why was it possible for a Briton to eat so well in Germany?**

Q **How do you think that this German would react to the situation described by the Englishman in the restaurant? Give your reasons.**

An argument with Hitler, as reported by his supporter Otto Strasser:

'Power,' screamed Adolf. 'We must have power.'
'Before we gain it,' I replied firmly, 'let us decide what we propose to do with it . . .'
Hitler . . . thumped the table and barked: 'Power first! Afterwards we can act as required.'

Otto Strasser: *Hitler and I*

WHO WERE THE NAZIS?

In 1923 Hitler and the Nazi Party were one of the extremist groups that tried to take power. Ten years later they would succeed. But who were they and what did they believe in?

Their full title was the NSDAP, the German National Socialist Workers Party. They were a nationalist party that wanted to make Germany great again. This meant that they wanted to destroy the Treaty of Versailles (see page 58). They believed that Germany should stop paying reparations and should take back all the land taken from them by the treaty. However, the Nazi demands went much further than this. They wanted to set up a German *Reich*, an empire made up of all the German-speaking people. They would continue the work begun by Bismarck. Yet their policies were not merely nationalist, they were also racist. They believed that the Germans were superior to all other people. Non-German people would not be allowed to be citizens of the *Reich*. Jews were regarded as the lowest of all the non-German races. This **anti-Semitism** was not a creation of the Nazis. It was common among many of the extreme parties. It was especially common among Germans, like Hitler himself, who had not been born in Germany. (Hitler was born in Austria.) These people were often far more extreme in their German nationalism and in their hatred of other races than were Germans born in Germany. Yet this extreme nationalism was only part of the Nazi programme. They were also the German Workers Party. They wanted to remove money from the rich for the benefit of the workers. Any income not earned by work was to be abolished. All large industrial companies were to have their profits shared among the workers. However, it is doubtful that Hitler was committed to these improvements for the workers.

The Munich Putsch 1923

As we saw on pages 60–1 the Nazis were just one of a number of extreme groups who tried to seize power in the early years of the Weimar government. In late 1923 Hitler thought the time was right for a revolution in Germany. The new Chancellor Stresemann had just agreed to end the strike in the Ruhr and to start paying reparations again. Hitler felt sure that most Germans would feel disgusted by this. He hoped that they would support a party that promised to oppose France and stop paying reparations. Hitler even managed to gain the support of General Ludendorff who had commanded the German army on the Western Front in the First World War. He was a national hero. Hitler hoped that Germans who had never heard of the Nazis would follow Ludendorff. Hitler's first plan was to seize control of the government of Bavaria and then to march on Berlin. In fact Hitler never even managed to gain control in Bavaria. On 9 November he set off from a beer hall towards the Bavarian parliament building. He was accompanied by Ludendorff and 3000 Nazis. The Bavarian police stood in his way and fired on the Nazis. Sixteen of Hitler's supporters were killed and so were three policemen. Hitler was arrested and sentenced to five years' imprisonment. He only served nine months.

The *Sturm Abteilung*

The men who marched with Hitler to the Bavarian parliament were members of the SA, the *Sturm Abteilung* or storm troopers. They wore brown uniforms and so were also known as 'brownshirts'. When the SA was formed in 1921 the Nazi newspaper, the *Volkischer Beobachter*, described it as the party's gymnastic and sports section. In fact it was mainly made up of ex-soldiers, the *Freikorps*. These were men who felt betrayed by the Weimar government. The SA offered them a new uniform in which to fight for Germany. They would disrupt the meetings of Hitler's opponents and often beat up opposition supporters.

(below) The SA gave uniforms and purpose to many ex-soldiers who felt betrayed by the Treaty of Versailles.

GERMANY'S PROBLEMS 1929–33

The collapse of Weimar Germany

In 1923 the German government successfully overcame the terrible problems that it faced. By 1928 industrial production had almost doubled when compared to 1920. Yet in 1933 the democratic government ended as Adolf Hitler and the Nazis took control. Although Hitler was the leader of what was now the largest party in the Reichstag he did not believe in democracy and during 1933 and 1934 he set about destroying it and setting up a **dictatorship** with himself as the all-powerful leader, or *Führer*. Why did democracy survive the crisis of 1923 and yet fail to survive ten years later? What were the problems that made the difference?

'Work, Freedom and Bread'. A Nazi election poster of 1932. The Nazis are appealing to the German people with this poster, promoting the idea of bread and work before repayment of war reparations (see page 64).

Q In what ways do Hitler's argument with Otto Strasser on page 64 and this poster give a different picture of Nazi policies? Why do you think that the Nazis had such policies?

Some of the problems were still the same:

- **The Treaty of Versailles**. Many Germans felt humiliated by the Treaty of Versailles and the reduced level of reparations did not change these feelings. They would not be satisfied until the treaty had been destroyed. These people were upset by Stresemann's willingness to accept the treaty by continuing to pay reparations.

- **The Weimar Constitution**. The Weimar Constitution was still the same. No party could gain a majority and so there were coalition governments. After 1928, however, the SPD or Socialists (the largest party) joined the coalition government and so it was easier for the government to pass laws than it had been in 1923. The Socialists did not like some of the policies proposed by the other parties in the government. They did not want to spend money rebuilding Germany's armed forces once the Treaty of Versailles allowed it. This of course made the government unpopular with the armed forces. The Socialists did not want to see any cuts in the standard of living of working people either.

These two problems were present in both 1923 and 1933 and so they cannot be the only reason for the collapse of democracy.

World Depression

The Wall Street Crash happened on 24 October 1929. This immediately created serious problems for Germany. The German economic boom had been based on loans from American banks. These banks now faced crisis in America and needed money and so they demanded that Germany repay the loans. German industrial production slumped. Factories were producing less and so were forced to make some of their workers unemployed. This meant that there were fewer people with the money to buy goods and so factories sold still fewer goods and even more workers had to be laid off. In 1928, 1.4 million Germans were unemployed. By 1931 this figure had risen to 4.5 million. Many people lost faith in democracy because it could not provide them with a job. When elections were held in 1930 the extremist Nazis (see page 70) won 107 seats; a dramatic rise from just 13 in 1928.

'Our last hope'. A Nazi election poster. Hitler promised a solution to the problem of unemployment. As unemployment rose many people felt that the government parties had failed Germany.

Government reaction to the Depression

The Depression created serious problems for the government. So many people were without a job that they had to pay large amounts of money in unemployment benefit and with fewer people in work, there were fewer people who were paying taxes to the government.

The government simply did not have enough money. To print money would have risked the return of hyper-inflation, so the government had to either cut unemployment benefit or raise the taxes of those people who still had a job. In March 1930 Chancellor Brüning of the Centre Party proposed a two and a half per cent tax increase on those people employed by the government. The SPD refused to agree to this and so left the coalition. Brüning no longer had a majority in the Reichstag. Instead he introduced the increases using the Presidential Decree (see page 60). He also cut unemployment benefit by five per cent and cut the pay of government employees by 23 per cent. The Socialists would never have agreed to all these measures that were introduced by Presidential Decree. Whereas the government had remained united in the face of the hyper-inflation of 1923, it became divided when faced with the problems created by the Depression.

Faced with ever rising unemployment Brüning resigned in May 1932 and was replaced by Von Papen. Von Papen called elections in July. He hoped that those parties that supported the government would be able to win a majority so that they could make laws democratically rather than having to rely on Presidential Decree. It did not work. Democratic government had left many people unemployed and discontented and so the voters turned in large numbers to a party that did not support democracy: the Nazi Party. The Nazis won 230 seats, far more than any other party. However, they had not won 50 per cent of the seats and so could not govern on their own.

Von Papen continued as Chancellor and held new elections in November to try and win more seats. The tactic failed again and Von Papen was replaced as Chancellor by General von Schleicher. He resigned in January 1933 when Hindenburg refused to allow him to govern by Presidential Decree and Hitler became the new Chancellor of Germany. The leaders of the Centre Party, such as Von Papen, hoped to use the support of the Nazi Party to stay in power and thought that they could dominate Hitler. Von Papen became Hitler's Vice-chancellor. In fact Weimar Germany had only a few months to live.

SUPPORT FOR THE NAZIS

It was not simply because 38 per cent of the voters had chosen to support the Nazis in July 1932 that the Nazis were so powerful. They had also won the support of important sectors of society. Weimar Germany had seen a growth in the power of the trade unions and an increase in the wages and working conditions of working people. With Germany in a depression businessmen wanted to cut wages and benefits. Hitler promised to destroy the trade unions and give businessmen more power. Many powerful businessmen such as the steel boss Thyssen and the armaments manufacturer Krupp were now willing to lend their support to Hitler.

The army leaders were also attracted to Hitler and the Nazi Party because he promised to destroy the Treaty of Versailles and build up Germany's armed forces. The army might not openly support Hitler but they would not stop him coming to power. They would not stop Hitler from destroying democracy.

A Nazi supporter, Kurt Ludecke, remembers his reaction to a speech by Hitler:

'My ability to think was swept away . . . he was holding everyone, and me with him, under an hypnotic spell.'

Quoted in Lee: *Nazi Germany*

'The meaning of the Hitler salute'. An anti-Hitler montage by John Heartfield 1932.

Q **What is the artist suggesting about Hitler's support?**

By 1932 Hitler was a nationally-known politician whereas, in 1923, he had only been known in Bavaria. His trial after the Munich Putsch had made him famous. In jail he had written *Mein Kampf* ('My Struggle') which gave more people a chance to read his violent nationalist and racist views. During the election campaigns he used posters and mass meetings to press home his message. In the spring of 1932 he stood for the position of president against the now 84-year-old war hero Hindenburg. Although Hitler was defeated he gained a very respectable 13 million votes and as Hindenburg had not campaigned, Hitler had the whole of Germany listening to him.

Q

1 What reasons can you find to explain the growth in support for the Nazi Party?
2 Why was Hitler able to come to power in 1933 but not in 1923? To answer this question you will need to look at a number of areas such as: The Treaty of Versailles; the level of support for the Nazis; Hitler's tactics; the Weimar Constitution; the Depression and the actions of the other political parties. For each of these you will have to decide if they were significantly different in the two years. You could write up to 250 words for this answer.

► Who voted for the Nazis?

SOURCE 1:

Hugh Thomas, an English writer in 1995:

'But once . . . Hitler's rabble rousing . . . had fascinated the working class, and once they had been provided with ready scapegoats such as the Jews, Hitler's assumption of power was almost cascade-like [inevitable] in its certainty.'

Hugh Thomas: *Doppelgangers*

SOURCE 2:

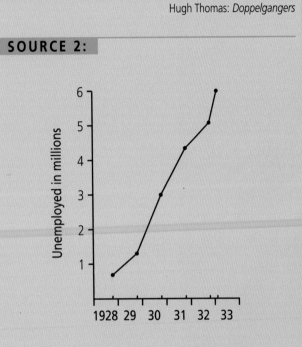

Unemployment in Germany 1928–33

SOURCE 3:

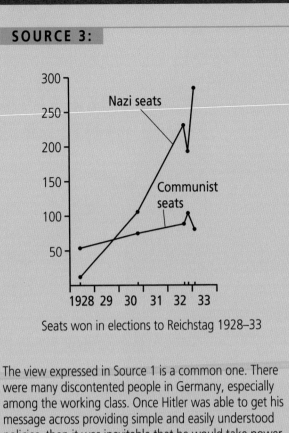

Seats won in elections to Reichstag 1928–33

The view expressed in Source 1 is a common one. There were many discontented people in Germany, especially among the working class. Once Hitler was able to get his message across providing simple and easily understood policies, then it was inevitable that he would take power. He appeared to be the right man in the right place. Yet historians must beware of such interpretations. If we look closely at the evidence we may find that Hitler taking power was not the only possible outcome of Germany's desperation at the beginning of the 1930s.

---

1 Look at Source 2. In which year is unemployment at its highest in Germany?
2 Look at Source 3. In which year is the Nazi vote at its highest?
3 Compare Sources 2 and 3. What impression do they give of the reasons that more and more people were voting for the Nazis?
4 Do Sources 2 and 3 confirm the point made by Source 1? Give your reasons.

5 In Source 1 Hugh Thomas says that the working class became 'fascinated' by Hitler's message. In other words he believes that they were more likely to be attracted to Hitler and the Nazis than other groups. Do you agree with this interpretation? Use the evidence from this chapter so far to support your argument.

It would seem from Sources 2 and 3 that as more people lost their jobs they were willing to turn to the Nazis. The failure of the German government to deal with the Depression meant that Hitler was bound to succeed. However, if we look more closely at the evidence, a different picture begins to appear. The workers who were losing their jobs had traditionally voted for the socialists because they had helped them gain better wages and working conditions. If these workers no longer wanted democracy, the Communist Party offered them a more obvious alternative than the Nazis. The Socialist Party, the SPD, wanted to bring about socialism by winning elections. The Communists stood for achieving socialism through revolution.

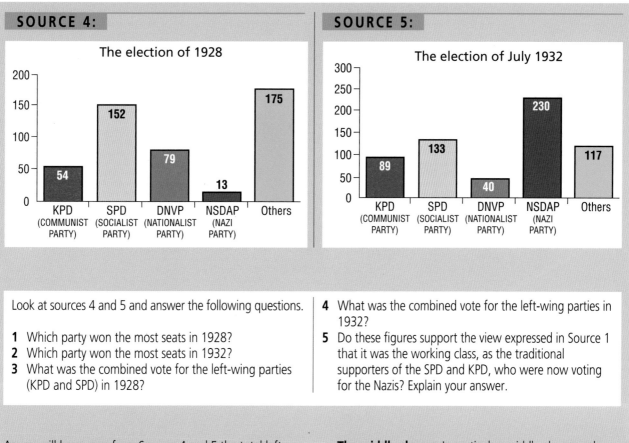

SOURCE 4:

The election of 1928

SOURCE 5:

The election of July 1932

Look at sources 4 and 5 and answer the following questions.

1 Which party won the most seats in 1928?
2 Which party won the most seats in 1932?
3 What was the combined vote for the left-wing parties (KPD and SPD) in 1928?

4 What was the combined vote for the left-wing parties in 1932?
5 Do these figures support the view expressed in Source 1 that it was the working class, as the traditional supporters of the SPD and KPD, who were now voting for the Nazis? Explain your answer.

As you will have seen from Sources 4 and 5 the total left-wing vote did not decline during the Depression. Therefore it was not the industrial working class in the big cities that voted for the Nazis. While the Nazis received 38 per cent of the vote in the whole of Germany in 1932 they only got 28 per cent in the Ruhr, the main industrial area of Germany. In contrast the Communists won as much as 70 per cent of the votes in some Ruhr towns. We need to look elsewhere for the new Nazis. They are to be found in three very different areas:

- **The countryside**. It was in rural areas of Germany that the Nazis first became popular after 1923. Although the German economy recovered quickly from hyper-inflation, agricultural prices slumped. Remember that food prices had been very high in 1923. Farmers were unhappy that they were suffering when other people were doing well. These farmers turned to the Nazis.

- **The middle classes**. In particular, middle-class people who worked for the government were likely to vote for Hitler. This is hardly surprising after the government of Brüning had cut their wages by 23 per cent at the same time as they had raised their taxes. Middle-class people who did not work for the government also voted for the Nazis. They feared that the unemployed working class might lead a Communist revolution which would destroy the middle class.

- **The working class outside the big cities**. We have seen that the workers in the cities did not vote for the Nazis in large numbers. These workers were usually members of trade unions who continued to support the SPD and Communists. However, most workers outside the big cities worked for small family firms. They did not belong to unions and were likely to vote for the Nazis.

Was it inevitable that Hitler took control of Germany?

Was it really inevitable that Hitler came to power? Remember the Nazis did not win more than 38 per cent of the vote at any stage. The vast majority of Germans did not vote for Hitler. The election of November 1932 finally led to Hitler becoming Chancellor. Yet in that election, the Nazis won just 196 seats, while the combined vote of the KPD and the SPD was 241 seats. If the left-wing parties had worked together they could have become the new government. However, the Communist parties in Europe were dominated by the Soviet Union. The Russian leader Stalin ordered the KPD not to work with the SPD. He saw the SPD as the main opponent in the struggle to gain the working-class vote.

In the early stages of the Depression Germany had been governed by the Grand Coalition of the SPD with the smaller centre parties. If the SPD had stayed in the coalition then Von Papen would not have had to turn to the Nazis for support.

There were other possibilities. A Socialist-Communist coalition could have occurred or the Grand Coalition could have been reformed. The leaders of the other parties failed to realise the danger that Hitler posed. Through the miscalculations of the leaders of the KPD, SPD and the Centre Party Hitler was allowed to come to power and he had no intention of letting go.

Q

1 Do you think that it was inevitable that Hitler became the ruler of Germany?
2 What reasons are given in the text to suggest that Hitler's rise to power was not inevitable?
3 Do you believe that Hitler could have been prevented from coming to power? Give your reasons. To answer this question look back at the material in the 'Collapse of Weimar Germany' on pages 65–7. Look at your answer to question 2 on page 69.

Part II: The Nazi State 1933–39

This section focuses on two key issues:

- *How did the Nazis control Germany?*
- *What was it like to live in Nazi Germany?*

SETTING UP A DICTATORSHIP

Although Hitler became the Chancellor of Germany he was only the leader of a coalition government. Only two members of his government were fellow Nazis – the First World War flying ace Hermann Goering and Wilhelm Frick. So Hitler called new elections in the hope that he could win more than 50 per cent of the vote and be able to rule without other parties. He did have advantages that no previous chancellor had enjoyed. Goering was the Prussian Minister of the Interior. He controlled the police in about two-thirds of Germany. The police were instructed to leave the SA alone. This meant that the Nazis were able to attack their opponents without being arrested. In February the Reichstag building burnt down (see page 76). Hitler used this as an excuse to arrest leading Communists and so make it far more difficult for the KPD to win. Despite all of these advantages the Nazis still won only 44 per cent of the vote in the election of March 1933.

In the next few months Hitler established a dictatorship in Germany. (A dictatorship is a government without opposition that is able to do whatever it wants.) One by one, Hitler removed all possible sources of opposition.

The Reichstag

There were 485 MPs in the Reichstag who belonged to parties that opposed the Nazis. Hitler could only rule with the support of the nationalists, the DNVP. He avoided this problem with the Enabling Act. The Act gave Hitler the power to make any law he wanted without needing a vote in the Reichstag. It might seem surprising that the members of the Reichstag would agree to this but it should be remembered that governments in Germany had been ruling in a similar way for the last three years through Presidential Decree. Hitler had also banned the KPD so that they could not vote against the Enabling Act. Many people were happy to see the Communists banned. They blamed the Communists for the increased violence on the streets of German towns, even though much of it was carried out by the SA and the similar nationalist group, the *Stahlheim*.

Political parties

The KPD were the first party to be banned. Other parties soon followed. In May the socialist SPD were banned. In July the other parties, some of whom had helped Hitler to become Chancellor, were also banned. The NSDAP was now the only party in Germany. The leaders of the Communists and the Socialists were arrested and put in concentration camps. The first of these camps was opened at Dachau in March 1933. It was not just the leaders who were arrested. Of the 300 000 Germans who were members of the KPD in January 1933 half would end up in the concentration camps. 30 000 of them would die there.

Trade unions

The trade unions were very closely associated with the left-wing parties and so they were natural opponents of the Nazis. In May all trade unions were abolished. Strikes were made illegal.

An election poster produced by the Socialists before Hitler came to power. It predicts that the Nazis would tie the workers in chains.

Q Was this an accurate prediction?

Regional goverment

Remember that Germany had only been founded in 1871. The once independent countries that joined the new Germany became states or *Länder*. These were run by elected governors, many of whom opposed Hitler's policies. In April 1933 Hitler replaced these elected governors with Reich governors who were appointed by Hitler. All 18 Reich governors were Nazis.

(above) 'They salute with both hands now.' A British cartoon about the Night of the Long Knives.

The Night of the Long Knives

Within just four months Hitler had removed most of the sources of opposition to Nazi rule. Hitler now turned on part of the Nazi Party, the SA. This might seem surprising but look back to page 64 and read Otto Strasser's report on Hitler. Hitler wanted total power. He was not concerned about policies. Many members of the SA, under their leader Ernst Röhm, expected Hitler to take wealth from the rich and give it to the workers. Hitler had no use for policies that frightened the rich. He had carefully won the support of rich businessmen like Krupp. Röhm also wanted the SA to take over the army but Hitler needed the support of the army; it had an important role in the new Germany if the Treaty of Versailles was to be overthrown. Now that he was in power Hitler had much less use for the SA. Their role had been to help him to gain power.

On 30 June 1933 'Operation Hummingbird' was launched. Under the direction of Goering the leaders of the SA were arrested and shot. Hitler used the opportunity to kill many other opponents, such as former Chancellor von Schleicher. This became known as the 'Night of the Long Knives'. As many as 1000 of Hitler's opponents may have died on this occasion.

The President

President Hindenburg had the power to choose another chancellor. He was the only person left who could oppose Hitler. However, in August Hindenburg died. No one opposed Hitler when it was announced that he would become President as well as Chancellor. He was now the all-powerful *Führer*. Hitler had won the support of the army by destroying the leaders of the SA. The army now swore an oath of allegiance to Hitler.

(below) A letter from Röhm to Hitler:

'I regard the Reichswehr (army) now as only a training school for the German people. The conduct of the war in the future is the task of the SA.'
Quoted in Lee: *Nazi Germany*

Röhm on Hitler. A report of a private conversation:

'Adolf is a swine . . . His old friends aren't good enough for him . . . Adolf knows what I want. I've told him often enough. Not a second edition of the old imperial army. Are we revolutionaries or aren't we?'
Quoted in Rauschning: *Hitler Speaks*

Q How do the quotations above help to explain why Hitler took the actions which are referred to in the cartoon on this page? What reasons for Hitler's actions are not referred to?

Who was responsible for the fire which burnt down the Reichstag?

The Reichstag was the German parliament building. It was a symbol of democracy in Germany. In March 1933 Reichstag elections were to be held. Hitler hoped to get 50 per cent of the votes so that the Nazis could rule Germany without coalition partners. On the evening of 27 February 1933 the Reichstag building burnt down.

Who was responsible?

The authorities were in no doubt. A young Dutch Communist, Marinus Van der Lubbe, was arrested at the Reichstag. He was carrying matches and firelighters. As Source 3 shows, Van der Lubbe admitted that he was guilty.

SOURCE 1:   The Reichstag in flames on 27 February.

SOURCE 2:

Van der Lubbe on trial for the Reichstag fire.

SOURCE 3:

Van der Lubbe in a statement to the police:

'As to the question whether I acted alone. I declare absolutely that this was the case. No one helped me at all'.

Quoted in Traynor: *Europe 1890–1990*

SOURCE 4:

Rudolf Diels, the head of the Berlin police:

'The voluntary confessions of Marinus Van der Lubbe prevented me from thinking that an arsonist who was such an expert in his folly needed any helpers. Why should not a single match be enough to set fire to the cold yet inflammable splendour of the chamber . . . and the bone dry wooden panelling? But this specialist had used a whole knapsack full of inflammable material. He had been so active that he had laid several fires.'

Quoted in Noakes and Pridham, *Nazism 1919–45*

The criminal had been caught red-handed and had confessed. Yet Van der Lubbe's story did not convince everyone. Hitler and Goering did not believe him. They declared that the fire was part of a Communist plot to overthrow democracy. Leading Communists were put in prison.

SOURCE 5:

Goering's opinion:

'The moment I heard the word "arson", I knew the Communist Party was guilty and had set the Reichstag on fire.'

Quoted from Mommsen in *Aspects of the Third Reich*

Look at Sources 3, 4 and 5.
1 In what way do the three sources agree?
2 Why does Diels say that he believed Van der Lubbe?
3 What evidence can you find in Diels' account that might lead to the conclusion that more than one person was involved?
4 At the time of his statement, do you think that Diels still believed that Van der Lubbe acted on his own? Give your reason.
5 Why might Diels have wished to change his opinion?
6 Do you think that Source 4 is reliable evidence if we wish to discover who burnt down the Reichstag?

Was it really a Communist plot? British newspapers of the time were not convinced, as the report of the trial given in Source 6 shows.

SOURCE 6:

The *Daily Telegraph*, 6 December 1933:

'The reasoned judgement in the Reichstag fire trial, which was read by the judge, Dr Bünger, at Leipzig on Saturday, fell into two sections . . . The first part of the judgement was a clear and even ruthless analysis of the evidence. This confirmed in full the impression which I had conveyed in my previous messages that many of the witnesses upon which the prosecution based their case were thoroughly unreliable. Among the points contained in the judgement were: Van der Lubbe is guilty of treason, the act being arson with intent to bring about a revolution . . . Lubbe could not possibly have fired the Reichstag alone but his accomplices are unknown . . . The second portion of the judgement was more like an election speech than a legal opinion. A highly controversial attack on the Communist party, it was evidently intended to appease the wilder Nazis. Their views have been put forward on more than one occasion during the trial and their spokesmen are General Goering and the notorious Breslau Chief of Police Lt Heines.'

7 Does Source 3 support the conclusion of Source 6? Give your reasons.
8 According to Source 6, does the court support the view of Source 5 or not?
9 Does the writer of Source 6 believe that the court had given the right verdict?

If the German court had got it right, just who were these unknown accomplices who had helped Van der Lubbe to start the fire? Did it require more than one person to set light to so many fires? The historian Professor Alan Bullock gives one view in Source 7. Support for his viewpoint came in some of the evidence given at the Nuremberg Trials. At the end of the war, important Nazis who had been captured were put on trial. After his trial Goering committed suicide. Halder also gave evidence but he was not a trusted advisor of Hitler by this time. In 1942 he had been replaced as Chief of Staff after disagreeing with Hitler over the invasion of Russia.

SOURCE 7:

Alan Bullock, writing in 1952:

'Goering and Goebbels were looking for some excuse to smash the Communist Party. After rejecting various plans – such as an attack on Hitler – they hit on the notion of setting fire to the Reichstag building.

An underground passage linked Goering's Palace of the President of the Reichstag with the main building across the street. Through this a small group of SA men under the command of Max Ernst, the leader of the Berlin SA, entered the deserted building on the evening of the 27th and scattered a chemical preparation with a delayed action effect over carpet, curtains and chairs. After doing this they made their way back to safety by the underground tunnel. As they were leaving, a half-crazed young Dutchman, who had been picked up by the SA after attempting to set fire to other buildings . . . climbed into the Reichstag from the outside and proceeded to start fires at a number of points.'

Bullock: *A Study in Tyranny*

SOURCE 8:

General Halder, in evidence to the Nuremberg War Crimes trials in 1946:

'On the occasion of a lunch on the Führer's birthday in 1943, the people around the Führer turned the conversation to the Reichstag building and its artistic value. I heard with my own ears how Goering broke into conversation and shouted: "The only one who really knows (about) the Reichstag is I, for I set fire to it."'

Quoted in Simkin: *The Rise of Hitler*

SOURCE 9:

Hermann Goering, in evidence to the Nuremberg War Crimes Trials in 1946:

'What the general (Halder) says is not true . . . The whole thing is preposterous. Even if I had started the fire, I would most certainly not have boasted about it.'

SOURCE 10:

The British historian, AJP Taylor, writing in 1961:

'The Nazis had nothing to do with the burning of the Reichstag. The young Dutchman, Van der Lubbe, did it all alone, exactly as he claimed.'

AJP Taylor: *Origins of the Second World War*

So exactly who did burn down the Reichstag? Is Source 10 right? Did Van der Lubbe tell the truth all along? Or is Source 7 correct? Did the Nazis merely want an excuse to ban the Communists and so win the next election? The evidence is far from complete but like any historian you have now got to decide which evidence you trust the most and which you will choose to discard.

10 Which source can you find to back up Bullock's interpretation that it was the Nazis who burnt down the Reichstag building?
11 i) According to Source 7, what was the Nazis' motive?

ii) What evidence is there in the text to back up this motive?
iii) Is Source 8 reliable? Is there any reason why General Halder might lie?
12 Do you believe the interpretation given in Source 9? Did Van der Lubbe burn down the Reichstag on his own?

Draw this table and then fill it in so that you can establish what evidence you have. Then write your own answer to the question backing up your views with reference to the evidence. Remember you will also have to explain why you are rejecting some evidence which does not support your

Theory	Sources in favour	Sources against
1 Van der Lubbe on his own		
2 Van der Lubbe backed by the Communists		
3 The Nazis		

Daily Telegraph *12 Jan 1934*:

'The reason why Van der Lubbe was executed by Ahrhardt and not the usual executioner, Grobler, . . . is said to be that Grobler recently resigned his post of executioner for Prussia owing to a nervous breakdown due to overwork. Fifty executions with the axe have been carried out since the Nazis came to power, says the Socialist statement. It adds that Grobler's nerve gave way after he had to behead three young workmen with the axe.'

Ⓠ **Who was Van der Lubbe? What evidence can you find that might lead you to doubt the reliability of this report?**

HOW DID HITLER MAINTAIN CONTROL OF GERMANY?

By August 1934 Hitler was in complete control of Germany. His task was to remain in control and prevent any opposition to his rule. This was done in three main ways, as the diagram on page 79 shows.

The Terror State

Nazi Germany was a police state. The Gestapo was founded in 1933. In the words of Gestapo Deputy Chief Werner Best, the job of the Gestapo was 'to discover the enemies of the State, watch them and make them harmless.' They could arrest and imprison anyone that they chose. The courts were also dominated by Nazis so that the people they arrested were bound to be found guilty. Anyone who opposed the Nazis would be arrested. People were asked to report their friends and family to the Gestapo. In 1936 the Gestapo came under the control of the SS. The SS were formed in 1925 as a bodyguard for Hitler. In contrast to the undisciplined mobs of the SA, the SS were highly disciplined and totally loyal to Hitler. In 1934 they had carried out the 'Night of the Long Knives' when so many of Hitler's opponents were murdered. As a reward they were put in control of both the Gestapo and the concentration camps. The SS operated with terrible brutality. Hundreds of thousands of people were imprisoned in the concentration camps where they were regularly tortured.

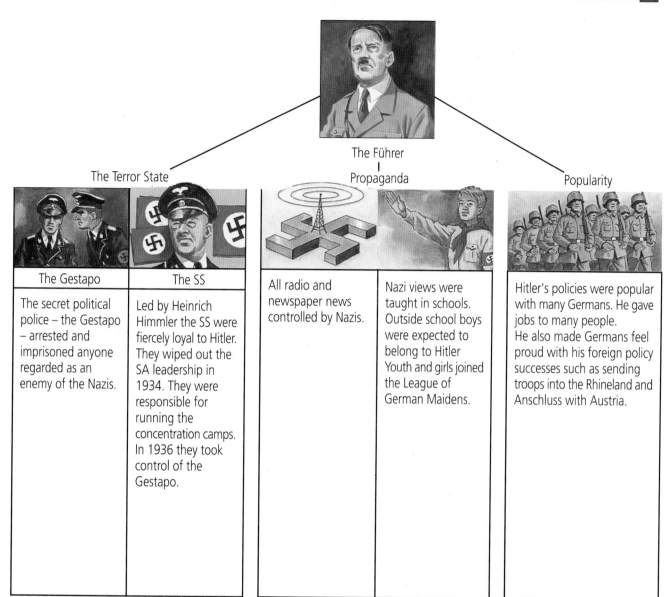

The Führer

The Terror State | Propaganda | Popularity

The Gestapo	The SS
The secret political police – the Gestapo – arrested and imprisoned anyone regarded as an enemy of the Nazis.	Led by Heinrich Himmler the SS were fiercely loyal to Hitler. They wiped out the SA leadership in 1934. They were responsible for running the concentration camps. In 1936 they took control of the Gestapo.

All radio and newspaper news controlled by Nazis.

Nazi views were taught in schools. Outside school boys were expected to belong to Hitler Youth and girls joined the League of German Maidens.

Hitler's policies were popular with many Germans. He gave jobs to many people. He also made Germans feel proud with his foreign policy successes such as sending troops into the Rhineland and Anschluss with Austria.

Controlling Germany.

Propaganda

More people in Germany had radios than in any other country in Europe, so Hitler used radio broadcasts, as well as huge open-air meetings, to get his message across. New buildings were added to many German cities to remind everyone that a new and powerful Germany was being created. Radio and newspapers were only allowed to report news that had been approved by the Nazi Propaganda Ministry, led by Joseph Goebbels. In 1936 the Olympic Games were held in Berlin. Germans were encouraged to feel proud as their superiority was shown to the world. The German people were disappointed as the most successful athlete of the games was the black American sprinter Jesse Owens. According to Nazi ideas he was from an inferior race. In schools, pupils were taught the Nazi version of history and biology. They were taught to hate the Jews and Jewish students were humiliated. Physical education was considered very important; for boys it prepared them for war and for girls it prepared them for having children. Outside school there were Nazi organisations for young people. The Hitler Youth was for boys from the age of 14 to 18 and it also placed great emphasis on physical fitness and military training. Girls of a similar age belonged to the BDM, the League of German Maidens.

A poster advertising the Nazi propaganda film SA man Brand – A biography of our time.

Q **Why do you think that the Nazis produced films like this? Does it give an accurate impression of the SA?**

German workers take part in a sack race on a cruise to the island of Madeira. Part of the policy to win the support of workers was KdF, 'Strength through Joy'. This provided a host of benefits for workers. Cruises on the ocean were granted to the most loyal and hardworking but there were operas, theatre visits and sporting occasions as well.

Q **Does this suggest that the Nazis kept the workers in chains, as the Socialists suggested in their poster on page 74?**

Popularity

Hitler's Germany gave people little chance to express opposition, not that many people wanted to. Hitler was very popular. When he had come to power six million Germans were jobless. By 1938 this figure had been reduced to a mere one million and wages had risen for many of those in work. In the years before he had become Chancellor he had promised to overthrow the hated Treaty of Versailles which is exactly what he did. He ignored the limits set on the size of the armed forces so that by 1936 the German army had 550 000 troops. In that year he also ordered German troops into the previously demilitarised Rhineland. Two years later German troops entered Austria and *Anschluss* (the union of Germany and Austria into a single country) was carried out. Many Germans felt that these successes were worth the price of the harsh Nazi rule because Germany was a strong and powerful country less than 20 years after the humiliation at Versailles.

German troops cross into the Rhineland. The Treaty of Versailles had declared this action illegal. The invasion showed the German people that Hitler was as good as his word. This was followed by the Anschluss with Austria and the invasion of Czechoslovakia. (See Chapter 6.)

The Church

There was one other reason why there was so little opposition to Hitler: people would be too frightened to speak out against Hitler unless they could join together with other people who felt the same way. In his first year in office,

(above) A Nazi poster, 'Build Youth hostels and camps'. These camps were part of the scheme to create young Germans who were strong and fit and also faithful believers in Nazi ideas.

Q **What sort of impression of young Germans does the poster above give?**

Hitler had removed nearly all the organisations that would have allowed people to join together, so there were no longer any political parties other than the NSDAP. There were no trade unions either. The only organisation that was allowed to survive was the Church.

There were two Christian churches in Germany, The Roman Catholic Church and the German Protestant Church. At first both churches accepted Hitler because they felt that Communism was a major threat to Christianity and Hitler was determined to destroy Communism. Many Nazis were very anti-Christian and so wanted to destroy the churches but in 1933 Hitler signed a Concordat (an agreement) with the Roman Catholic Church. They were allowed to keep their church schools and their own youth organisation providing that they did not oppose the Nazis. However, they soon found that Hitler was not to be trusted and in 1937 the Pope issued an encyclical (an open letter) against Hitler.

A group of Nazis set up their own German Christian movement but Protestants did not usually join because they objected to the terror tactics of the Nazis. Many of them were put in concentration camps. The most famous of these was the Protestant pastor Niemoller.

Q How far do the written and visual sources on pages 78–82 give an accurate picture of how Hitler managed to control Germany? To answer this question you will need to consider some aspects that have been left out.

Evening. A painting by Oskar Martin-Amorbach. Nazi paintings stressed the values of hard work and the simple peasant life. This was summed up in the phrase 'blood and soil'. This painting shows that the role of women was to produce babies. According to Paul Hermann, a Nazi expert on racial purity, it was considered good for a woman to have several children. A childless married woman was regarded as inferior.

The treatment of the Jews

In the section on the beliefs of the Nazis on page 64 you will have noted that anti-Semitism was an important belief although not one that was unique to the Nazis. However, the Nazis took their hatred of the Jews to a terrible level.

Poster for the film Jud Süss, c.1940.

Q **How can you tell that this film attacked Jews?**

As early as March 1933 Hitler ordered the SA to turn customers away from Jewish shops. People were also ordered to stop using Jewish lawyers. Jewish doctors and nurses were ordered to attend only Jewish patients. Things soon got worse. In 1935 the Nuremberg Laws were passed. This made it illegal for Jews to marry non-Jews, or even to have sexual intercourse with them. Jews were deprived of German citizenship and so they lost the right to vote. They were also stopped from using swimming pools, restaurants and other public facilities.

GROSSE POLITISCHE SCHAU IM BIBLIOTHEKSBAU DES DEUTSCHEN MUSEUMS ZU MÜNCHEN · AB 8. NOVEMBER 1937 · TÄGLICH GEÖFFNET VON 10-21 UHR

Poster for the exhibition 'The Eternal Jew'.

Q How does this poster portray Jews? Why is money shown in the Jew's hand and why is the hammer and sickle shown on the other side?

In 1938 a German diplomat in Paris was shot dead by Herschel Grynszpan. Grynszpan had heard that 17 000 Jews, including his own family, had been deported from Germany but left stranded on the border with Poland when the Poles refused to accept them. The German response to the murder was to launch an organised attack on Jews and Jewish property. This took place on the night of 9 November. It became known as *Kristallnacht*, a reference to all the broken glass caused by the violence.

Q

An eyewitness account of *Kristallnacht*

The *Daily Telegraph* 12 November 1938:
'Mob law ruled in Berlin throughout this afternoon and evening, and hordes of hooligans indulged in an orgy of destruction. I have seen several anti-Jewish outbreaks during the last five years, but never anything as sickening as this. Racial hatred and hysteria seemed to have taken complete hold of otherwise decent people. I saw fashionably-dressed women clapping their hands and screaming with glee, while respectable mothers held up their babies to see the "fun". The fashionable shopping centre of the capital has been reduced to a shambles, with the streets littered with the wreckage of sacked Jewish shops and offices. No attempt was made by the police to stop the rioters.

The attacks on Jews and their property started all over Germany, as if by a signal, soon after midnight, when the beer-halls closed . . . The caretaker of the synagogue in the *Prinzregentenstrasse* is reported to have been burnt to death together with his family. It is learned on good authority that two Jews were lynched in Berlin's East End early this morning and two more in the West End.'

1 What evidence can you find in this extract to suggest that *Kristallnacht* was centrally organised?

2 What evidence can you find in this extract to suggest that Hitler's anti-Semitic policies were popular?

3 Do you think that official posters or newspaper reports are more useful to the historian trying to find out about anti-Semitism in Germany? Explain your answer.

Once the Second World War had begun the situation worsened. In 1941 the decision was taken to introduce the 'Final Solution'. All Jews in the areas of Europe controlled by the Nazis were to be exterminated. Between 1942 and 1945 approximately six million Jews perished in extermination camps such as Auschwitz and Sobibor.

(below) The disposal of bodies that had perished in the gas chambers of Auschwitz.

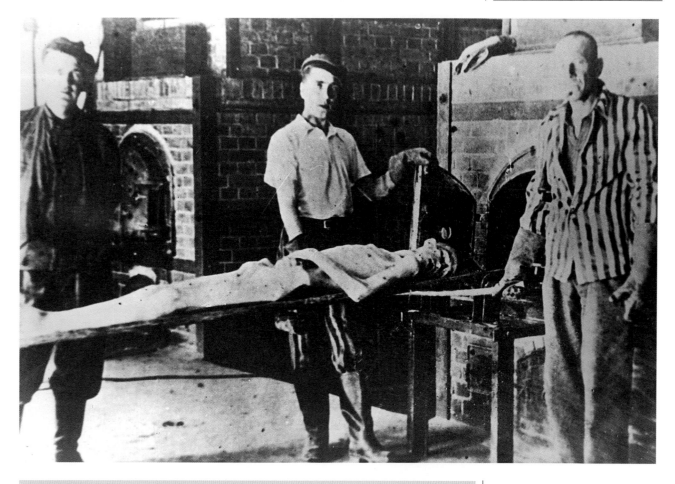

HITLER'S ECONOMIC POLICY

In the 1930s there was an economic depression throughout most of the world. The high unemployment it created was an important reason why the Nazis came to power. In his election campaigns Hitler promised to provide 'Bread and work' for the German people. He would overcome the Depression. Could he succeed? He needed to make good his promises if he was to remain popular with the German people.

▶ Did Hitler produce an economic miracle?

SOURCE 1:

'Our building blocks of work, freedom and bread'. A Nazi election poster. The Nazis promised a better standard of living for the German people. This poster contrasts the simple and good policies of the Nazis with the corruption, unemployment and lies of their opponents.

SOURCE 2:

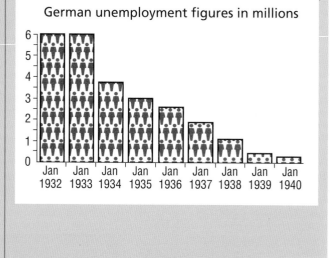

German unemployment figures in millions

SOURCE 3:

As well as the *autobahns*, huge public buildings were constructed. The photograph below shows the opening ceremony of the Olympic Games in 1936 at the newly built Olympic Stadium in Berlin. Such buildings not only created jobs but also impressed people. They were a visible sign that Hitler was making Germany 'great' again.

SOURCE 4:

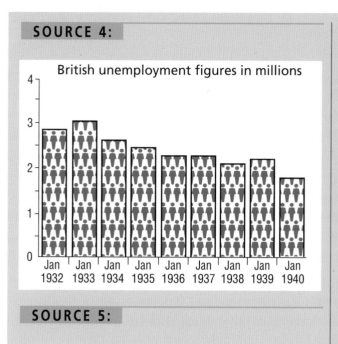

British unemployment figures in millions

(x-axis: Jan 1932, Jan 1933, Jan 1934, Jan 1935, Jan 1936, Jan 1937, Jan 1938, Jan 1939, Jan 1940)

SOURCE 5:

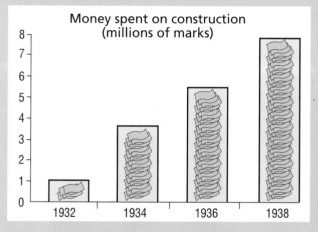

Money spent on construction (millions of marks)

(x-axis: 1932, 1934, 1936, 1938)

SOURCE 6:

5 Mark die Woche musst Du sparen – willst Du im eignen Wagen fahren!

KdF-Wagen: Über Anschaffungspreis und Zahlungsweise erteilen Auskunft alle Betriebswarte und Dienststellen der NS.-Gemeinschaft „Kraft durch Freude" Gau München-Oberbayern

The Volkswagen. The 'people's car' was a symbol of how the Nazis were seeking popular support. In 1938, 300 000 Germans paid a regular subscription so that they could own one of these cars as soon as they became available. However, only a few had been produced by the time that war broke out and then the production line was turned over to the needs of the armed forces.

1 Look at Sources 2 and 4.
  a Which country had the greater unemployment in 1932?
  b What would explain this?
  c Which country had the greater unemployment in 1938?
  d What reasons can you find to explain this?
2 Look at Source 1. Does it accurately sum up Hitler's policies? Give your reasons.
3 Draw a poster of your own which illustrates the economic policies that Hitler carried out.
4 Look at Source 5. How does this source help to explain why Hitler was successful in reducing unemployment?
5 Look at Source 6. What does this suggest was the main purpose of the car industry? What other purposes were there?
6 How valuable are Sources 5 and 6 in helping to understand Hitler's economic policies?

Source 2 shows just how successful Hitler was in reducing German unemployment. Look at Source 4 and you will see that he was far more successful than the British government during the same period. Was this a miracle? How was Hitler able to achieve such a dramatic fall in German unemployment?

There were four main reasons for this success:

- **Reparations.** Hitler stopped paying reparations when he came to power. This meant that money which had been going to France and Belgium could now be invested in the German economy and so create more jobs.
- **Government spending.** Hitler sought to create jobs through government spending on construction. Germany built a network of motorways, known as '*autobahns*', across the country. The *autobahns* not only created jobs, they also helped make German industry more efficient by increasing the speed at which goods could cross the country. Of course they also increased the speed at which troops could cross the country.
- **Wage and price controls.** Hitler had promised jobs but he also destroyed the power of the trade unions. Wages were then kept low. This was a reward for the industrialists who supported Hitler. It helped them to make big profits. This made sure that industrialists would want Hitler to stay in power.
- **Rearmament.** This was only really significant after 1936. Before this Hitler concentrated on providing the bread and work which he had promised. From 1936 onwards Hitler changed the aims of the economy. A Five Year Plan was introduced to develop an army which would dominate much of Europe. (See Chapter 6 for details of Hitler's foreign policy.) Before 1936 the economy had been in the hands of the economist Schacht. After 1936 it was under the control of the First World War hero Goering. The drive for rearmament created still more jobs and so unemployment fell further.

Advertisement for the Volkswagen as the KdF 'Strength through joy' vehicle. An expanded German car industry created jobs by cutting the imports of foreign cars. Car factories were also useful as they could quickly switch production to military needs.

Autarky

Bread and work were not Hitler's only aims. He also wanted to establish 'autarky', that is, to make Germany economically self-sufficient. He wanted to stop Germany being dependent on imported goods, especially raw materials. Hitler did not want Germany to be held to ransom by the countries that supplied Germany with food and vital raw materials. Modern armed forces were dependent upon oil. So companies like the chemical company IG Farben were paid to develop a method of extracting oil from coal. Attempts were also made to develop an artificial rubber. Although these experiments did create jobs they did not reduce the amount of goods that Germany had to import.

A brigade of the Reich Labour Service parading with spades at a party rally at Nuremberg in 1937. Hitler established the Reich Labour Service for all school leavers and unskilled workers. They carried out projects such as draining marshes and building sea walls.

Farmers had been important supporters of the Nazis in the late 1920s and early 1930s. Hitler's Minister of Food, Darre, sought to reward German farmers and protect them from the effects of the Depression. He cut the taxes that farmers had to pay and also ordered them to reduce the amount of land under cultivation. This cut food overproduction and so caused food prices to rise. This was good for the farmers. However it also meant that more food had to be imported and so did not help to create autarky.

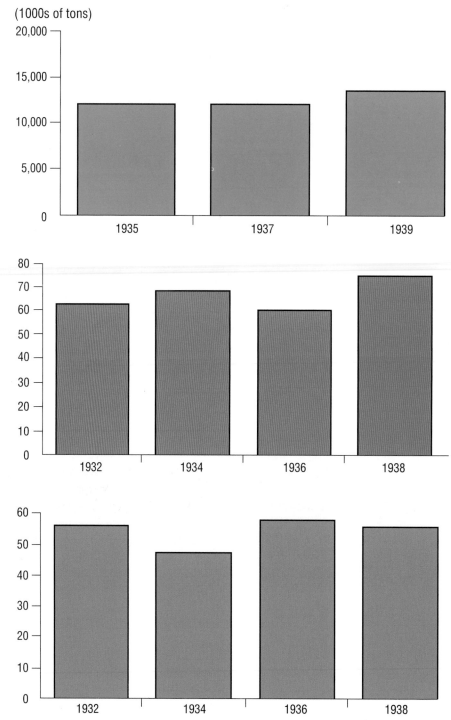

German agricultural production 1935–9

These import figures (above) and export figures (right) represent a comparison with German trade in 1913, before the First World War. The figures for 1913 are given a value of 100. So a figure of 50 in the export column would mean that Germany was exporting half as much produce as had been the case in 1913.

In 1938, a Cambridge University lecturer gave this opinion of Germany:

'No-one who is acquainted with German conditions would suggest that the standard of living is a high one, but that the important thing is that it has been rising in recent years.'

Das Vollbad und das Brausebad

so ist es richtig. Für eine gesunde Lebensführung in modernen Wohnungen müssen beide Badegelegen-

'Bath and shower – yes. Both are a must for a healthy lifestyle in a modern apartment.' An advertisement showing the consumer goods available in Nazi Germany.

Q

1 Why did Hitler wish to make Germany self-sufficient?

2 Look at the production, import and export figures on page 90. Do they suggest that Germany was becoming self-sufficient? What other evidence can you find to back up your answer?

3 Was there an economic miracle in Germany? To answer this question you will need to decide how successful Hitler's policies were in three areas: unemployment; autarky; preparing for war. For each of the three areas you will need to back up your decision with evidence from sources as well as the text.

1920	**Prohibition introduced; women get the vote**
1922	**First advertisement on radio**
1927	**First talking film**
1928	**Hoover elected President**
1929	**St Valentine's Day Massacre; Wall Street Crash**
1932	**Roosevelt becomes President**
1933	**Prohibition ends; New Deal programme begins; unemployment at 13 million**
1935	**Second New Deal begins; Supreme Court declares NRA illegal**
1936	**Roosevelt re-elected President**
1940	**Roosevelt re-elected for a second time**
1941	**USA enters the Second World War after Pearl Harbor**

This chapter focuses on four key issues:

- *Why was there a boom in the 1920s?*
- *How prosperous were the 1920s?*
- *What were the causes and effects of the Depression?*
- *How successful was Roosevelt's New Deal?*

Between 1919 and 1941 the USA went through two decades of dramatic change in its political, economic and social life. During this period Americans experienced a decade of great prosperity in the 1920s, followed by one of real poverty for many in the 1930s.

Americans changed their political attitudes as well. In the 1920s they were reluctant to let their political leaders have too much power; by the end of the 1930s they accepted the idea that governments have the duty to influence peoples' lives.

Some social attitudes changed for the better – women campaigned for and won greater rights and recognition. Others changed for the worse – Americans became less tolerant of foreigners coming to the USA and some became more racist towards minority groups already living there.

THE 1920S: THE SECOND INDUSTRIAL REVOLUTION

America's first industrial revolution in the late nineteenth century had made the USA the world's greatest economic power. The second industrial revolution of the 1920s would be a **consumer** revolution and would make sure that Americans also had the world's highest standard of living. The booming industries of the 1920s were mostly ones producing consumer goods: cars; radios; refrigerators; vacuum cleaners and rayon stockings. These were just a few among the many new, mass-produced goods available to improve the quality of people's lives.

Advertisers made sure that the public knew about these and other products. Advertising played a major role in making Americans want things. The *National Advertiser* declared that 'One reason there's so much success in America is because there's so much advertising of things to want.' Mail-order companies sprang up, making it even easier for Americans to spend their money. Now they didn't even have to leave their own homes.

'Only the rich will burn candles...'

Technology was at the heart of these dramatic changes. New methods of production and new inventions meant that goods became cheaper and more varied. People wanted to buy and they had a lot of enticing new goods to spend their money on. Samuel Insull, the owner of an electricity generating company, boasted: 'We will make electric light so cheap that only the rich will burn candles.' Keeping production costs down and prices low were the best ways to create demand for goods and services.

By the mid-1920s RCA was marketing radios with advertisements like this one. The radio itself was a new consumer item and by 1929 12 million American families owned one and 350 000 a year were being sold.

Any colour, as long as it's black

The industry and individual that most symbolised the spirit of this decade of invention and prosperity was the automobile industry and Henry Ford. Ford pioneered the technique of the moving assembly line to mass-produce cars. Each worker performed a single task on the car as it moved past him. The work was repetitive and boring but well paid – as much as $5 a day and more than twice that of Ford's competitors.

Output increased dramatically, production costs dropped and so did prices. Ford's cheapest and first assembly-line-built car, the Model T, cost $1200 in 1909 but only $295 in 1925 – less than three months' wages for an average worker. Ford's assembly lines could turn out one Model T every 10 seconds. To keep costs low Ford offered any choice of colour that the buyer wanted as long as it was black!

Those who did not have the ready cash could buy in instalments – another invention of the 1920s. Advertising took off as companies worked hard to persuade consumers to buy their products. Cars became a status symbol that had to be changed every few years. As one housewife told her interviewers at the end of the decade: 'We'd rather go without clothes than give up the car.'

By 1929 there were 26 million car owners in the USA. The automobile industry caused a boom in a host of related industries which fed off and into it. Steel, glass, rubber and paints are all obvious examples. But these cars also needed roads, asphalt, petrol, petrol stations and insurance.

There was a darker side to Henry Ford. He hated Jews and used his newspaper to launch attacks on Jews in America and he did not allow trade unions in his company. He also described history as 'bunk' and 'one damn thing after another'. Clearly, he was better suited to making motor cars than to philosophy.

The booming motor industry was at the heart of the prosperity of the 1920s and advertisers played their part in making it happen. This advertisement, in 1929 in the Saturday Evening Post, shows a woman driver. Advertisers had realised that women bought cars too.

Q

Why was there a boom in the 1920s?

The chart on page 95 lists five important reasons in Column A that explain why there was an economic boom in the USA in the 1920s. In Column B there is an explanation of these reasons but they are in the wrong order. Your first task is to copy out the chart and match the explanation in Column B with the right reason in Column A. Make sure that you read through all the explanations before you start to match them up.

Your second task is to give each of these five reasons a mark out of five as to how important you think it was in creating the boom. Put the mark in Column C and then your reason in Column D. Try to explain your reason *in relation* to one or more of the other reasons. You could give buying in instalments, for example, two out of five and give as your reason: 'It did contribute to the boom because it meant that more products were sold even if they weren't fully paid for straight away. However, they needed to be cheap in the first place so instalment buying can't be that important.'

Reason (Column A)	Explanation (Column B)	Mark out of 5 (Column C)	Explanation for mark (Column D)
Mass-production of goods	because other industries quickly developed to keep these new industries supplied with the materials that they needed		
Buying in instalments	because people were keen to buy the new products that would improve the quality of their lives		
Advertising	because it allowed people to buy products even if they didn't have the full purchase price		
New consumer inventions	because it made goods cheaper and so more people could afford to buy them		
Mass-production of goods	because it drew people's attention to the new products and made them want to buy them		

THE OTHER AMERICA

While advertisers were busy creating demand for new products – 'The greatest gift of electricity to the modern housewife is the Conover Electric Dishwasher' – other, older industries were struggling. Electricity and oil were replacing coal; artificial fibres such as rayon were overtaking cotton. Fashion also played a part here. In 1913 it took 19 metres of cloth to dress a woman but only seven metres in 1928. As these traditional industries (such as mining and cotton) declined, unemployment increased. Unemployed workers could not afford to buy the new consumer goods and so workers in these industries would, in their turn, also be laid off.

Farmers

The worst affected industry of the 1920s was agriculture. Demand for crops dropped rapidly after the war as the Europeans produced more of their own food and bought less from America. Less cotton was needed and American consumers ate fewer cereal products. In 1920 the price of wheat plunged from $2.50 a bushel to just $1.00.

This photograph shows Jackie Coogan's Relief Train providing free milk for 'starving children' in 1925. Jackie Coogan was a child actor of the period and was aged 11 when this picture was taken. The picture suggests that the booming 1920s were not a decade of prosperity for everyone.

Q Can you think which communities in the USA would have particularly welcomed free milk at this time?

To make matters worse, even though demand was falling, production continued to increase. The introduction of the tractor, for example, (in place of the horse or mule) allowed more crops to be grown because the tractor was more efficient. It also meant that fewer acres were now needed to provide animal feed and these could be used to grow more food for people.

Unfortunately, for American farmers, they were producing more than they could sell and as a result prices (and their income) continued to fall throughout the decade. In 1932 wheat reached a new low of $0.38 a bushel, and the average income of a farmer in 1929 was $273 compared to the national average of $681.

The Fordney-McCumber Act 1922

The government's response was to introduce 'protection'. Protection is an economic policy that involves taxing foreign goods coming into the country to force their prices up. This 'protects' the economy from foreign competition by making foreign goods much more expensive and encouraging consumers to buy the equivalent products made in their own country.

In 1922 the Fordney-McCumber Act was passed by Congress, the equivalent of Britain's parliament. It imposed heavy taxes or tariffs on 28 foreign agricultural products including wheat, corn and beef. But this did not solve the basic problem of over-production and it simply encouraged the European states to put similar tariffs on US produce. This meant that American farmers now had even less chance of selling their surplus food abroad.

Q

1 What evidence is there in the text that mass-production led to a fall in prices?
2 Why was the automobile industry such a vital part of American industry in general?
3 What evidence is there in the text that falling demand leads to lower prices?
4 Why do you think that the demand for *new* consumer goods was so high in the 1920s?
5 How did the Fordney-McCumber tariff make those problems facing American farmers worse?

Blacks

If times were hard for American farmers in the 1920s, they were worse still for black Americans. Blacks were the victims of legalised discrimination in the southern states where 75 per cent of them lived. The 'Jim Crow' laws segregated them and forced them to use separate, inferior facilities, such as separate buses, hotels, schools and even water fountains.

The racist and terrorist organisation, the Ku Klux Klan, tried to make sure that blacks knew and kept their 'place' in southern society. The KKK also included Jews and Catholics on their list of undesirables and saw themselves as 'defenders' of the Protestant religion. Those African Americans who tried to claim the equal rights promised to them in the Constitution, were terrorised by the Klan. Blacks such as these faced death by castration, burning, and lynching. The white Klan members responsible for these violent crimes were never brought to trial.

Many blacks went north in search of better treatment and opportunities. In the northern states there was less prejudice but still only menial jobs as cleaners, street cleaners or dishwashers. Nonetheless, these were better than the grinding poverty that African Americans faced trying to scratch a living on southern farms. The black population of New York, Chicago and other northern cities more than doubled in the 1920s.

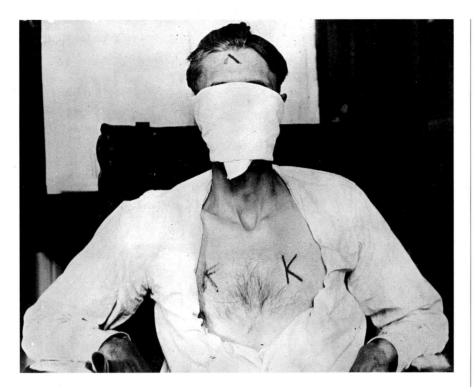

In July 1924 Nelson Burroughs, a Catholic, was kidnapped by the Ku Klux Klan and branded with red hot irons because of his religious views.

> **Q What evidence is there in the photograph of the KKK's handiwork? Why were Catholics a target for the Klan's terror?**

Immigrants

Between 1900 and 1914, 13 million 'new' immigrants arrived in the USA. They were described as new because they did not come from the traditional Protestant Anglo-Saxon countries of Europe like Britain, Germany or Scandinavia. They were mostly Catholics or Jews from southern or eastern Europe. They included Italians, Poles and Greeks. Very soon they were made to feel unwelcome because of their different religions, their poverty and their lack of education. Even worse, many of them had socialist ideas and believed in trade unions. This was not the 'American Way'.

This photograph shows a 1927 protest demonstration against the execution of two Italian-American anarchists, Sacco and Vanzetti (see page 98). It was taken in Massachusetts, USA.

The earlier, well-established immigrants from northern Europe believed that these newcomers had little to offer the USA. A series of immigration laws were passed in the early 1920s to cut immigration from southern and eastern Europe while continuing to allow it from Britain, Germany and Scandinavia. Such official, government-backed policies simply encouraged greater intolerance of minorities and the Klu Klux Klan prospered.

Sacco and Vanzetti: 'ashes in the winds of God'

Two Italian socialists, Sacco and Vanzetti, were victims of this prejudice. Their status as new immigrants with left-wing views made them easy targets. They were convicted in 1921 of the murder of a security guard during a robbery. The case against them was flimsy and confused but they were still sentenced to death. Six years of protest and appeals followed as America was torn apart over the case. In 1927 they were electrocuted. One poet promised Sacco and Vanzetti 'to spread your name abroad like ashes in the winds of God'.

Women

In 1920 the women's suffragette movement won a right for which they had fought since 1869: the right to vote. This was approved in the Nineteenth Amendment to the US Constitution. But gaining the vote hardly changed

Women were an obvious target for advertising. Here, Edna's case is described as a 'pathetic one': 'Like every woman her primary ambition was to marry.' But Edna could not marry because she had smelly breath and now she was nearly 30!

Q Why might feminists have considered such advertising as very sexist?

women's lives. They continued to occupy the lower-paid jobs and found it difficult to have careers in the well-paid professions. In 1930 there were, in the whole of the USA, only 151 women dentists and less than half that number of women accountants.

For most women, especially working-class women, the only alternative to low-paid jobs was life as a housewife and mother. This was in sharp contrast to the types of skilled and challenging jobs that women had done during the war – jobs no longer available once the war was over and the men had returned. Nonetheless, the percentage of women with jobs in the 1920s increased by 25 per cent with 10.6 million at work in 1929.

'Shapes while you sleep'

As a result, women became a target for advertisers who were keen to sell their new products to them. In 1930 the cosmetics industry sold $200 million worth of lipsticks, face powders, perfumes and other beauty aids. The makers of the 'Anita Nose Adjuster' promised those who could not afford a face-lift that it 'shapes while you sleep'.

Some women, mostly from the middle and upper classes, were determined to break away from the traditional role that society expected them to fulfil. They set out to shock conventional attitudes by wearing short skirts above the knee, smoking in public and taking up energetic sports. They flattened their busts and wore short hair in a bid to reject the traditional, feminine appearance. Such women were known, unflatteringly, as 'flappers'.

Some middle- and upper-class women in the 1920s set out to challenge traditional ideas about how women should behave. This photograph shows several features of the 'flapper' of the 1920s. She is wearing a short skirt, has short hair and smokes.

Q Can you think of anything else in this photograph which would have shocked traditional views at the time?

However, on the whole, the traditional view of women as carers, mothers and housewives did not significantly change during the 1920s. This was a disappointment for those women who had hoped that their valuable service in the First World War would open up new opportunities for them. Supporters of women's rights were also disappointed by how little political life changed after women got the vote in 1920. Many women, it seems, continued to see politics as a matter for men. In 1928 there were only two women members of Congress and over 500 men.

'It may leak, shake and sag but...'

The 1920s was a difficult decade for women. In some respects attitudes and behaviour did change. Women made more use of divorce to escape from bad marriages. The divorce rate increased from one in every ten marriages to one in every six with two-thirds of the divorces started by the wife. More than 90 per cent of women born after 1900 made use of contraception. Women had much greater sexual freedom as a result but most traditional attitudes refused to die.

The film and advertising industries bombarded women with images that told them to look attractive and find a husband at all costs. Marriage remained the ambition of most women. One female novelist, Fannie Hurst, commented that the marriage structure was 'leaky, the roof sags, the timbers shake. . .We don't feel comfortable in it. . . but we don't dare get out of it.'

Q

1 Why do you think that the members of the KKK were never brought to trial for the crimes against blacks?
2 Why were the 'new' immigrants unwelcome in the USA?
3 What evidence is there in the text that women found it hard to have professional careers?
4 Why do you suppose that the behaviour of the 'flappers' was so shocking to more traditional Americans?
5 What do you think Fannie Hurst meant by the quotation above?
6 Do you think the 1920s really was a decade of change for women? Explain your answer.

The camera never lies? This photograph seems to show a woman operating a film camera in 1925, suggesting that new opportunities had been opened up for women in the 1920s. In fact, it is a picture of a glamorous actress, Pauline Frederick, taking a peep behind the camera while on the set of her film 'The Woman in Room Thirteen'.

PROHIBITION

Women who campaigned for a change in attitudes had more success in the Women's Christian Temperance Union (WCTU). The WCTU and the Anti-Saloon League both campaigned to have the sale and manufacture of alcohol declared illegal or 'prohibited'. Prohibitionists (supporters of the ban on alcohol) achieved their aims in 1920 when the Volstead Act made the sale or manufacture of alcohol illegal – though it was not actually against the law to drink it.

Supporters of a 'dry' or alcohol-free America argued that Prohibition would put a stop to drunkenness and violence in the family. Men would no longer spend their wages on drink, leaving families hungry. The WCTU also argued that alcohol was against Christian teaching and businessmen hoped that sober workers would produce more in their factories. Patriots pointed out that the owners of the big brewing companies in the USA were of German descent and the USA had just fought a war against Germany. So drinkers were guilty of not only un-Christian behaviour but also a lack of patriotism.

The Prohibition movement tended to be supported by white, Anglo-Saxon Protestants (WASPs) from the south and rural west of the USA. Its opponents, 'wets', were often Catholics, Jews, immigrants and poor. Prohibition, therefore, was not just a moral issue but also a racial and religious one and it sharply divided the country.

'Sir, your horse has diabetes'

Many Americans wanted to drink beer, spirits and wine and organised crime saw an opportunity to make money by providing them. 'Bootleggers' sold redistilled industrial alcohol which might have been intended for paint, cosmetics or hair tonic. (The term 'bootlegger' came from 17th century smugglers who hid bottles of alcohol in their boots.) 'Moonshiners' made their own alcohol in secret stills at home, while rum-runners smuggled in genuine liquor from across the Canadian or Mexican borders or by sea.

The OVERSHADOWING CURSE
THE LEGALIZED SALOON

HAS SHE A FAIR CHANCE?

"Our religion demands that every child should have a fair chance for citizenship in the coming Kingdom. Our patriotism demands a saloonless country and a stainless flag."---P. A. Baker, General Superintendent Anti-Saloon League of America.

This Anti–Saloon League poster was produced in 1922. The appeal to patriotism in the text is a reference to the fact that many breweries were owned by Americans of German descent and America had just fought a war against Germany.

Q Can you suggest why this would have been an effective poster against alcohol?

Some redistilled and home-brewed stuff was lethal while other liquids proved to be non-alcoholic. One story tells of how a customer took his bottle of bootleg 'alcohol' to a chemist for analysis because he was suspicious of its yellow colour and smell. 'Sir', the chemist told him, 'your horse has diabetes'.

Beer Wars

The Treasury Department never employed more than 3000 agents to enforce Prohibition. Their task was hopeless. They were told to shut down an illegal two-billion-dollars-a-year industry and patrol 18 000 kilometres of coastline and border. They probably only managed to destroy ten per cent of the illegal alcohol manufactured in the USA.

They were also expected to enforce an unpopular law. Most public sympathy went with those who set out to satisfy the average American's thirst for a glass of beer or wine. The criminal underworld quickly spotted a good business opportunity and branched out from its traditional illegal activities of supplying prostitutes and gambling casinos.

It is ironic that a law which was intended to improve morality and the behaviour of Americans actually had the opposite effect. Many millions of ordinary Americans now became accomplices to crime by continuing to drink

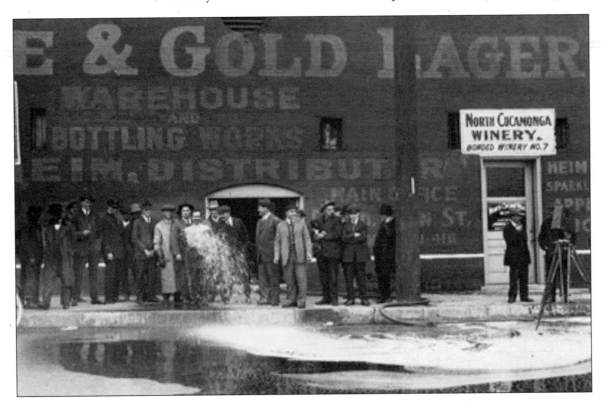

150 000 litres of wine is being poured down the drain in this photograph in Los Angeles from February 1920. The Prohibition agents responsible look enthusiastic about their task.

◐ Why might they have looked a little less happy a few years later?

in illegal 'Speakeasies'. Inevitably, the price of whisky shot up from $4 per gallon to $24, in the first six years of Prohibition. The price of bootleg alcohol did mean that less was drunk by the poor but it became fashionable for the middle and upper classes to offer a drink at parties.

Prohibition encouraged a disrespect for the law. It increased corruption as the police and judges were easily bribed to turn a blind eye to the bootleggers' activities. In some cases, criminals like Al Capone were seen as popular heroes by providing the public with what it wanted. Nobody minded the occasional gangland killing as rival gangs fought for the control of this very profitable industry, as long as they were murdering their own kind.

This unemployed worker is shown next to a sign advertising the nearest 'speakeasy'.

Q Why is it likely that this photograph was taken during the Prohibition era?

Public opinion was shocked, however, by the St Valentine's Day Massacre in February 1929 in which seven members of the Bugs Moran gang were killed. Moran's men were 'arrested' by five of Capone's men dressed as policemen. They were ordered to face the wall with their hands up and calmly mowed down by machine-gun fire. The public's shock was probably due to the fact that Capone's men were dressed as policemen but the memory was quickly washed away with a few drinks.

The St Valentine's Day Massacre February 1929. Seven members of the Bugs Moran gang were killed by Al Capone's gang. Americans were not much concerned by gangland killings – as long as only gangsters were being murdered.

Q Do you think this was a healthy attitude for the public to adopt?

In 1933 Americans asked themselves whether America was now a less violent, more honest and moral country than it had been before Prohibition. Prohibition encouraged a rise in gangsterism, corruption and did nothing to reduce violence in the family. In March 1933 one of the new President Roosevelt's first steps was to legalise the sale of beer. Prohibition was over.

How prosperous were the 1920s?

The 'Roaring Twenties' is one of those convenient terms that seems to sum up a whole decade. It suggests that the decade was a prosperous one. However, as with all easy generalisations, such descriptions can be misleading. The point of this exercise is to establish just how prosperous the 1920s were.

SOURCE 1:

America's Gross National Product, 1920–29. GNP is a measure of how prosperous a country is – the greater the figure, the richer it is. The figures are in billions of dollars.

1920:	$90 billion	**1921:**	$74 billion
1922:	$74 billion	**1923:**	$86 billion
1924:	$88 billion	**1925:**	$91 billion
1926:	$98 billion	**1927:**	$96 billion
1928:	$98 billion	**1929:**	$104 billion

SOURCE 2:

Farm prices – the price of wheat per bushel in dollars. This is what American farmers got for the wheat they sold by the bushel.

1920:	$1.83	**1921:**	$1.03
1922:	$0.97	**1923:**	$0.93
1924:	$1.25	**1925:**	$1.44
1926:	$1.22	**1927:**	$1.19
1928:	$1.00	**1929:**	$1.04

SOURCE 3:

Farm prices – price per head of cattle in dollars.

1920:	$53	**1921:**	$39
1922:	$30	**1923:**	$32
1924:	$32	**1925:**	$32
1926:	$37	**1927:**	$40
1928:	$51	**1929:**	$58

SOURCE 4:

Average yearly income per head in dollars.

1922:	$672	**1929:**	$857

SOURCE 5:

American economists believed that an income of $2500 a year was the minimum needed in the 1920s for a reasonable standard of living for a family.

In 1929, 72 per cent of families had an income below $2500.

28%

72%

1 Did GNP rise or fall in the 1920s and by roughly what percentage?

2 In what way does Source 4 confirm the general impression of Source 1?

3 Would it be fair to say that the 1920s was a difficult decade for American farmers? Explain your answer using Sources 2 and 3.

4 'These sources prove that the 1920s were a decade of prosperity.' Explain whether you agree or disagree with this view, using the sources given here. What other statistics would help you arrive at an answer?

THE GREAT DEPRESSION

The Wall Street Crash

In the space of a week from 24 October 1929 the value of the New York Stock Market fell by about 50 per cent and it continued to fall. The Dow-Jones Index, which measures the value of the market, stood at 106 points in 1924. During 1929 it had risen by five times its value in 1924 to 542 points. In 1932 it stood at just 41 points and shares were worth less than ten per cent of their 1929 values.

What made matters worse is that many investors had borrowed the money to buy the shares. This is called buying 'on the margin'. Now they found themselves unable to pay the bank or the stockbroker and were forced to sell their possessions to find the money.

Not that many Americans had shares (perhaps only two million) and only a small percentage of the population was directly affected. But the banks were forced to stop making further loans to businesses and had to tell their customers to pay back the money they had lent them immediately. This made the economic situation even worse and in this sense the Wall Street Crash did have an effect on the Depression but it did not cause it. The huge profits which could be made on the stock market had also led investors to speculate in shares. Some of this money would normally have been invested in setting up new businesses and would have created new jobs, boosting the economy.

Over-production

The basic cause of the Depression was over-production. American companies had simply been making more goods than people could buy. The market had become 'saturated' with goods. Either they had all the vacuum cleaners and refrigerators they wanted, or they could not afford them.

American factories had become much more efficient during the 1920s (productivity went up by 43 per cent) but wages had increased by only 11 per cent. If workers' wages had gone up more they would have been able to continue buying consumer goods. Instead, employers laid off more workers to cut costs, or they lowered wages and this meant that even fewer goods were sold.

This led to a downward spiral in the economy with more workers losing their jobs in order to reduce costs and lower prices. Unemployment increased to 4.3 million in 1930 from just 1.5 million in 1929. In 1933 it reached a peak of 13 million. Twenty-five per cent of the adult population in the USA were unemployed.

Under-consumption

There is another way of looking at over-production and this is to see the Depression as a crisis of *under-consumption*. In this view the Depression was not caused by too many goods being produced but because people were too poor to afford them. If employers had increased wages more and shared company profits more fairly with the workforce then people would have had the money to buy the goods produced. This explanation is popular with socialist historians. They see the workers as the victims of the employers' search for greater profit.

What were the causes of the Great Depression?

One of the most important tasks that historians have is to explain why certain events in history took place. It is an important and difficult task because events like the Great Depression of the 1930s have many different causes. These causes are also linked with each other. Some historians describe this as 'the inter-linking of causal factors' or as 'the web of causation'.

The diagram below shows how several different causes of the Depression link in with each other like a spider's web. Each of the causes listed here has been explained earlier in the chapter.

1 The first thing that you have to do is copy the diagram into your file. Then explain how each of these factors helped to cause the Depression and show how they link in with the next box by following the arrow. For example, you could say this for the box labelled 'Advertising': 'Advertising persuaded people to buy things by bringing their attention to the products available even if they didn't really need them. This led companies to turn out even more goods, adding to over-production.'

2 Not all causes are equally important in helping to bring about a particular event. If you can take a cause away and still think that an event would have happened sooner or later, then it is obviously not essential. There are probably at least two causes listed in this diagram that are not essential for the Depression to have happened. Which ones are they and why?

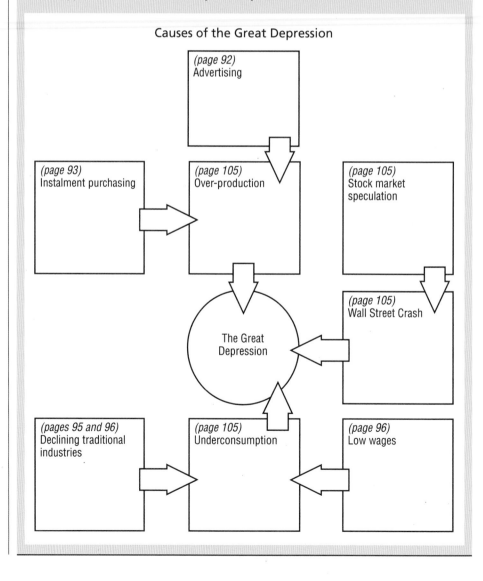

Causes of the Great Depression

▶ The Spiral into Depression

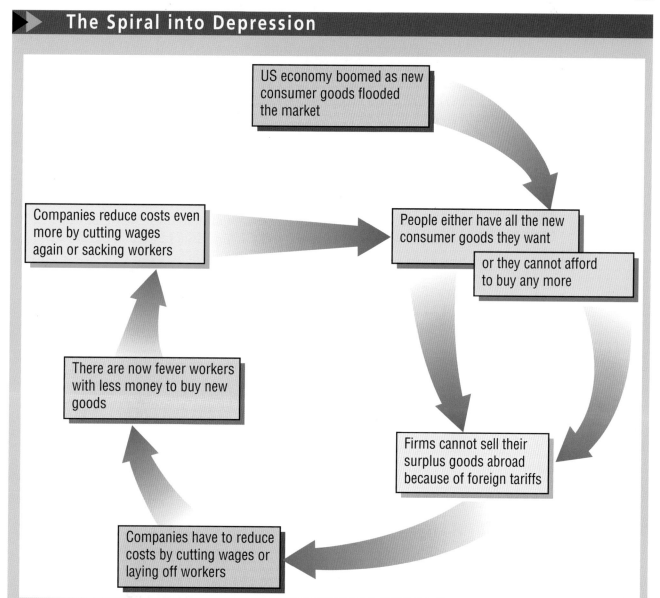

US economy boomed as new consumer goods flooded the market

Companies reduce costs even more by cutting wages again or sacking workers

People either have all the new consumer goods they want

or they cannot afford to buy any more

There are now fewer workers with less money to buy new goods

Firms cannot sell their surplus goods abroad because of foreign tariffs

Companies have to reduce costs by cutting wages or laying off workers

The statistics below show the impact of the Depression on three key areas of the US economy between 1929 and 1933: prices; employment and wages. Study them and the diagram above and then answer the questions which follow.

These statistics come from the US Bureau of Labor. They use 1926 as the base year and give it an index value of 100. So, for example, wages in 1930 were just 81% of what they were in 1926 and there was 15% more unemployment (100 – 85 = 15) than there was in 1926. The average income in 1926 was $678 so 81% of that gives an average income of $549.

		Prices	Employment	Wages
1929	(average)	95	97	101
1930	"	86	85	81
1931	"	73	72	62
1932	"	65	60	42
1933	"	66	65	44

1 Which year represents the worst year of the Depression and why?

2 Explain why (a) prices; (b) employment and (c) wages all fell after 1929. (Refer back to the 'Spiral into Depression' diagram for help, if necessary.)

3 Explain how these three areas of the economy were all linked together during this period. For example, think about why an increase in wages paid out would lead to an increase in jobs and prices.

4 Do the figures on wages and unemployment support the interpretation that the Depression was caused by under-consumption?

5 Design the opposite of a 'Spiral into Depression' diagram. This would show how an economy can 'spiral into prosperity' once workers have some money to spend. It could start with the following box:

The government provides jobs for workers and so employment increases and they can afford to buy products.

Rugged individualism

Herbert Hoover was President from 1929 to 1933 and these were the worst years of the Depression. He has been heavily criticised for doing nothing because of his belief in 'rugged individualism'. He believed that Americans were at their best when the government did not control their activities, especially their economic activities. He believed that Americans should rely on their own abilities and not government handouts to see them through crises. This was the standard policy of the Republican Party that Hoover led.

However, he did make some efforts to help those in need by encouraging charitable help through the President's Organisation for Unemployment Relief. But he was reluctant to spend federal (government) money to do this. When he did eventually agree to spend taxpayers' money, through the Reconstruction Finance Corporation, most of it went to big businesses and not to poverty-stricken workers. The public did not forgive him for doing so little. By 1931 mocking phrases based on his name had entered the language: 'Hooverville' was a shanty town of cardboard and corrugated iron homes; 'Hoover blankets' were newspapers used by people to keep warm; 'Hoover flags' were empty trouser pockets turned inside out as a sign of poverty.

Q

1 Why was 'buying on the margin' such a risky way to buy shares?
2 How did the Wall Street Crash make the Depression worse?
3 Why were phrases such as 'Hoover blankets' and 'Hoover flags' such bitter and mocking ones?
4 Why do you think 'rugged individualism' led Hoover to do so little to get Americans out of the Depression?
5 Why was over-production a major cause of the Depression?
6 Why do you think under-consumption is more popular with socialist historians as an explanation of the Depression?

The Depression was not Hoover's fault and it was his bad luck that he was President when it was at its worst. It was also his bad luck to be replaced as President by a man who had so many of the qualities that Hoover lacked. Franklin Delano Roosevelt (or FDR, as he was popularly known) had a charming, easy-going manner that Hoover did not. He was also firmly committed to the idea that it was the government's duty to help end the Depression. He would do this by spending as much federal money as was necessary to provide jobs and hope.

Roosevelt came from a very wealthy family. But despite his privileged background he had a deep concern for the welfare of ordinary Americans. His enemies said he was really a socialist. In fact, Roosevelt understood that the worst enemy of the private-enterprise system was poverty. Hungry and jobless people are, he said, 'the stuff of which revolutions are made'.

NEW DEAL, NEW FUTURE

Roosevelt, a Democrat, defeated Hoover in the 1932 election, winning seven million votes more than his Republican opponent. He promised a 'New Deal' to the American people. He gave himself 100 days to put them back to work and deal with the worst aspects of the crisis.

His first task was to save the nation's banks. More than one in every five banks had already gone out of business with their customers losing all their savings. Panic had gripped the other banks' customers as they demanded to get their money out before their bank collapsed as well. If customers tried to

Men queuing for bread in New York City. This might seem like a fairly typical photograph from Depression America in the early 1930s except that it was taken in 1938.

Q Can you suggest why this might make it even more interesting to an historian?

withdraw all their money at the same time, it would lead to the collapse of the entire banking system. One customer in Ohio told his bank: 'If my money's there, I don't want it. If it's not, I want it.'

Roosevelt's Emergency Banking Act in March 1933 closed all the banks in the USA for ten days. Federal officials checked through the accounts of all these banks. They only allowed the ones in a sound financial position to re-open. The Act closed the weak banks and others were given federal grants to help them. Seventy per cent were allowed to carry on trading and this restored American confidence in banks. By the end of March over one billion dollars in hoarded bank notes had been deposited with the banks.

Some of FDR's measures were temporary and others were more permanent. The Federal Emergency Relief Act (FERA) was an emergency, temporary measure which provided $500 000 000 of benefits to be given to the unemployed and poor. But the FERA was not the approach Roosevelt favoured. He wanted to give men useful work which would give them back their dignity rather than federal 'handouts' that were little more than government charity. The FERA was replaced in November 1933 by the Civil Works Administration (CWA) which found men jobs. The CWA built 410 000 kilometres of roads, 33 000 kilometres of sewers and over 400 airports.

The Tennessee Valley Authority was also set up during the Hundred Days and its benefits were similarly long-lasting. The TVA tackled the problem of poverty and backwardness along the valley of the River Tennessee. The soil had been overcultivated, eroded and was often flooded. The TVA brought seven US states together to build 20 dams that would provide electricity, reforestation and irrigation for the farms along the valley. By 1943 the TVA increased the number of farms with electric power from two in every 100 farms to 80 in every 100.

A family in Depression America.

> **Q** What guesses could you make about when this photograph was taken and in which area of the USA? Why is a photograph like this of limited value to an historian?

The blue eagle

Two other important Hundred Days programmes were provided by the National Recovery Administration and the Agricultural Adjustment Act. The first tried to improve industry by bringing together government, employers and workers in a patriotic scheme to boost the economy. The NRA encouraged fair competition to benefit the employers by setting limits on how much each company could produce and the prices it could charge. This was intended to reduce the surplus of goods. It also set down a maximum number of hours that workers could be made to work and set a minimum wage of $12 for a 40-hour week. All companies that agreed to take part in this voluntary scheme could display a blue eagle and stamp it on their products.

The NRA was not a great success since employers resented the right it gave workers to join a union. Henry Ford refused to join the scheme, declaring that he wouldn't have 'that Roosevelt buzzard on my cars'. Workers were initially very enthusiastic about the NRA but grew disillusioned when FDR, in a typical compromise, allowed firms to set up their own 'tame' unions which workers were 'invited' to join. Those who joined proper unions often found themselves sacked. Relations between workers and employers became very bitter and violent. In 1934, one and a half million workers took part in over 1800 separate strikes in protest.

The **Supreme Court** put an end to the NRA in 1935. It decided that the NRA was unconstitutional because it broke the laws of the American **Constitution**. This meant that much of Roosevelt's New Deal was illegal because it allowed too much power to the federal government in controlling business in America. FDR was furious about this ruling but waited until victory in the 1936 election before hitting back (see page 115).

The Triple A

The Agricultural Adjustment Act (AAA) was just as controversial but probably more successful. The Triple A asked farmers to produce fewer crops and less food and paid them money not to raise livestock and to destroy their crops. Over-production was the key reason for the poor state of American agriculture. Output would have to be reduced so that prices would rise. This would allow farmers to start making profits again which was difficult to do when a wagon-load of oats could be worth less than a pair of shoes. This was bound to be controversial at a time when many in the cities were going hungry.

Ten million acres of cotton and six million pigs were destroyed in 1933 to ensure higher prices. Prices did rise and so did farmers' incomes, but mostly for the bigger farmers and mostly because of government subsidies rather than higher prices. Nonetheless, the price of wheat in 1941 was 94 cents a bushel – up from its 1932 price of 38 cents. In an economic sense, the Triple A can be seen as reasonably successful but many have questioned its morality.

The second New Deal

In 1935 Roosevelt began another New Deal programme designed to improve the rights of workers and provide some social security benefits. The Social Security Act began the first national system of pensions and these were first paid in 1940. States were also made to provide unemployment benefit. By European standards, the payments were not generous. An unemployed worker could expect only $15 a week and then only for four months. But the Act did represent an important change in American attitudes to the role of the state. Americans no longer saw these benefits as charity to be ashamed of but as a right that the federal government had a duty to provide.

Q

1 In what ways was Roosevelt a very different President from Hoover?
2 Why do you think Roosevelt had such an easy election victory over Hoover?
3 What do you think the bank customer in Ohio meant by the quotation on page 109?
4 Why was the National Recovery Act unpopular with employers and then workers?
5 Why was the Triple A such a controversial policy?
6 What do you suppose Roosevelt meant by the phrase that hungry and jobless people 'are the stuff of which revolutions are made'?

The sit-down strike

The Wagner Act went some way to restoring the faith of American workers in the New Deal after the disappointment of the NRA. The Act gave the workers the right to choose their own union in a secret ballot and forced the employers to recognise it. However, employers resented this 'interference' in the way that they ran their companies. Workers would have to fight bitter and violent battles to gain rights promised by the Act.

Goodyear tyre workers invented a new form of strike in 1936 to force the company to recognise their union. They sat inside and occupied their factory, refusing to work or to leave until Goodyear agreed to negotiate wages and conditions with their chosen union. The 'sit-down' strike was born. It was immediately successful not only because tyres were not produced, hitting hard at company profits, but also because Goodyear could not bring in newly-hired workers to replace the strikers as the factory was already full of men on strike.

Employers had not thought twice about hiring thugs to attack workers on picket lines outside factories. They hesitated about doing the same inside a factory with so much valuable machinery at risk. The number of workers in unions rose from three million in 1933 to ten million in 1941.

The Workers Progress Administration was another part of the second New Deal. In its eight years of existence it provided work for eight million Americans (about 20 per cent of the working population) at a cost of some $11 billion. The WPA built schools, hospitals, roads and airports. It did not neglect writers, artists, musicians or actors either. All of these found work with the WPA.

Women and the not-so New Deal

The 1930s was a mixed decade for women. In some respects women did become more prominent: in sport; politics; the cinema and in aviation. Amelia

Earhart proved that women could be resourceful and brave. She was the first person to fly solo from Hawaii to the Pacific coast. She was killed in 1937 when her plane crashed as she tried to fly solo around the world. Actresses such as Mae West, Joan Crawford and Bette Davis made a name for themselves as strong independent women. Women no longer had to play the cinema role of the vulnerable 'sex kitten' to have a film career. Frances Perkins, Secretary of Labour, was the first woman member of the government. She was among several women appointed by FDR to jobs previously only held by men, such as ambassadors and federal judges. But progress for women in politics was slow. Only one woman was elected to the Senate in the 1930s.

Clara Bow in a scene from her 1927 film 'It'. Clara Bow became the symbol of the new woman of the 1920s; confident, sexy and not afraid to challenge traditional views about women's behaviour. She became known as the 'It Girl' after this film and whatever 'it' was she seemed to have it.

Women workers continued to find jobs during the 1930s and the percentage of women in work rose from 22 per cent to 25 per cent but this was mostly because they were cheaper to employ. Women earned approximately half the income of men in 1937 ($525 a year compared to $1027 for men). The jobs were typically female ones in low-status occupations such as clerical, sales and domestic service. The percentage of women in professions such as medicine, higher education and law actually fell.

The notion that a married woman's place was in the home and that the role of the male breadwinner had to be protected at all costs remained strong. Most states passed laws excluding married women from public-service jobs. Any women who turned to the New Deal to defend their rights were to be disappointed. The NRA allowed employers to pay women less than men for the same job. The Civilian Conservation Corps was able to find jobs for 2 750 000 men but only 8000 women. While it is true that there was nothing in the New Deal specifically for women, they did benefit as workers in the same way as men because they gained the right to join a trade union. But only a tiny proportion of women (perhaps only one in 15) where in jobs that allowed unions.

Blacks and the very old deal

If women did not do well out of the New Deal then black women did even worse. Forty per cent of black women had a job but for much less pay than white women. The New Deal did nothing to get rid of the two worst forms of discrimination against blacks. They were not allowed to vote in most southern states (a policy known as 'disenfranchisement') and they were separated from whites and made to use different facilities (a policy known as 'segregation').

The number of black women workers in this photograph paints a typical picture of 1930s America: women in low-paid, low-status jobs. Roosevelt has been criticised for doing little for black workers but at least the New Deal gave some of them the confidence to take on their employers.

Roosevelt needed the support of southern white Democrats in the Senate to get his policies through. As they were opposed to black rights, he refused to upset them by supporting equal-rights proposals in the south.

The New Deal mostly benefited skilled, unionised workers and most blacks were unskilled and not in unions. One black worker later told an interviewer that the Depression 'only became official when it hit the white man'. Nonetheless, FDR did try to change attitudes to blacks by appointing the first black federal judge, William Hastie. The WPA had over one million blacks working for it in 1939. Roosevelt may not have done much for America's 20 million blacks but it was more than any US president since Lincoln.

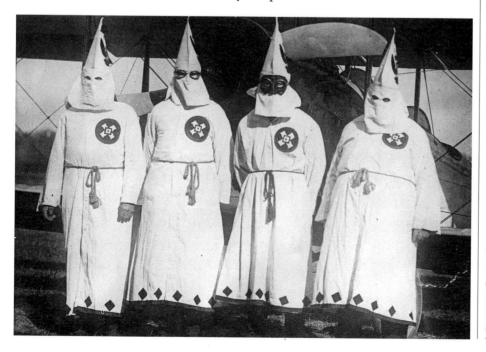

A photo of four members of the Ku Klux Klan taken in 1935. After this photograph was taken, these KKK men flew off to drop propaganda leaflets – though the one on the right may have had problems getting into his seat.

Did the New Deal benefit American blacks?

SOURCE 1:

A modern historian's view of the impact of the New Deal on American blacks:

'Roosevelt did not attempt to alter the two most obvious forms of oppression against the majority of black citizens in the south: segregation and disenfranchisement . . . Black Americans could list other grievances against Roosevelt's government. They called the NRA [National Recovery Act] the ''Negro Run Around'' because it forced the shutdown of many small black-run businesses and the layoff of black employees. The Triple A proved to be an economic disaster for nearly a million black poor farmers. Both the Civilian Conservation Corps and the Tennessee Valley Authority used racial segregation policies.'

Adapted from M E Parrish: *The Anxious Decades*

SOURCE 2:

Robin Langton was a black child during the Depression years. His father ran a restaurant and his mother was a teacher. He was interviewed by Studs Terkel for the book *Hard Times* published in 1970. This is part of his memories of that time:

'Roosevelt caught the mood of the black community. You did not look on him as being white, black, blue or green. He was President Roosevelt . . . The WPA and other projects introduced black people to handicrafts and trades. It gave Negroes a chance to have an office to work out of with a typewriter. It made us feel that there was something we could do . . . I don't remember any serious black opposition to Roosevelt.'

SOURCE 3:

Ed Nixon worked as a railway sleeping car porter during the Depression and was a member of the black porters' union, the Brotherhood of Sleeping Car Porters. He was fined eight day's pay by the Pullman Company for talking to his wife while at work:

'The Chicago office of the company said eight days. The local man [supervisor] made it read: eighteen days. So I said to my wife, ''They're askin' for a fight and they're gonna get it.'' The Brotherhood appealed to the Relations Board [the National Labour Relations Board set up under the New Deal]. I was not found guilty and the Pullman Company had to pay me for all the time lost. And that my record be clear of all charges.'

Studs Terkel: *Hard Times*

SOURCE 4:

(left) Blacks queuing for government relief in 1937.

1 What did 'segregation' and 'disenfranchisement' (Source 1) mean for blacks?
2 What else does Source 1 criticise Roosevelt for?
3 Does Source 2 support this critical view of Roosevelt? Explain your answer with evidence from the source.
4 Why might Nixon in Source 3 be grateful to the New Deal?
5 The text on page 113 says 'The New Deal mostly benefited skilled, unionised workers and most blacks were unskilled and not in unions.' How can you explain the support seen in Sources 2 and 3 for Roosevelt if blacks did not benefit from his policies? (Think carefully about the occupations of the blacks in these two sources.)
6 The historian in Source 1 clearly has a different interpretation from Sources 2 and 3. How can you explain this?

Opponents of the New Deal

The Supreme Court consisted of nine judges appointed for the rest of their life. Six of these were conservatives who opposed Roosevelt's New Deal. They declared that the federal government was interfering with the rights of each state to carry out their own policies dealing with the Depression. This issue is known as 'states' rights'. Because several of Roosevelt's New Deal programmes, like the TVA and AAA, interfered with states' rights, the Supreme Court declared them illegal.

In 1937 Roosevelt threatened to force all judges over the age of 70 to retire and appoint new ones. This would allow FDR to appoint two new judges and so give him a five-to-four majority in the Court. This was legal, but 'court-packing' (as it was called) was not popular. Many Americans, even members of Roosevelt's own Democratic Party, valued the role of the Supreme Court as a check on the power of the federal government. Fortunately the President never had to force the issue because the Court suddenly began to approve controversial New Deal programmes like the Wagner and Social Security Acts. Now that the judges were more co-operative Roosevelt ditched his plans to force judges over 70 to retire.

Roosevelt also faced opposition from other groups for very different reasons. A Louisiana senator, Huey 'Kingfish' Long, led a successful 'Share Our Wealth' campaign to force the rich to pay more taxes to help the poor. Long claimed that Roosevelt was not doing enough. Long was shot dead by an assassin's bullet in 1935 just before his bodyguards emptied 61 bullets into the killer's body. Wealthy businessmen, on the other hand, protested that Roosevelt was doing too much. Some of them set up the American Liberty League to defend their interests against government interference in the way that they ran their businesses. They complained about the 'waste' of tax-payers' money and the New Deal policies that favoured workers.

"Mother Wilfred wrote a bad word!"

'Mother, Wilfred wrote a bad word.' This cartoonist reflects the concerns of some rich Americans about Roosevelt and his New Deal policies – though the cartoonist doesn't seem to share them.

Q Why did some wealthy Americans think 'Roosevelt' was a dirty word?

Q

1 Why did the 1930s do little for women's employment prospects?
2 Why was the New Deal a disappointment for women?
3 Why was Roosevelt unwilling to do much to help the cause of black civil rights? Do you think his reason is understandable?
4 Why was 'court-packing' likely to cost Roosevelt support?
5 How justified do you think businessmen were in their reasons for opposing Roosevelt's New Deal?
6 What do you suppose the black worker meant by the phrase quoted on page 113 that the Depression 'only became official when it hit the white man'?

An evaluation of the New Deal

The New Deal lasted a brief five years and most of its measures came during two flurries of activity in the spring of 1933 and the summer of 1935. Its impact on politics, society and economy in the USA was huge but it was less successful in ending the economic problems caused by the Depression. There was little economic recovery by the end of the decade. American output in 1939 barely reached its 1929 level. Unemployment stood at nine and a half million, higher than it had been in 1931.

It was the Second World War that finally ended the Depression because of the massive increases needed in output for the war. The start of the Second World War had an immediate impact on the US economy. The value of American exports rose from $3.2 billion in 1939 to $5.1 billion in 1941. This provided a massive boost for export companies as they supplied the Allied nations who were at war with Germany.

More lasting and significant change came about in social and political attitudes. For the first time, the government accepted its responsibility to provide help for the sick, poor, old and unemployed. Americans also accepted that the government had a duty to control aspects of business and society. 'Rugged individualism' quietly faded away. Above all, Roosevelt provided hope for millions of people at a time of despair and ensured that America's democratic system survived this turbulent decade.

Q

Extended writing

Write at least 300 words on each of the following questions:

1 How far did the New Deal
  a change people's attitudes to the role of government?
  b change the lives of workers, women and blacks in American society?

To answer **b** it is important to discuss the situation for these groups of people before the New Deal. What rights did they have? How well off were they? How were they treated? Then compare this part of your answer with their situation in 1941. What has changed and what has not changed? Were the changes really significant or just on the surface? You should use the same approach for attitudes to the role of government before and at the end of the New Deal.

2 How successful was the New Deal in solving the problems of the economy?
  Begin by setting out the condition of the economy in 1933 and its problems e.g. unemployment, falling prices, ruined farmers, low output. Then compare your assessment with the situation in 1941. How much has changed?
  You should use all the relevant information you have read in the chapter as well as the statistics on page 117 on the US economy during the New Deal years.

Unemployment 1933–41 in millions of workers:

1933: 12.8	1934: 11.3	1935: 10.6
1936: 9.0	1937: 7.7	1938: 10.4
1939: 9.5	1940: 8.1	1941: 5.6

Gross National Product in billions of dollars. GNP is a measure of how much wealth a country produces – the higher the figure, the more prosperous the country.

1933: 56	1934: 65	1935: 72
1936: 83	1937: 91	1938: 85
1939: 91	1940: 101	1941: 126

Price of wheat per bushel in dollars. This is an indication of how well American farmers were doing – the higher the price for their produce, the better off the farmers were.

1933: 0.74	1934: 0.85	1935: 0.83
1936: 1.03	1937: 0.96	1938: 0.56
1939: 0.69	1940: 0.68	1941: 0.94

5 Britain 1906–51

1908	**Old-age pension introduced**
1914	**Outbreak of First World War**
1918	**End of war; women get the vote**
1926	**General Strike**
1931	**Formation of National Government**
1936	**Jarrow March**
1939	**Outbreak of Second World War**
1945	**End of War**
1947	**Nationalisation of the coal industry**
1948	**NHS introduced**

This chapter focuses on three key issues:

● *How did Britain change in the twentieth century?*

● *What were the causes and effects of the Depression?*

● *How did the Welfare State develop?*

The picture above right shows Parliament Street, Harrogate, Yorkshire, in 1907. You can see that the horse is the main form of transport.

Guildford High Street, Surrey, in 1923. Less than 20 years later and the internal combustion engine has made a big impact. There are no horses to be seen.

At the beginning of the twentieth century Britain was one of the world's great powers. Indeed with an empire which stretched across the globe it thought of itself as the greatest. In 1900 Britain produced 18 per cent of the world's industrial goods. By 1950 Britain's wealth and empire had dwindled and it was no longer a great power.

As the two photographs on page 118 show, the twentieth century has seen dramatic technological developments. This chapter looks at how Britain has changed politically, economically and socially.

THE CHANGING POLITICAL SCENE

As the twentieth century began Victoria was still queen and British politics were dominated by just two parties – the Conservatives and the Liberals. The big issue that divided the two parties at the start of the century was free trade. The Liberals supported free trade; they believed that Britain's wealth depended on trade. Goods would remain cheap and trade would boom as long as there were no import or export duties. The Conservatives however believed that British industry faced strong competition from countries such as America and Germany and would not be able to compete unless **tariffs** were imposed. This would make foreign goods more expensive than British products. As a result British people would choose to buy British goods and so British industry would thrive.

The Conservatives were often known as the 'Unionist Party'. This is because they wished to preserve the union of Britain and Ireland. They did not want to allow the Irish to rule themselves. The Liberals supported Home Rule for the Irish, and after 1906 they also supported social reform, seeking to improve the working and living conditions of ordinary people.

The voting system was rather different at the beginning of the twentieth century. The only people who could vote in elections were men who were over 21 and owned a house. This meant that about seven million people could vote out of a population of about 45 million.

The rise of the Labour Party

In the nineteenth century **socialist** societies had formed in Britain. As poverty and dangerous working conditions in industry became increasingly common these societies became popular. In 1893 James Keir Hardie formed the Independent Labour Party (ILP) to try and get socialists elected to parliament. This meant that it was a democratic socialist party, unlike the Communists in Russia, who believed that socialism could only be achieved through a revolution. In 1899 the party gained the support of the Trade Union Congress (TUC) and the Labour Representative Committee (LRC) was formed as a result. In 1900 two LRC MPs were elected. One of these was Keir Hardie himself.

Over the next three years the membership of the LRC trebled. The main reason for this was a court decision in 1901 known as the 'Taff Vale Judgement'. In 1900 railway workers on the Taff Vale Railway in south Wales went on strike. During the strike the company lost money as no trains were running. The company sued the union and the court declared that the union would have to pay the company's losses. Before Taff Vale, most union members and leaders supported going on strike to improve working conditions. After Taff Vale, it appeared that unions could no longer afford to go on strike, and so getting MPs elected to parliament became a much more popular option. In 1906 the LRC became known as the Labour Party.

The problem of the third party

The British voting system is not one of **proportional representation** like in Germany after the war (see page 60). The British system divides the country into constituencies and whoever wins the most votes in that constituency is elected. This tends to produce a two-party system. Those people who are content with the government will vote for the party which is in power. Those people who are not happy with the government will vote for the party who are likely to win enough seats to replace them. Therefore third parties, which the voters believe are not likely to win enough seats to form a government, tend to win few votes. In the early years of the twentieth century the Labour Party was the third party. In 1906 they attempted to overcome this problem by making a deal with the Liberal Party so that in certain constituencies the two parties did not oppose one another. This resulted in 29 Labour candidates being elected.

After the war, the 1918 Representation of the People Act gave the vote to all men over 21 and all women over 30 who were house owners. Veterans of the war were allowed to vote at 19. This increased the number of voters from seven million to 21 million. The new leader of the Labour Party, James Ramsay MacDonald, was determined to make people think of his party as the official opposition party. Then they would vote for Labour when they were fed up with the government. The chart below shows just how successful he was and in January 1924 he became the first ever Labour Prime Minister.

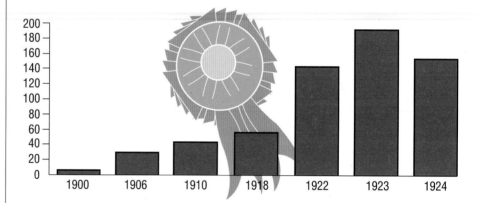

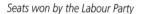

Seats won by the Labour Party

A poster produced by the Unionist Party in 1924. The poster asks voters to choose between the Bolshevist 'rag' or the British flag. The Unionists tried to make voters connect the Labour Party with Russian Communists rather than the British people.

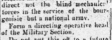

MOSCOW ORDERS TO OUR REDS.

GREAT PLOT DISCLOSED YESTERDAY.

"PARALYSE THE ARMY AND NAVY."

AND MR. MACDONALD WOULD LEND RUSSIA OUR MONEY!

DOCUMENT ISSUED BY FOREIGN OFFICE

AFTER "DAILY MAIL" HAD SPREAD THE NEWS.

A "very secret" letter of instruction from Moscow, which we publish below, discloses a great Bolshevik plot to paralyse the British Army and Navy and to plunge the country into civil war.

The letter is addressed by the Bolsheviks of Moscow to the Soviet Government's servants in Great Britain, the Communist Party, who in turn are the masters of Mr. Ramsay MacDonald's Government, which has signed a treaty with Moscow whereby the Soviet is to be guaranteed a "loan" of millions of British money.

The letter is signed by Zinoviev, the Dictator of Petrograd, President of the Third (Moscow) International, and is addressed to A. McManus, the British representative on the executive of this International, who returned from Moscow to London on October 18 to take part in the general election campaign.

Our information is that official copies of the letter, which is dated September 15, were delivered to the Foreign Secretary, Mr. Ramsay MacDonald, and the Home Secretary, Mr. Arthur Henderson, immediately after it was received some weeks ago. On Wednesday afternoon copies were officially circulated by the Executive authorities to high officers of the Army and Navy.

A copy of the document came into the possession of *The Daily Mail*, and we felt it our duty to make it public. We circulated printed copies to other London morning newspapers yesterday afternoon. Later on the Foreign Office decided to issue it, together with a protest, dated yesterday, which the British Government has sent to M. Rakov-

...paign of disclosure of the foreign policy of MacDonald.

ARMED INSURRECTION.

The IKKI [Executive Committee, third (Communist) International] will willingly place at your disposal the wide material in its possession regarding the activities of British imperialism in the Middle and Far East. In the meanwhile, however, strain every nerve in the struggle for the ratification of the Treaty, in favour of a continuation of negotiations regarding the regulation of relations between the S.S.S.R. and England. A settlement of relations between the two countries will assist in the revolutionising of the international and British proletariat not less than a successful rising in any of the working districts of England, as the establishment of close contact between the British and Russian proletariat, the exchange of delegations and workers, etc., will make it possible for us to extend and develop the propaganda of ideas of Leninism in England and the Colonies. Armed warfare must be preceded by a struggle against the inclinations to compromise which are embedded among the majority of British workmen, against the ideas of evolution and peaceful extermination of capitalism. Only then will it be possible to count upon complete success of an armed

Zinoviev, whose real name is Apfelbaum.

insurrection. In Ireland and the Colonies the case is different; there there is a national question, and this represents too great a factor for success for us to waste time on a prolonged preparation of the working class.

But even in England, as in other countries where the workers are politically developed, events themselves may more rapidly revolutionise the working masses than propaganda. For instance, a strike movement, repressions by the Government, etc.

...letariat and desire in the future to direct not the blind mechanical forces in the service of the bourgeoisie but a national army.

Form a directing operative head of the Military Section.

Do not put this off to a future moment, which may be pregnant with events and catch you unprepared.

Desiring you all success, both in organisation and in your struggle,

With Communist Greetings,

President of the Presidium of the IKKI,

ZINOVIEV.

Member of the Presidium,

McMANUS.

Secretary, KUUSINEN.

FOREIGN OFFICE PROTEST.

REPLY WITHOUT DELAY REQUESTED.

The following is the text of the letter sent yesterday by Mr. J. D. Gregory to M. Rakovski, the Chargé d'Affaires in London of the Soviet Union:—

Foreign Office, October 24, 1924

Sir,—I have the honour to invite your attention to the enclosed copy of a letter which has been received by the Central Committee of the British Communist Party from the President of the Executive Committee of the Communist International, over the signature of Monsieur Zinoviev, its president, dated September 15.

The letter contains instructions to British subjects to work for the violent overthrow of existing institutions in this country, and for the subversion of his Majesty's armed forces as a means to that end.

2. It is my duty to inform you that his Majesty's Government cannot allow this propaganda and must regard it as a direct interference from outside in British domestic affairs.

3. No one who understands the constitution and the relationships of the Communist International will doubt its intimate connection and contact with the Soviet Government. No Government will ever tolerate an arrangement with a foreign Government by which the latter is in formal diplomatic relations of a correct kind with it, while at the same time a propagandist body organically connected with that foreign Government encourages and even orders subjects of the former to plot and plan revolutions for its overthrow.

Such conduct is not only a grave departure from the rules of international comity, but a violation of specific and solemn undertakings repeatedly given to his Majesty's Government.

4. So recently as June 4 of last year the Soviet Government made the following solemn agreement with his Majesty's Government:—

The Soviet Government undertakes not to support with funds or in any other form persons or bodies or agencies

 Q

1 What does the bar chart on page 120 show you about the Labour Party in the early twentieth century?
2 What effect does the First World War have on the fortunes of the Labour Party? What explanation can you find for this?
3 Look at the Unionist poster on page 120. What impression does it give?
4 **a** What evidence can you find to support the view given in the poster?
 b What evidence can you find to oppose the view given in the poster?

The decline of the Liberal Party

In 1906 the Liberal Party won a massive election victory with 399 seats against the Conservative Party's 157. Yet in 1924 they won just 40 seats and they have remained the third party of British politics ever since. Why did this happen?

Before the First World War both the Labour and the Liberal parties supported social reform. However, the Liberal Party was the only one likely to be able to form a government and the Labour Party won very few seats. The First World War changed this. At the beginning of the war Britain had a Liberal government led by Asquith but the war did not lead to the quick victory that had been expected and Asquith was blamed. In December 1916 he was replaced by another leading Liberal, Lloyd George. He set up a coalition government which included Conservatives as well as the Labour leader Arthur

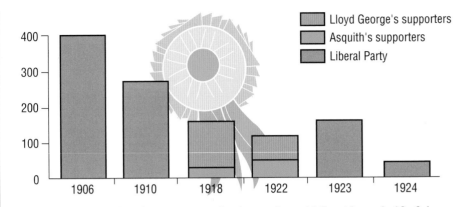

(right) Seats won by the Liberal Party

Henderson. The Liberal Party was split down the middle. About half of the Liberal Members of Parliament supported Lloyd George. However, half of them continued to support Asquith who remained the official party leader. The split continued after the war and so there were now two Liberal parties. Voters who wanted social reform turned to the Labour Party. Those who could not face socialism turned to the Conservatives.

'The Locust Years': the British economy in the Twenties and Thirties

At the end of the war the soldiers returned to Britain. You might expect this to produce high unemployment but this did not happen. Many of the women who had worked during the war lost their jobs to some of the returning soldiers and an economic boom created jobs for others. People had been unable to spend much money during the war years and so they had managed to save a lot of money. Now they wanted to be able to buy the sorts of things that had not been available during the war. However, the boom was temporary. Prices shot up so that people were buying foreign goods as well as British goods. British factories found that they could not sell all of the goods that they were producing. By 1921 the boom was over. Britain had not seen the dramatic economic growth that had been experienced in the USA in the 1920s. Why was this? There were four main reasons:

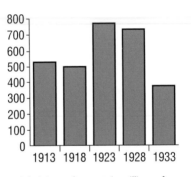

Britain's total exports in millions of pounds

- **Exports.** The figures for total exports (on the left) show that Britain's exports grew in the 1920s. However, the figures for textile exports (below, left) show that it was not every industry that enjoyed this expansion. The traditional industries of Britain, such as coal and textiles, were faced with new competition from countries that produced the same goods for less money. For instance India used to be a major market for cotton goods produced in Britain. In the 1920s India began to buy cotton goods from Japan. By 1935 they were buying more from Japan than Britain. In Europe Italy had been a major importer of British coal. After the war Germany needed to export coal to earn money to pay reparations and so they undercut British prices (by making their coal very cheap) and Italy bought their coal from Germany.

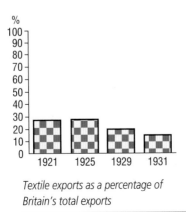

Textile exports as a percentage of Britain's total exports

- **The return to the Gold Standard.** In 1925 the government decided to return to the Gold Standard. This meant that the pound was now worth a fixed amount of gold equivalent to $4.86. Returning to the Gold Standard gave the impression that the pound was once again the most important currency in the world but setting its value at such a high level had disadvantages. It meant that British exports became more expensive, making it more difficult for British companies to sell their goods abroad. Britain was already facing competition from countries like Germany and Japan and returning to the Gold Standard made the problem worse.

• **Consumer goods.** As the figures on the previous page indicate the industries that produced consumer goods, such as cars and washing machines, were growing. Wages rose in the 1920s and people wished to buy modern consumer goods. However, expansion in the production of consumer goods was nothing like as great as that of the United States. Jobs were being created in these new British industries, but not nearly as many as in America.

• **The General Strike** (see page 124). The General Strike and the continued dispute in the coal industry caused a dip in industrial production due in particular to a shortage of coal.

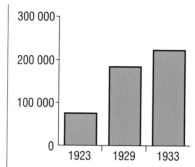

Numbers of cars produced in Britain.

Percentage of the workforce who were unemployed

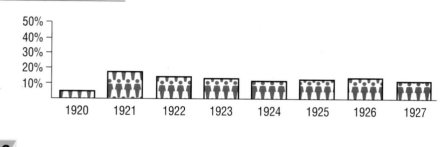

1920 1921 1922 1923 1924 1925 1926 1927

Q

1 Look at the bar chart above. In what year was the level of unemployment at its lowest? Why is this?
2 What reasons can you find to explain why the boom did not last for long?
3 What do you notice about the level of unemployment throughout the 1920s?
4 What reasons can you find to explain this?

(below) The original Hoover vacuum cleaner produced in 1907. It was expensive and large.

All the awkward cleaning is more easily done with Electrolux

Electrolux
The New Cleanness

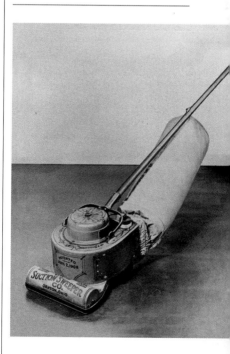

Q Why do you think such a machine was much more popular than the machine from 1907?

(left) An advertisement for an Electrolux vacuum cleaner of the 1920s.

WHY WAS THERE A GENERAL STRIKE IN 1926?

During the First World War the government had taken control of the coal mines to ensure that the war effort would not suffer from lack of supply of such a vital fuel. In 1921 the mines were returned to their owners. Since the First World War coal prices had fallen. This meant that the coal mine owners were not making as much profit as they were used to. They wanted to cut the miners' wages. This would help the owners to make more money.

The Miners' Federation was regarded as the strongest union. Other workers were worried that if the Miners' Federation could not protect miners' wages then in time the wages of most other workers would also be cut. Other unions would want to help the miners to win their struggle by going on strike as well. On 'Red Friday', 31 July 1925 a general strike was threatened when the mine owners announced cuts in the miners wages.

The government did not want the strike to happen and so they agreed to top up the miners' wages. This meant that the mine owners cut the money that they paid to the miners but the government made up the difference so that the miners still got the same amount of money. They agreed to do this for nine months. At the same time the government set up a Royal Commission to look at the coal industry and suggest a solution to the problem.

In 1926 the Royal Commission made its report. It recommended improvements in the working and living conditions of the miners but also said that wages had to be cut. The Miners' Federation rejected the report. It asked for the support of the other trade unions. The General Council of the Trade Union Congress (TUC) called for a general strike to begin on 3 May. Printers, rail and bus workers and dockers all took part. The TUC hoped that the strike would create so many problems for the owners of other industries that they would force the government and the mine owners to give in. Essential services such as refuse collectors were asked not to join so that public health was not put at risk. Oddly enough, the miners were unable to strike. They had been locked out of the mines by the owners because they would not accept the pay cuts.

While the strike lasted it received great support from union members. However the armed forces had made sure that food got to the shops. Anti-strike volunteers helped to run public transport. On 11 May Sir Herbert Samuel, who had chaired the Royal Commission, offered to resolve the strike. On 12 May the TUC General Council accepted his ideas, which included pay cuts for the miners. The strike was over. The miners continued to hold out but without the support of the other unions they had little chance of success. They had no wages coming in and so in December 1926 they finally accepted defeat.

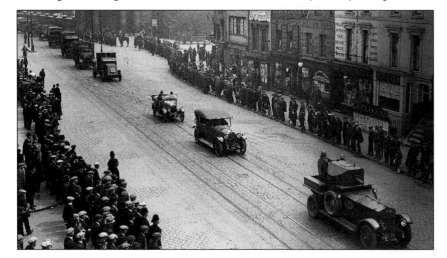

A food convoy protected by armoured vehicles travels down the East India Dock road in London during the General Strike.

Who supported the General Strike?

SOURCE 1:

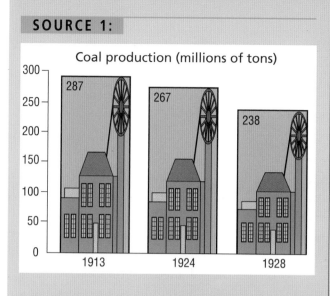

Coal production (millions of tons)

287   1913
267   1924
238   1928

SOURCE 2:

A miner's cage in Frog Lane Pit, Bristol, 1905. These lifts dropped at high speed down to the coal face far below. Caged birds were still used to detect the presence of any poisonous gases.

SOURCE 3:

Working underground at Frog Lane Pit, Bristol, 1905. Miners had to work in dangerous and cramped conditions. The only safety measure was the wooden pit props that supported the roof. Although coal was an important export and vital to the wealth of the nation, miners were poorly paid.

SOURCE 4:

Workers at the *Daily Mail* refused to print this editorial attacking the strikers on 3 May.

'The General Strike is not an industrial dispute; it is a revolutionary movement, intended to inflict suffering on the great mass of innocent persons in the community, and thereby put pressure on the government.'

SOURCE 5:

The *British Worker*, 10 May 1926. With the printers on strike there were no daily papers being produced. However, workers on the *Daily Herald* produced the *British Worker* to get the strikers' message across.

'A procession of transport workers, be-medalled and in Sunday clothes, marched in fours to Brockwell Park. the immense crowd in the park gave a clear indication of where the sympathies of the British nation lie in this dispute. Many of the crowd were trade unionists, including strikers and their families. But at least a third of them were of a class which the press loves to call "the general public" – bank and insurance clerks, small shopkeepers, holders of season tickets, dwellers in suburban villas.'

SOURCE 6:

THE LEVER BREAKS.

(*above*) 'The Lever breaks.' A cartoon in the magazine *Punch*, 19 May 1926. This magazine was read largely by the middle class and which supported the employers during the General Strike.

SOURCE 7:

(*above*) 'The real victims.' A cartoon from the magazine *Punch*, 21 July 1926:

'WORKER (*thrown out of employment through coal strike, to miner*). "I haven't said much so far; but I've got a wife and family to support the same as you, and I'm beginning to find you a bit of a nuisance."'

SOURCE 8:

Margaret Murray, a British historian, writing in 1994:

'There was widespread middle-class sympathy for the miners as well as an outstanding act of solidarity by the working class.'

1 Source 8 suggests that the middle class supported the General Strike.
  a What evidence can you find to support this view?
  b How reliable is this evidence? Explain your answer.
2 a What evidence can you find which does not support this view?
  b How reliable is this evidence? Explain your answer.
  c Do you agree or disagree with Source 8? Give your reasons.
3 Source 5 and Source 7 give very different views on the attitude of working people to the strike. How can you explain how these two publications could give such different interpretations?

Why did the TUC abandon the strike?

Why did the General Strike only last nine days? The miners did not give up the struggle for many months. They felt betrayed by the TUC. The leaders of the TUC were divided. Some believed that going on strike would bring success but others felt that strikes could not work. They felt that the miners must make a deal with the owners. Half of the General Council of the TUC were also MPs. They feared that the General Strike would portray the Labour Party as revolutionaries and this would drive away middle-class voters.

The aftermath of the strike

When they returned to work the miners were forced to accept longer hours and lower wages. At first sight it looks as though the miners lost the most along with the TUC, while the government and the mine owners gained. In 1927 the government passed the Trade Disputes and Trade Union Act. This made it illegal for unions to hold sympathy strikes on behalf of other workers. In other words general strikes were made illegal. In the years before 1926 about one million workers a year went on strike. In the years after 1926 this figure fell to 300 000. However this was largely because the union movement was controlled by leaders like Ernest Bevin who did not believe in going on strike.

Q

Who won the General Strike?

1 The statement issued by the Miners' Federation at the top of this page suggests that the mine owners lost the General Strike. Do you agree with this interpretation? Explain your answer using the evidence from the statement and from the quotation from AJP Taylor, below it, to support your answer.

2 So who do you think were the winners and losers in the General Strike? Fill in the table below and then write an answer based on the table, explaining who you think won and who lost. Give your reasons.

Group	Evidence that suggests this group won	Evidence that suggests this group lost
Miners		
Mine owners		
TUC		
Government		

Statement issued in January 1927 by the Miners' Federation:

'If we were deserted and forced to fight a lone fight, it was not by the workers that we were abandoned. Their hearts beat true to the end . . . On Tuesday evening, the 11th of May, The Miners' Executive were sent for by the General Council and were informed that they (the Council) had agreed upon and accepted proposals [to end the strike].'

The British historian AJP Taylor, writing in 1965:

'In the end, the owners were destroyed by their victory. The class war continued in the coal districts when it was fading elsewhere, and the miners insisted on nationalisation [see page 134] as soon as power passed into their hands [the Labour victory in 1945].'

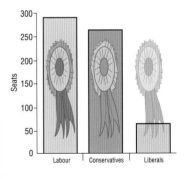

The election result of 1929

THE DEPRESSION

In May 1929 the Labour Party won the General Election and so Ramsay MacDonald formed a government for the second time. Labour did not have an overall majority, and they needed the support of Liberal MPs to pass any new laws. This made governing the country difficult. In October the economy was hit by the Wall Street Crash, adding to the Labour Party's problems. As unemployment spread in the United States so demand fell and British exports to America fell. The picture was the same in other European countries and so all trade declined producing unemployment everywhere. This caused demand to fall still further and produced still more unemployment.

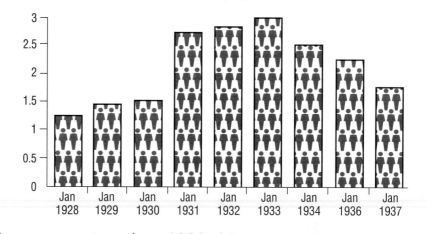

(Left) British unemployment (figures in millions)

Government action 1929–31

Rising unemployment created two particular problems for the government; it got less money from taxes because only people with a job paid tax and, at the same time, the government had to pay more money in unemployment benefit. The Labour government decided that the best way to solve this problem was to cut unemployment benefit. It also decided to pay lower wages to people who worked for the government, such as civil servants and teachers.

Many Labour MPs did not agree with these cuts, although they did agree with increasing income tax to 22.5 per cent. This did not solve the problem, however, and so the Liberals and Conservatives joined forces and voted together. They forced the government to set up a committee, known as the May Committee, to look at the problem. This committee recommended a cut in the wages for all people employed by the government as well as a 20 per cent reduction in unemployment benefit. Ramsay MacDonald resigned because he was faced with a Labour Party that did not want to introduce these measures. On the very same day, 24 August 1931, he formed a coalition government with the Conservatives and Liberals. This government was known as the National Government.

The National Government 1931–37

The majority of the Labour Party opposed MacDonald's decision to form a coalition government. However, when an election was held in October 1931, those parties supporting the National Government won 554 seats while the anti-MacDonald Labour Party won just 52.

The National Government carried out the recommendations made by the May Committee. All government employees had their wages cut by 10 per cent, except for teachers, who had their wages cut by 15 per cent. The government also raised import duties to try and protect British industries and so prevent more unemployment. This didn't really work. It forced foreign

George Orwell, writing in 1937:

'When you see unemployment figures quoted at two millions, it is fatally easy to take this as meaning that two million people are out of work . . . This is an enormous underestimate because . . . the only people shown on unemployment figures are those drawing the dole – that is, in general, heads of families.'

From The Road to Wigan Pier

industries to look for new countries to sell their goods in and meant that British industries faced even more competition if they wanted to sell goods abroad. British exports fell but Britain did abandon the Gold Standard, making British exports cheaper compared to American and French goods. These two countries did not leave the Gold Standard until 1936.

One further result of the May Committee's report was the introduction of the Means Test. This meant that if an unemployed person had some savings they would get less benefit. Anyone who had been careful and saved a little money would be paid less than someone who had spent all their money.

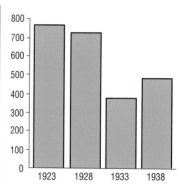

(above) A bar chart showing British exports in millions of pounds (1923–38).

(left) The National Government pose for a photograph in the garden of 10 Downing Street. The Prime Minister, Ramsay MacDonald, is in the centre of the front row. To his left is the Conservative leader Stanley Baldwin and to his right is the Liberal leader Sir Herbert Samuel.

Q Why did MacDonald prefer to lead a coalition rather than a Labour government?

(left) Labour versus the rest. A Labour election poster from 1931.

Q Why was this the Labour election slogan for 1931? How does this poster help to explain the enormous election victory of the National Government?

'Mates! Help me get a job.' A National Government election poster from 1931.

Q **Why did Labour disagree with the policies of the National Government? Create a Labour poster which shows these views.**

The Means Test was hated by working people and many Labour-controlled local councils refused to use it. In 1934 the government took unemployment benefit out of the hands of local authorities and set up the Unemployment Assistance Board. This action was even more unpopular than the Means Test as the amount of money it offered was even lower than before. However, in the same year the Conservative Chancellor of the Exchequer, Neville Chamberlain, restored the wages of government employees to their old level and returned unemployment benefit to its previous figure.

Unlike America and Germany, Britain did not spend huge amounts of money creating jobs. The British government believed that a large government debt would produce far worse problems in the long term.

Q

1 Look at the bar chart on page 128. In what year was unemployment at its worst in Great Britain?
2 What does George Orwell (page 128) suggest about the accuracy of this figure?
3 In 1933 Neville Chamberlain said that Britain had been the country that had coped with the Depression 'with the greatest measure of success'.
   a What evidence can you find to suggest that the National Government was successful in dealing with unemployment and the economic crisis?
   b What evidence can you find to suggest that the government was unsuccessful?
   c Do you agree or disagree with Chamberlain? Explain your answer.

The effects of the Depression

Marches by the unemployed became common. This one, held in London in 1930, led to clashes with the police. The desperation of the unemployed led to marches (especially in the East End of London) in support of the British Union of Fascists led by the ex-Labour Cabinet Minister Oswald Mosley.

The most obvious effect of the Depression was unemployment. However, even for those in work, wages could be very low. Health care was not free in the 1930s and so the poverty produced by the Depression led to a rise in ill-health, especially among children and the elderly. A survey carried out in Newcastle in the mid-1930s revealed that poor children were far more likely to suffer from ill health than rich children. Pneumonia was eight times more common, and bronchitis ten times more common among the poor. A survey carried out in York in 1935–6 found that 43 per cent of the working class were living in poverty and York did not suffer from as much unemployment as many other northern cities.

Poor people often lived in terrible, overcrowded housing. In 1935 it was estimated that 12 per cent of the population lived more than two to a room so a family of four lived in just two rooms. It was worse in many areas of London. In Finsbury 60 per cent of families lived in either one or two rooms. Liverpool had the worst slums in the country. In the St Anne's district of Liverpool 20 000 people lived more than three to a room. The toilets for the houses would be outside and the whole district would be full of rats.

Hunger marches by the unemployed became common. The most famous of these occurred in 1936 when many of the people of Jarrow, a north-eastern shipbuilding town, marched to London to protest that the government was doing nothing to solve unemployment. At least two-thirds of the working population of Jarrow were unemployed.

Frank Cousins, who later became a union leader, reports an incident in a café. A couple were walking from the north-eastern town of South Shields to London in search of work:

'They came into the café and sat down, and they fetched a baby's feeding bottle out, and it had water in it. They fed the baby with water and then lifted the kiddy's dress up – it was a small baby – and it had a newspaper nappy on. They took this off, and wiped the baby's bottom with it and then picked up another newspaper and put that on for a fresh nappy.'

The Listener 26 Oct 1961

Q

1 Read the extract on the right. Why is Frank Cousins so surprised that there is water in the feeding bottle?
2 What does Cousins' report tell you about conditions in north-east England?
3 What evidence can you find to suggest that what Cousins reports was typical of the 1930s?

Did everyone suffer during the Depression?

As Source 1 shows, not everywhere in Britain suffered equally from unemployment. It was in the old manufacturing areas that unemployment reached such terrible levels. Jarrow was a shipbuilding town that suffered when the Palmer's Shipyard, the only big company in the town, closed down in 1934. Merthyr was a Welsh mining town. In 1926 there had been over one million miners in Britain. By 1934 there were less than 800 000. In contrast Source 4 shows that many new consumer industries were booming. If you had money you were better off. Prices fell in the 1930s. Source 5 shows that well off families had the money to buy these consumer goods.

SOURCE 1:

This graph shows the percentage of workers unemployed in these towns in 1937.

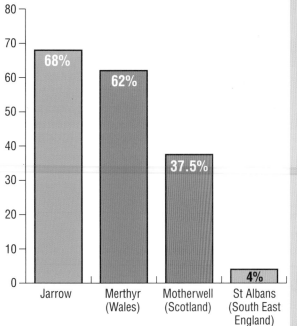

Regional unemployment in Britain in 1937

- Jarrow: 68%
- Merthyr (Wales): 62%
- Motherwell (Scotland): 37.5%
- St Albans (South East England): 4%

SOURCE 2:

An advertisement for new housing in south east England. During the 1920s and 1930s tree-lined suburban developments had grown around the outside of London, offering family houses with large gardens.

SUPER 1933 HOMES

9/6 WEEKLY

BARNEHURST PARK ESTATE
BARNEHURST, KENT £395 FREEHOLD

Estate Office : Station Approach, Barnehurst, Kent.
Telephone : Bexleyheath 406.

NEW IDEAL HOMESTEADS LTD
BRITAIN'S BIGGEST BUILDERS

SOURCE 3:

Unemployed men (below) singing for money in front of people queuing to go in to the theatre in London's West End.

SOURCE 4:

THREE-SPEED TWO-SEATER
£100

FOUR-SPEED MODELS
from **£105**

An advertisement for the Morris Minor. Car ownership increased dramatically in the 1930s. In 1929 the industry produced 180 000 cars. By 1938 production had almost doubled to 340 000.

SOURCE 5:

Dick Cunningham describes the middle-class house in which he was brought up in the 1930s:

'When my father bought the house it had no electricity, just gas for lighting and cooking . . . and coal fires in every room. Before we moved in my father had electricity installed for lighting and plugs for lamps and electric fires . . . In the mid-Thirties an electric heater was installed in a water tank . . . In the late Thirties my mother had a small refrigerator, made by a reputable company, installed in the pantry. She discovered she was the first in her circle of friends to do so . . . We had two live-in servants, a cook and a housemaid, who shared the back bed-sitting room on the attic floor . . . the housemaids were aged fourteen to sixteen. As they usually had little or no experience they began on a monthly wage of 12/6 – 15 shillings (62½ – 75 pence).

From Horseman: *Growing up in the Thirties*

SOURCE 6:

J Stevenson and C Cook, writing in 1994:

'It would be silly to suggest that the 1930s were not for many thousands of people a time of great hardship and personal suffering. But beside this picture of the unemployed must be put the other side of the case. There were never less than three-quarters of the population in work during the 1930s and for most of the period considerably more. Alongside the pictures of dole queues and hunger marches must also be placed those of another Britain, of new industries, prosperous suburbs and a rising standard of living.'

From *Britain in the Depression* 1994

---

1 What do Sources 2 and 4 tell you about the 1930s?
2 What evidence can you find to suggest that the image created by these advertisements is correct?
3 Look at Source 1. Which two towns suffered from the worst unemployment? Why was this?
4 The 1930s have been described as 'the hungry Thirties'. Which sources support the view that the 1930s were a decade of poverty and suffering?

5 Source 6 refers to a decade when many people were well off and living standards rose. Which sources support this view?
6 The historian AJP Taylor has written that the 1930s was a decade when over one million people were unemployed whilst one million people owned cars. Was this a decade of prosperity or poverty? Explain your answer by using the sources on pages 132–3.

Nationalisation of industry in post-war Britain

In April 1945 Germany finally gave in and the war in Europe was over. In July 1945 Labour won a huge majority in the General Election. Although Winston Churchill had been the great hero of the war, voters wanted to give the Labour Party the chance to make changes. Many people had given their lives in the war and the survivors did not want to return to the poverty and desperation of the 1930s.

The new Labour government was led by Clement Attlee. It wanted to take over the main industries of the country. This was called 'nationalisation'. It was not new to Britain. During the First World War the railways and the mines had been taken over by the government. In 1926 the Central Electricity Generating Board had been created as a government-controlled company to produce electricity. These nationalisations had occurred either to make sure that the industries served the needs of the country in war, or to ensure that the economy functioned efficiently.

In 1945 Labour had another motive to nationalise British industry. As a socialist party they believed that privately-run industry could lead to the needs of the workers being ignored. This would only stop if the government actually owned the factories, mines and transport systems. This belief was set out in Clause Four of the constitution of the Labour Party. High profits for company owners would no longer be the country's main concern. Safer working conditions and less unemployment would be more important.

In 1947 the coal industry was nationalised and this was followed in 1948 by the nationalisation of the railways. Both needed huge amounts of money to replace their old equipment and only the government could afford this. In 1948 the supply of electricity and gas was also nationalised. By 1945, ten per cent of British workers were employed in the nationalised industries. Only the nationalisation of the steel industry led to serious opposition. Unlike the coal industry, the steel industry had made big profits in the 1930s and the Conservatives opposed its nationalisation. They accepted nationalisation where it made the economy more efficient, but not when the only reason seemed to be the Labour Party's belief in socialism. The Conservatives believed that government ownership of the steel industry would make it less efficient, and so after the Conservatives had won the election in 1951 they returned the steel industry to private ownership.

THE CHANGING ROLE AND STATUS OF WOMEN

Votes for women

At the beginning of the twentieth century women were not able to vote and the only men who could vote were those that owned their own house. In the nineteenth century the National Union of Women's Suffrage Societies (NUWSS) had been set up to demand the vote for women. It was mostly supported by women who had good jobs or were wealthy. The NUWSS was led by Millicent Fawcett and by 1914 had become a large organisation of 53 000 members. The union's main objective was to allow women to vote on the same terms as men. It was not campaigning for all adults to have the vote, only those who owned houses. The members of the NUWSS were commonly known as 'suffragists'.

In 1903 Emmeline Pankhurst, the daughter of a wealthy cotton manufacturer, set up another women's organisation that wanted more than this. It was called the Women's Social and Political Union (WSPU) but its

THE CAT AND MOUSE ACT

PASSED BY THE LIBERAL GOVERNMENT

THE LIBERAL CAT
ELECTORS VOTE AGAINST HIM!
KEEP THE LIBERAL OUT!

BUY AND READ 'THE SUFFRAGETTE' PRICE 1D.

A suffragette poster against the 'Cat and Mouse' Act of 1913. Many suffragettes had been arrested and then gone on hunger strike to continue their protest. The Act allowed them to be released so that they did not die in prison, but they were re-arrested once they had recovered their strength.

Q **Why do you think that the suffragettes hated this Act?**

members were usually known as the 'suffragettes'. Their slogan was 'Deeds not Words'. The WSPU engaged in direct action; they disrupted political meetings, chained themselves to railings, slashed paintings in the National Gallery and even planted a small bomb in Westminster Abbey. The purpose was to gain people's attention. Their actions were shocking in an age that believed that a woman's main purpose was to be married and obey her husband. The most famous protest occurred in 1913 when Emily Davison ran out in front of the King's horse during the Derby race. Her funeral was watched by a large audience and her death created enormous publicity.

Emmeline Pankhurst talking to crowds in Hyde Park, London, in 1917.

Despite all the publicity women were still not given the vote. MPs who agreed with votes for women introduced bills into parliament in 1907, 1908 and twice in 1910, but they were all defeated. While some Conservative MPs agreed with the demands of the suffragists only the Labour Party supported the suffragettes.

The breakthrough came with the outbreak of war. Women were able to prove their worth by helping in the war effort. The London branch of the NUWSS used its organisation to train women to take on jobs previously held by men. They set up training classes in welding and munitions work. The suffragettes were divided. The majority, led by Emmeline Pankhurst and her daughter Christabel, supported the war because it gave women a chance to

"What's the disturbance in the market-place?"
"It's a mass meeting of the women who've changed their minds since the morning and want to alter their voting-papers."

A cartoon from Punch, *18 December 1918*

Q What does this tell you about men's attitudes to women in 1918?

"WHAT'S THE DISTURBANCE IN THE MARKET-PLACE?"
"IT'S A MASS MEETING OF THE WOMEN WHO'VE CHANGED THEIR MINDS SINCE THE MORNING AND WANT TO ALTER THEIR VOTING-PAPERS."

prove that they were as good as men. They demanded the 'Right to Serve', so that women could play a full part in the war effort. Emmeline's other daughter, Sylvia, opposed this point of view. She believed that women should not support a government that women had not been able to vote for. The majority view won. Many thousands of women joined up as nurses in the Voluntary Aid Detachments while others worked in factories and in other jobs (see pages 138–9).

Women were able to use the war to prove that they could play a full part in the life of the country. The result was partial victory. The Representation of the People Act of 1918 gave the vote to all women who were over the age of 30 and who also owned a house or were married to a house owner. In the 1918 General Election Countess Markiewicz became the first woman to be elected to parliament although she and 72 other Sinn Fein MPs refused to take up their seats as a protest against the English refusal to grant independence to Ireland. But it was not until 1928 that all women over the age of 21 were given the right to vote that had been given to all men in 1918.

In September 1914 Christabel Pankhurst made a speech which spelt out the suffragette position:

'If we are needed in the fighting line, we shall be there. If we are needed to attend the economic prosperity of the country, we shall be there. What it is best in the interests of the country to do, women will do.'

Q

1 Look at the *Punch* cartoon on page 136. How does it explain why it was so long before women were granted the vote?
2 What other reasons can you find to explain why women were not given the vote until 1918?
3 Lloyd George said that he felt that the violent tactics used by the suffragettes 'poisoned' the public and the government. In other words, they lost support for the campaign. Do you agree with this interpretation? Do you think that the campaign of the suffragettes won the vote for women? To answer this question try and work out which of these three factors was the most important in gaining the vote for women:
  a the suffragists;
  b the suffragettes;
  c the First World War.
For each of the three find evidence to show their influence. Then decide which is the most important and explain your choice using the evidence that you have found.

Women's work at the start of the century

At the beginning of the century most women did not have paid work. The 1911 government **census** revealed that over 11 million adult women did not have a paid job, in contrast to fewer than five million women who did. The reason for this was that women were expected to marry and become housewives; their job was to care for their husbands and bring up a family.

Many working class women, however, did not have the choice. Their husbands did not earn enough and so wives had to have a paid job as well as being a housewife. The commonest jobs were as servants and cooks. Look back to Source 5 on page 133 and you will see that these jobs were still important in the 1930s. In the industrial areas of Britain in the north and midland regions women worked in factories and throughout the country many poor women worked in what were known as the 'sweated' trades such as hat and dress making. They were forced to work long hours for very little money.

Middle-class women might work as shop assistants or in an office but they were expected to give up their job as soon as they married. Indeed some jobs, such as teaching and bank work, demanded this. However, as the chart on page 140 shows, women were paid much less than men, even when they were doing similar work.

Joan Dobson describes the difficulties of finding a teaching job in the 1930s:

'There were thirty or more applicants at each interview, plus many more who had not been put on the short list . . . my young man of the time quickly obtained a job in his own county of Kent, but then he had been given a loan and they were anxious to get their money back. I had been given a London Senior Scholarship for my training and had nothing to repay . . . I finally obtained a job in Surrey . . . but in 1938 I left to get married to a fellow student who had taken a similar course to mine.'

From Horseman: *Growing up in the Thirties*

When the war was over the men once more returned to their jobs. However, not everything returned to the way it had been before. Many more married women were in work in 1951 than before the war. The 1944 Education Act finally allowed married women to teach, although they did not receive the same pay as men.

Women manufacturing a barrage balloon. With so many men fighting in the war, women had to work in factories in the Second World War just as they had in the First World War.

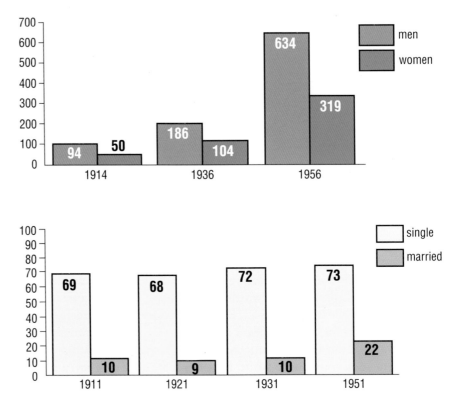

Average earnings in Britain (£).

Percentage of women in paid work. (Figures adapted from Halsey, British Social Trends)

Q

1 Read the extract from Joan Dobson on page 140. What reasons does she give for the difficulties she experienced in finding a job? What other reasons might there have been?
2 Look at the bar chart showing the percentage of women in paid work on page 140. What do you notice about the percentage of married women in work between 1911 and 1931? What reasons can you think of to explain this?
3 Look at the bar chart showing average earnings on page 140. What does this source tell you about women's wages between 1911 and 1951?
4 Did the role and status of women really change between 1911 and 1951? Use the evidence from this section to back up your answer.

HEALTH AND WELFARE

A nineteenth-century slum in Kensington, London.

Q How can you tell that these houses belong to the poor?

At the beginning of the twentieth century Britain was arguably the richest country in the world as Lloyd George maintained (below, right). Yet many of the working class lived in terrible conditions. They were often laid off when there was no work and this meant that there was no money coming into the house. Living conditions were often unhealthy.

The Liberal reforms

In the period 1906–11 the Liberal government introduced a number of major reforms to improve the situation:

- **Old Age Pensions.** In 1908 an act gave a pension of five shillings (25p) a week to those people over 70 who earned less than ten shillings a week. This was paid for by higher taxes on the rich. Income tax for those earning £3000 a year or more was raised from one shilling (5p) to 1s 2d (6p) in the pound, and a super tax of 6d was introduced for those earning more than £5000. Death duties were also doubled.
- **Children.** In 1906 an act was passed which meant that local councils had to provide school meals for children. The following year another act introduced medical inspections for all school children.
- **National Insurance.** In 1911 the National Insurance Act was introduced. This had two parts. Part One set up a fund to help pay for medical care for low paid workers. Better paid workers were still expected to pay for their own medical care. Everyone who had a job but earned less than £160 a year

Lloyd George, the Liberal Chancellor of the Exchequer, speaking in 1909:

'Help for the aged and the deserving poor – it is time it was done. It is a shame that a rich country like ours – probably the richest in the world – should allow those who have toiled all their days to end in poverty and starvation.'

had to pay 4d (1½p) a week into a fund. Employers had to pay another 3d for each worker and the government added a further 2d. In return workers could go and see a doctor for free. They also received ten shillings (50p) a week if they could not go to work because they were too sick. Part Two set up another fund to which workers and employers paid 2½d (1p) a week. This money would then be used to give seven shillings (35p) a week to anyone who was unemployed, though only for the first 15 weeks. However, this was limited to certain industries like building where workers were regularly laid off work. It should be noted that since women were unlikely to have a job, most could not contribute or benefit from these schemes.

As can be imagined these reforms were only passed after a great deal of opposition. The rich resented having to pay for the pensions of the poor and the Lords initially rejected the measures. The Labour Party opposed the changes from the opposite standpoint. They believed that pensions should be provided by the government. Finally, many workers resented having to make contributions from already thin wage packets.

Why did the Liberals introduce these reforms?

The creators of this 'New Liberalism' were Lloyd George and Winston Churchill. Both hoped that this concern for the poor would win votes. Lloyd George had visited Germany, the country that was quickly developing into the new industrial leader of Europe. Germany already had health insurance and old age pensions. It was hoped that the reforms would produce a stronger and fitter workforce who would be able to meet the challenge of Germany.

Between the wars

The system set up by the Liberals was gradually extended between the wars. In 1919 health insurance was extended to cover people who earned between £160 and £250 a year. In 1924 pensions were doubled to 10 shillings a week but the Depression revealed that this was simply not enough. Ill-health was still common among the poor and of course in 1931 unemployment benefit was cut and the Means Test introduced. Although the benefit level was restored in 1934 the Means Test remained until 1941.

The Beveridge Report

During the war the coalition government commissioned a number of reports to draw up plans for rebuilding Britain after the war. The period after the First World War had not produced the 'Land fit for heroes' that had been hoped for. This time the sacrifice of those who died would lead to a new Britain. The horrors of the 1930s had made many realise that the government needed to do much more to help its people. The most important of the reports was drawn up by William Beveridge. It proposed free health care and free unemployment benefits for everyone. The State would look after its citizens 'From the cradle to the grave'.

The Welfare State

A Labour government was elected to power in 1945. It carried out the Beveridge proposals despite the fact that the country's economy needed to be rebuilt after six years of war. The reforms fitted in well with socialist beliefs. Wealth should be shared out more equally. A free health service would be available for all regardless of wealth. It would be paid for by taxation. The richer you were the more you would contribute. In 1946 the National Health

Act was passed and in 1948 the National Health Service came into being. Free health care was provided for all. However in 1951 a charge of one shilling (5p) was introduced for prescriptions. Many doctors were opposed to the National Health Service. They feared that the government would tell them how to treat their patients. The doctors also thought that they would earn less money if they worked for the government. The Health Minister, Aneurin Bevan, managed to produce a solution to the problem. He allowed doctors to work privately as well as for the government. By 1949, 92 per cent of doctors had agreed to join the NHS.

The National Insurance Act of 1946 gave women pensions from the age of 60 and men from 65. Everyone who worked was also able to claim benefit when they were ill or unemployed. The scheme was financed by contributions from both workers and employers. The National Assistance Act of 1948 gave benefits to those who failed to qualify under the National Insurance scheme. By the mid-twentieth century Britain had achieved a welfare system for the entire nation.

▶ Was the Welfare State a success?

In its first year of operation 95 per cent of the population joined the NHS. However the historian Correlli Barnett has suggested that, despite its undoubted popularity, the NHS has not been a success. If you look back at the Liberals' motives for introducing social reforms at the beginning of the century you will see that they wanted to produce fitter workers so that British industry could compete with foreign industry. Barnett says that this is how the NHS should be judged. At the end of the war Britain spent huge amounts of money on the NHS. It cost £400 million in its first year. Barnett believes that this money should have been spent on updating British industry, as happened in Germany. Only when the modernised industry had created wealth should money have been spent on a health service. Instead an increasingly uncompetitive British industry was having to fund an increasingly expensive Health Service.

SOURCE 1:

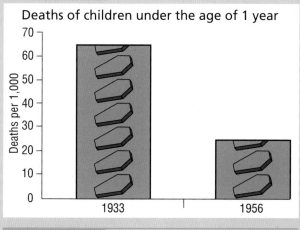

Deaths of children under the age of 1 year

SOURCE 2:

Gallup Poll, October 1950:

71 per cent believed that the National Health Service had been a success.

SOURCE 3:

Gallup Poll, May 1953:

70 per cent felt that they received a good service from the NHS.

SOURCE 4:

British share of world trade in manufactured goods

---

1 Look at Sources 1, 2, 3 and 4. Which sources support the view that the NHS has been a success and which do not?

2 Why do you think that the NHS was so popular in the years after the war?

3 Barnett believes that the government was wrong to spend so much money on the National Health Service after the war. Using the sources and your own knowledge explain whether you agree or disagree with this interpretation.

The Treaty of Versailles

Germany was heavily punished in the Treaty of Versailles. Thirteen per cent of German land was taken away along with six million people. Some of these people were given a choice. The people of Eupen and Malmedy, for example, were allowed to vote whether they wanted to be part of Germany or Belgium. This type of vote on a single issue was called a **plebiscite** or a 'referendum'. The voters of Eupen and Malmedy decided to join Belgium. Many other people were not given the choice. West Prussia and Posen were given to the new country of Poland. Their people were not allowed a plebiscite.

Germany's **colonies** were also taken over by the League of Nations. The League did not have the resources to run these countries and so the Allies ran these countries on behalf of the League. These countries were known as **mandates**. German East Africa, for example, was ruled by Britain as a mandate.

Germany received other punishments. France had been invaded twice in 45 years by Germany and they wanted to make sure that it did not happen again. Germany was not allowed to keep any troops or weapons in the Rhineland (the area of Germany which was nearest to France) and the German army was not allowed to be larger than 100 000 men. There was to be no German airforce at all.

Finally the Germans were blamed for starting the war. This meant that Germany would have to pay to repair all the damage done by both sides in the war. These payments were known as **reparations**. The Treaty of Versailles did not set the actual amount that the Germans would have to pay but in 1921 it was decided that the Germans should pay £6 600 000. The British economist John Maynard Keynes, who had been an advisor to Lloyd George at Versailles, suggested that £2 000 000 was the most that Germany should be expected to pay; a higher amount would make Germany too poor.

Eastern Europe after the treaties. (See page 146.)

The Treaties of St Germain and Trianon

The Treaty of St Germain dealt with Austria and the Treaty of Trianon dealt with Hungary. Eastern Europe had been dominated by the Austro-Hungarian Empire before the war as the map on page 144 shows. The Austro-Hungarian Empire had contained many different **national minorities** and many of them wanted to rule themselves rather than be part of an empire. The treaties attempted to set up national states for these people. Yugoslavia was provided for the Serbs and Croats, and Czechoslovakia was created for the Czechs and Slovaks. However no one was given the chance to vote about which country they were put in. There were three million Germans in the new state of Czechoslovakia. The Germans in the former Austrian province of South Tyrol were handed over to Italy and were not allowed to remain as part of Austria. Italy was given South Tyrol because it had been promised a reward for joining the war in 1915.

The Treaty of St Germain reduced Austria to a small country of just six and a half million people. The areas of Austria that had contained most of the country's industry, Bohemia and Moravia, had been given to Czechoslovakia and Austria was not allowed to unite with Germany even if it wanted to. The Allies feared that a united Germany and Austria would quickly become powerful again.

Hungary suffered as badly as Austria. Before the war Hungary had a population of 21 million. The Treaty of Trianon took away so much land that the population of Hungary was left at just seven million people. The best agricultural land was given to Romania who, like Italy, also needed to be rewarded for fighting on the winning side.

The results of the treaties

As the maps on pages 144, 145 and 146 show, Europe was very different after the war to what it had been in 1914. New countries had appeared, especially from the wreckage of the Austro-Hungarian Empire; the Poles had their own country now, as did the Serbs and the Croats with the new Yugoslavia. This was not really self-determination at work. New national minorities had been created throughout Europe. There were Germans in Poland and Czechoslovakia and there were 400 000 Slavs in Istria who were not allowed to join the Slav nation of Yugoslavia but were forced to be part of Italy.

These were not the only problems. Germany was made to pay reparations but many of the areas that it needed to create the necessary wealth were taken from it. Germany, Austria and Hungary all believed that they had been treated unfairly and they wanted the chance to change the treaties. Yet the Germans had behaved in the same way in 1918. If you turn to page 41 you will see that

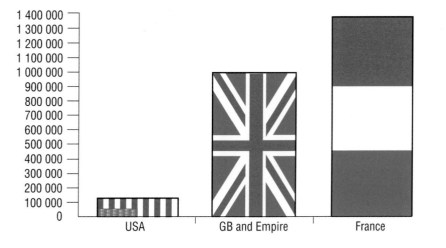

Number of First World War dead.

the Germans forced the Russians to sign a very unfair treaty at Brest-Litovsk.

President Wilson had hoped that a treaty based on his 'Fourteen Points' would make future wars in Europe less likely. Instead the treaties left a number of countries determined to have revenge for the way that they had been treated.

Q

1 Why were the Germans not allowed to keep troops in the Rhineland?
2 What two reasons can you find to explain why Britain did not want to punish Germany too harshly?
3 How does the map on page 145 help to explain France's attitude at Versailles?
4 Do you think that the Treaty of Versailles was fair to Germany? To answer this question make a list of the actions taken at Versailles using the map and the text. Then divide this list into those points that you feel were fair and those that were not. For each list work out why you believe a decision was fair or unfair. Then decide overall whether you think the treaty was fair or unfair.

THE LEAGUE OF NATIONS

President Wilson wanted to create 'a world safe for democracy' at the end of the war. The last of his 'Fourteen Points' proposed that an organisation would be set up so that countries would settle their differences through peace rather than war. This was not a new idea and was not even Wilson's own idea. However the time was now right. With the horror and destruction of the war fresh in everyone's mind there was a belief that something positive should emerge from the Great War, as it was already being called. It should become 'a war to end war'.

The League had two main aims:

• **Collective security.** This meant that all countries would become safe from attack. The members of the League would join together against any nation

The structure of the League of Nations.

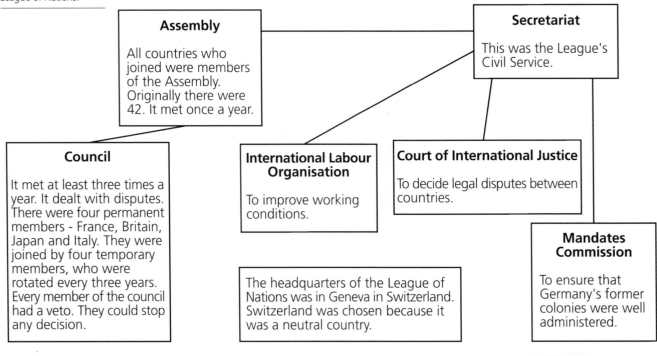

Assembly

All countries who joined were members of the Assembly. Originally there were 42. It met once a year.

Secretariat

This was the League's Civil Service.

Council

It met at least three times a year. It dealt with disputes. There were four permanent members - France, Britain, Japan and Italy. They were joined by four temporary members, who were rotated every three years. Every member of the council had a veto. They could stop any decision.

International Labour Organisation

To improve working conditions.

Court of International Justice

To decide legal disputes between countries.

Mandates Commission

To ensure that Germany's former colonies were well administered.

The headquarters of the League of Nations was in Geneva in Switzerland. Switzerland was chosen because it was a neutral country.

that attacked another nation. The League could take two types of action. Economic **sanctions** would mean that League members would refuse to trade with the attacking country. Military sanctions would mean that League members would launch a military attack on the attacking country.

- **Solving the world's economic and social problems.** This meant that the League's members would join together to help to wipe out such problems as disease and poverty.

The weaknesses of the League

When the League first met in January 1920 it was hoped that it would end war forever. However, there were major weaknesses that soon undermined its hopes.

- Not every nation was a member. Germany was not allowed to join until 1926 and Russia did not join until 1933, but the most important non-member was the USA. Despite the fact that President Wilson had been so involved in setting up the League, the people of America did not want their country to have to play the role of the world's policeman. Therefore the American Congress (parliament) voted to stay out of the League.
- If a country disagreed with a League decision it was free to leave the League. It could then ignore the decision. This is what Japan did in 1933.
- Britain and France did not want the League to be able to control their policies. After the war the victors had set up the Conference of Ambassadors to ensure that everyone obeyed the treaties of Paris. Once the League was set up there was no longer any need for the Conference of Ambassadors. However, Britain and France kept it in operation because they were able to use it to overturn League decisions which they did not agree with.
- Although the League had the power to use military sanctions, it did not do so.

Despite these weaknesses the League did achieve some important successes. It did not, however, end war. Within a generation Europe would once more be engulfed in a world war.

How successful was the League of Nations in the 1920s?

Successes:

- **Upper Silesia.** The people of the former German province of Silesia were allowed a plebiscite to decide whether they wanted to be part of Germany or the new state of Poland. The plebiscite was organised by the League. The vote did not produce a clear decision but the League managed to sort this out by splitting Upper Silesia between the two countries.
- **The Washington Conference 1922.** The League organised this conference to try and prevent another arms race of the type that had helped to cause the Great War. Britain, France, the USA, Italy and Japan all agreed to limit the size of their navies. Even though the USA was not a League member it still took part so that its non-membership did not weaken the move towards disarmament. It was hoped that this agreement would help prevent a future war.
- **The Kellogg-Briand Pact 1928.** The move to end war was continued by the Kellogg-Briand Pact. Kellogg was the US Secretary of State (foreign minister) while Briand was the French Foreign Minister. 15 major countries signed and agreed that they would give up war and seek a peaceful solution to all disputes in the future. Germany was one of the 15 and later another 31 countries added their names.

- **The International Labour Organisation (ILO).** This was one of the special commissions of the League. Its aim was to improve the wages and working conditions of ordinary people and end poverty. Even countries that were not members of the League were allowed to join and so the USA was a member of the ILO. The ILO soon gained the respect of most countries and it still exists today.

Failures:

- **Vilna.** In 1920 the new state of Poland captured the city of Vilna, the capital of Lithuania. The League demanded that Poland should hand Vilna back to Lithuania. However the Conference of Ambassadors supported Poland. The League felt unable to act since the major European powers, Britain, France and Italy, were members of the Conference and so Poland was allowed to keep Vilna.
- **The Ruhr.** When Germany fell behind with reparation payments to France and Belgium these countries did not leave it to the League to deal with the matter. Instead they invaded the Ruhr, Germany's main industrial area. They did not leave until Germany had agreed to restart payments (see page 62 for further details).
- **Corfu.** In 1923 the Italian general Count Tellini was killed while attempting to map the border between Greece and Albania. The Italians sent their fleet to bombard the Greek island of Corfu and threatened to keep up the shelling until the Greeks agreed to pay compensation. The League ordered the Italians to withdraw. The Italians obeyed. However the Conference of Ambassadors again intervened and ordered the Greeks to pay the compensation that the Italians were demanding.

'The Gap in the Bridge.' A cartoon from the British magazine Punch.

Q

1 Which country in the cartoon above is not a member of the League according to the cartoonist?
2 Why do you think that the cartoonist calls this country the 'keystone'?
3 Do the events of the 1920s support the view that the League could not work without this country?
4 What were the main failures of the League in the 1920s?
5 What do you think were the main reasons for these failures?

How successful was the League in the 1930s?

Successes:

- **Iraq.** The role of the Mandate Commission was to govern the former colonies of Germany and Turkey until they were ready for independence. Since 1918 the former Turkish colony of Iraq had been controlled by Britain on behalf of the League. In 1932 it became independent. However, most of the other colonies did not become independent until after World War Two.
- **The Saar.** The Saar was an area of Germany that contained important coalfields. Since 1919 it had been governed by the League, and its coal given to France to help to pay reparations. In 1935 a plebiscite was held, the people voted to return to Germany, and were allowed to do so peacefully.

Failures:

- **Manchuria.** In the nineteenth century Japan had begun to develop its industry. It was determined to become a great power. In 1904–5 it surprised the world by defeating Russia.

   However, Japan was short of land to grow food for its expanding population. It also lacked raw materials for its industries. In 1929 the world was hit by economic depression (see pages 105–7). All over the world unemployment grew. This meant that fewer people were able to buy goods and so companies went bankrupt and still more people became unemployed. Japan was hit as badly as any country by this depression. The young officers of the Japanese armed forces regarded war as noble and they believed an invasion of China would allow them to serve Japan's needs. The Japanese army attacked the Chinese province of Manchuria in 1931.

   Manchuria was rich in farming land and raw materials. The Chinese forces were no match for the Japanese and Manchuria soon fell to the invaders. Japan was ordered to withdraw its forces but they refused. In 1932 the League sent the British diplomat Lord Lytton to investigate. He suggested that the League should rule Manchuria. The Japanese resigned from the League in 1933 and then, four years later, they invaded the rest of China. The League took no action. Britain and France were too afraid to attack Japan. They felt that it was too far away from Europe. The Japanese would find it much easier than Britain and France to fight a war in China.

The Manchurian crisis.

- **1932–4 Disarmament Conference.** The 1922 Washington Conference was a success. The same could not be said of the conference that took place in Geneva ten years later. Hitler had come to power in Germany in January 1933 and he refused to agree to limit the size of Germany's armed forces. He left the Geneva Conference in October and then followed this by leaving the League of Nations. Germany was now outside the control of the League.

A cartoon showing the Japanese attacking China.

Q Does the cartoonist support Japan or China? How does he make this point?

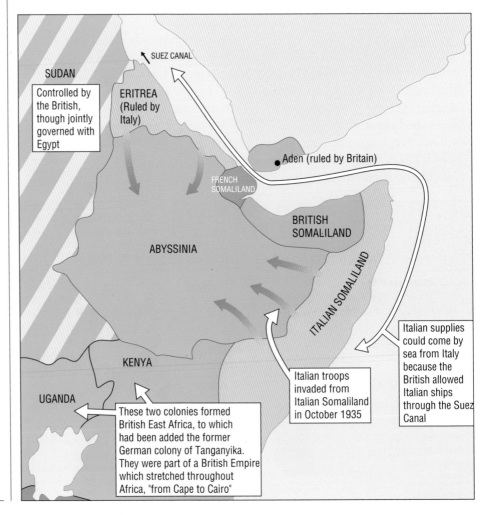

Abyssinia.

- **Abyssinia.** The Italian dictator Mussolini had promised the Italian people that he would turn Italy into a great power. At the treaties of Paris the Italians had felt that they had not received all of the land that they had been promised by the other powers.

  Britain and France had huge African empires but the Italian Empire was very small. Mussolini believed that an empire was necessary for Italy to appear great. He had also invested large amounts of money in his army because he felt that he needed military victories to prove Italy's greatness to the world and the Italian people. Mussolini chose Abyssinia, which is now called Ethiopia, as his target. It was the last country in Africa that was not controlled by a European country. It could be easily invaded from Italy's existing colony of Italian Somaliland.

  The attack was launched in October 1935. The poorly-armed Abyssinian army was no match for the modern weapons of the Italians. This time the League took action and ordered countries to stop trading with Italy. However, countries were still allowed to supply oil, which was vital to the Italian war effort. The USSR demanded oil sanctions but Britain and France refused. They were afraid of Germany and wanted Italy as an ally against Germany. Britain even allowed Italy to use the Suez Canal to transport weapons and supplies to Italian Somaliland. It was Britain and France, not the League, that proposed a solution to end the war. This was known as the Hoare-Laval Pact after the two politicians who drew it up. Italy was to be given two-thirds of Abyssinia and the Emperor of Abyssinia, Haile Selassie, was to be allowed to rule just one-third of his own country. The people of Britain and France were so horrified by this unjust treatment of Abyssinia that the two politicians were forced to resign. In 1936 Haile Selassie went to the League of Nations and appealed for support. The League did not help him and Mussolini was able to take control of the whole country.

*Abyssinians give the **Fascist** salute to a picture of the Italian leader Mussolini that had been hung on some trees.*

> **Q What does this tell you about the success of Mussolini's invasion?**

- **The Spanish Civil War 1936–9.** In 1936 the extreme right-wing Nationalists, led by General Franco, launched a rebellion to overthrow the Spanish government. Franco received help from both Italy and Germany. The German airforce provided the Condor Legion that bombed Spanish cities. The world was horrified when they bombed the town of Guernica in

1937, killing hundreds of civilians. The League stood by helpless. Eventually the USSR sent weapons to the Spanish government but it was too little and too late. Britain and France did nothing. In 1939 Franco finally took control of Spain.

(above) La Guernica *painted by the Spanish artist Pablo Picasso. Picasso was not living in Spain at the time and he refused to allow the painting to hang in Spain until Franco had died. (See page 155 for a photograph of Guernica.)*

THE DOORMAT.

(right) 'The Doormat.' A British cartoon by David Low.

Q

1 Why is the word 'Geneva' shown on the pillar in the cartoon above?

2 The kneeling figure is meant to represent Britain. What does the 'face saving outfit' refer to?

3 What point is being made by the cartoonist?

4 Do you think that the cartoon would be equally appropriate if the figure of Mussolini was shown instead of that of Japan? Explain your answer.

5 In the 1930s the League failed to prevent the aggressors winning in Manchuria and Abyssinia. Why was this?

6 a Look at the weaknesses of the League given on page 149. Which of these weaknesses do you believe was the most important in leading to the failure of the League to stop war in the 1930s? Explain your answer.

  b Was this weakness apparent in the 1920s? Explain your answer.

A photograph of Guernica after the bombing.

WHY DID ANOTHER WORLD WAR BREAK OUT IN 1939?

Hitler's war?

One understanding of the outbreak of the Second World War in 1939 is to blame Adolf Hitler's ambition. He came to power in 1933 determined to follow a policy of aggressive **nationalism**. He also believed that war was good. The result can clearly be seen in the map below. Hitler overturned the Treaty

US President Wilson, speaking in 1919:

'I can certainly predict with absolute certainty that within another generation there will be another world war if the nations of the world do not produce methods to prevent it.'

Ⓠ Why was President Wilson so accurate in his prediction? In the last section we have seen how the League of Nations failed to prevent attacking countries from succeeding. Does that mean that it was Britain and France who were to blame for the outbreak of the Second World War?

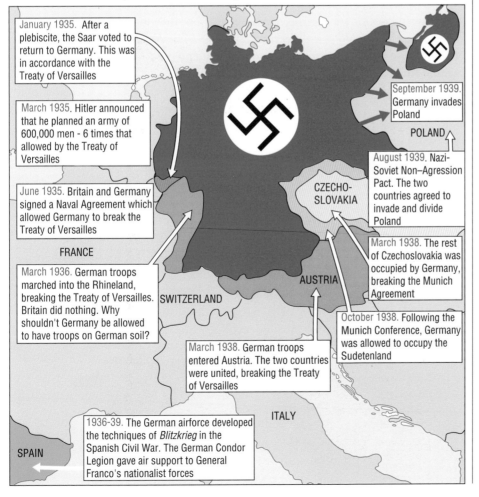

January 1935. After a plebiscite, the Saar voted to return to Germany. This was in accordance with the Treaty of Versailles

March 1935. Hitler announced that he planned an army of 600,000 men - 6 times that allowed by the Treaty of Versailles

June 1935. Britain and Germany signed a Naval Agreement which allowed Germany to break the Treaty of Versailles

FRANCE

March 1936. German troops marched into the Rhineland, breaking the Treaty of Versailles. Britain did nothing. Why shouldn't Germany be allowed to have troops on German soil?

SWITZERLAND

March 1938. German troops entered Austria. The two countries were united, breaking the Treaty of Versailles

SPAIN

1936-39. The German airforce developed the techniques of *Blitzkrieg* in the Spanish Civil War. The German Condor Legion gave air support to General Franco's nationalist forces

September 1939. Germany invades Poland

POLAND

August 1939. Nazi-Soviet Non–Agression Pact. The two countries agreed to invade and divide Poland

CZECHO-SLOVAKIA

March 1938. The rest of Czechoslovakia was occupied by Germany, breaking the Munich Agreement

AUSTRIA

October 1938. Following the Munich Conference, Germany was allowed to occupy the Sudetenland

ITALY

The expansion of Germany in the 1930s.

of Versailles stage by stage. He then set about conquering areas of Europe. He wanted to create a Greater Germany. This would contain all the German-speaking people of Europe in a single country. He also wanted to claim *Lebensraum.* By this he meant 'living space' which would provide food and raw materials for the growing German population. To the east of Germany lay lands occupied by the Slavs, a people that Hitler regarded as inferior to the Germans. They would serve the needs of the German master race.

The Rhineland

The Treaty of Versailles had not allowed Germany to place troops in the Rhineland. In March 1936 Hitler ordered German troops into the Rhineland. The troops were under orders to retreat if the French army marched to meet them. France was not willing to act without British support and Britain refused to cooperate. The British were not willing to go to war and they felt that it was fair for Germany to be able to place its own troops on its own land. Hitler had won and he now moved on to see what other areas of Europe he could gain.

Austria

The Treaty of Versailles had banned Germany and Austria (the two major German-speaking countries of Europe) from uniting. Wilson's principle of self-determination did not extend to those countries blamed for starting the war. Hitler was born in Austria and wanted unification with Germany. He had tried to unite the two countries in 1934 but had been stopped by the Italian leader Mussolini. However, by 1938 Mussolini was a close ally of Germany and so only Britain and France could prevent the union, or *Anschluss.* In March 1938 the Austrian Chancellor Schuschnigg decided to hold a plebiscite. The Austrian people would decide for themselves whether or not they wanted to be a part of Germany. Hitler could not allow this to happen. The Austrian people would probably vote against *Anschluss.* If they did, Hitler would not be able to claim that the Austrian people wanted to unite with Germany. This was exactly what Schuschnigg hoped would happen. Hitler demanded Schuschnigg's resignation and that the plebiscite be cancelled. Schuschnigg appealed for help from Britain and France. Yet when German troops invaded Austria on 12 March Britain and France did nothing.

German troops march into the Austrian city of Salzburg in March 1938. The civilians are giving the Nazi salute.

Austrian citizens celebrate the arrival of German troops in Salzburg in March 1938.

Q

1 What do the photographs on pages 156–7 appear to show?
2 Do you believe that all Austrians felt like this? Explain your answer.
3 What does this tell you about the use of photographs as evidence?

Czechoslovakia

The Treaty of Versailles had placed the area known as the Sudetenland in Czechoslovakia despite the fact that it contained three million Germans. After his success in Austria, Hitler believed that Britain and France would not stop him from taking over the Sudetenland. He met with the British Prime Minister Neville Chamberlain at Berchtesgaden. Hitler made what seemed a reasonable demand; he wanted a plebiscite in the Sudetenland. The people of the Sudetenland should be allowed to choose. Did they want to be part of Czechoslovakia or Germany? After all, the people of Upper Silesia had been allowed to choose between Poland and Germany in 1921. Chamberlain agreed that the people should be allowed a plebiscite. He left Germany to meet the French and the Czechs because the plebiscite could only take place with their agreement. When Chamberlain returned to Germany eight days later he met Hitler at Bad Godesberg. He had a shock when Hitler now demanded that the Sudetenland be given to Germany.

War seemed likely but it would not be an easy war for the Germans. France had a treaty with Czechoslovakia promising to help defend Czechoslovakia against invasion. The Czech army was almost as big as the German army and the Sudetenland contained strong defences. The Italian dictator Mussolini suggested that Italy, Germany, France and Britain should meet to decide what should be done to prevent war from breaking out. The meeting took place in the German city of Munich. The four countries agreed that Germany could take over the Sudetenland and in return Hitler promised that he would not ask for any other areas of Europe. The Czechs were not even consulted. Chamberlain returned to Britain and claimed that he had won 'peace for our time'. Six months later German troops invaded the rest of Czechoslovakia. Aggression had won again.

Chamberlain arrives back in England holding the piece of paper that he promised would deliver 'peace for our time'. Chamberlain was following a policy of **appeasement**. He was giving in to Hitler's demands so that war did not break out.

Poland

The invasion of the rest of Czechoslovakia had finally shown Chamberlain that Hitler could not be trusted. So Chamberlain announced that Britain would defend Poland if Germany tried to take it over. But this would not be easy. Britain was a long way from Poland. The Soviet Union was much nearer and so Britain tried to make a deal with Stalin, the leader of the Soviet Union. Chamberlain wanted both countries to agree to protect Poland.

Hitler was certain that Chamberlain would back down over Poland in the same way that he had backed down over Czechoslovakia. Hitler's main worry was Stalin because an invasion of Poland might provoke a Soviet attack. So Hitler also began secret talks with Stalin.

Stalin was afraid that Germany was planning to invade the Soviet Union and was certain that his army was not yet strong enough to defeat the Germans. Stalin felt that he could not trust Britain and France to help him, as the events in Czechoslovakia proved that Britain and France could not be trusted to try and stop Germany. In August 1939 the world was astonished when the Nazi-Soviet Pact was announced. Germany and the USSR agreed not to fight one another for ten years. The pact also contained a secret agreement to invade Poland and divide it between themselves. There was now nothing to stop Hitler and on 1 September 1939 German troops invaded Poland. Two days later Britain and France declared war on Germany.

Polish cavalry are mobilised to meet the German tanks and bombers. The Germans were far too strong for the Polish army and it was quickly defeated.

Who was to blame for war breaking out?

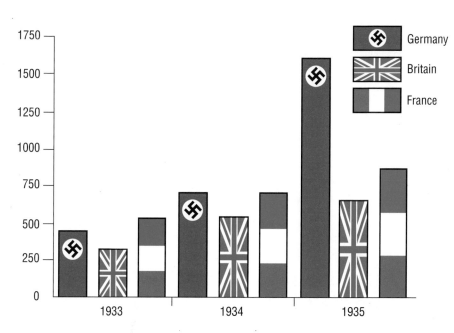

Defence spending. (Figures in millions of dollars.)

So was the war simply the result of German aggression? The bar chart above shows that the Germans were building up their armed forces at a much greater rate than the other European powers. Hitler's aggressive policies were obviously a major cause of the war, but were they the only cause and indeed were they the most important cause?

Q

1 What evidence can you find to suggest that Hitler was responsible for the outbreak of war?
2 What evidence can you find to suggest that others were also to blame?

WHAT WERE THE OTHER CAUSES OF THE SECOND WORLD WAR?

Appeasement

We have already seen that the actions of Britain and France stopped the League of Nations from solving some problems. If you consider the material on German aggression you can also see that Britain and France's attitude encouraged Hitler. Each time they failed to stop him Hitler demanded more. When Hitler's troops invaded the Rhineland they only advanced because they were not met by French troops. The French were not willing to defend the Rhineland because Britain refused to back such an action. In 1939 the British Prime Minister Chamberlain gave in to Hitler's demands. This policy of appeasement sought to prevent war from breaking out by giving in to demands that could be seen as reasonable. The policy led Hitler to assume that Britain and France would behave in a similar way over Poland. It is possible to argue that Hitler would not have invaded Poland if he had known that it would lead to war with Britain and France. He would surely not have invaded if Britain and France had already secured an alliance with the USSR as well.

▶▶ Why did Chamberlain follow a policy of appeasement?

Read Chamberlain's own explanation for his actions at Munich in Source 1 below. He was part of a generation that had seen the horrors of modern warfare and did not wish to see it again. It was this spirit that had led to the League of Nations. As Sources 2 and 3 show, Chamberlain had the support of the majority of the British population who did not want another war either. Like Chamberlain they found it a 'horrible, fantastic, incredible fact that Britain was preparing for war because of a quarrel in a far-away country between people of whom we know nothing'. A survey showed that two-thirds of the British people wanted the countries of the world to agree to get rid of all their weapons. The same survey revealed that only about one third of all men were willing to volunteer if war broke out. Contrast this to the reaction of men in 1914 when Kitchener asked for volunteers to fight in the First World War. Chamberlain was in tune with the wishes of the British people.

SOURCE 1:

A speech by the British Prime Minister Neville Chamberlain in 1938:

'When I think of those four terrible years, and I think of the millions of young men who were cut off in their prime, the 13 million who were maimed and mutilated . . . then I am bound to say to all in the world: "In war, whichever side may call itself victor, there are no winners but all are losers".'

SOURCE 2:

The British attitude to disarmament. The result of a gallup poll carried out in December 1937:

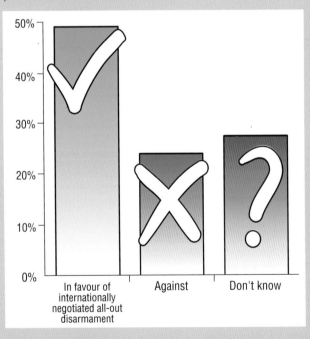

SOURCE 3:

Result of a by-election in East Fulham in 1933:

The Labour candidate won by 4480 votes, overturning a Conservative majority of 14 521. The Labour candidate was a pacifist while the Conservative candidate had called for rearmament in the face of growing aggression abroad.

SOURCE 4:

Would you volunteer if war broke out? The result of a gallup poll of British men carried out in December 1937:

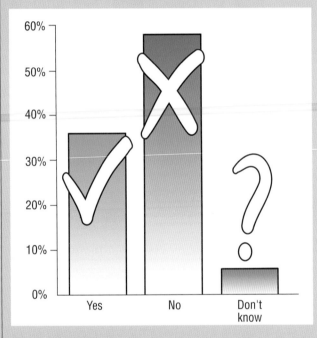

SOURCE 5:

Winston Churchill, speaking to the House of Commons after the Munich Agreement:

'All is over. Czechoslovakia recedes into the darkness. She has suffered in every respect from her association with the western democracies. She has suffered in particular from her association with France. I think you will find that in a period of time which may be measured in years, but may be measured only by months, Czechoslovakia will be engulfed in the Nazi regime.'

SOURCE 6:

A British cartoon from July 1936 by David Low.

1 How does Source 1 help to explain Chamberlain's attitude at Munich?

2 What was the attitude of the British people to Chamberlain's policy suggested in Sources 2 and 3?

3 Look at Source 6. What do the people who are bent over represent?

4 Look at the map on page 155. If Low had drawn his cartoon in 1939 which other names could he have written on the backs of the 'spineless leaders'?

5 What is Source 6's attitude to Chamberlain's policy?

6 Do you think that appeasement was the correct course to follow in the 1930s? Use the evidence from Sources 1–6 and your own knowledge to support your argument.

The peace treaties of 1919–20

The policy of appeasement and Hitler's aggression cannot be the sole causes of the war. After all, the war was a world war and not just a European one. In 1937 Japan invaded China and in 1941 they attacked the Americans at Pearl Harbor. The Italians also took the war to North Africa. The treaties must take some of the blame for these actions. Japan and Italy were both victors in the First World War and yet their leaders felt ignored by the Big Three (see page 144) in Paris. These countries felt that they had not received the rewards they deserved. When aggressive leaders took control of these countries they found that the people supported them.

The Treaty of Versailles had punished Germany. This had left many Germans wanting revenge and this had helped Hitler to gain power. It also made Hitler's actions, like putting troops in the Rhineland, seem reasonable. This encouraged appeasement. Leaders failed to see the threat posed by Nazi Germany.

The treaties had replaced the Austro-Hungarian Empire with a series of small countries such as Czechoslovakia. None of them were strong enough to stand up to an aggressive Germany. They needed the help of countries like Britain and France. However, Britain and France did not want to fight Germany.

The Treaty of Versailles had set up the League of Nations to try to stop war. But the world's strongest country, America, had not even joined the League of Nations. It would not help to stop Germany, Italy and Japan.

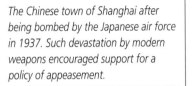

The Chinese town of Shanghai after being bombed by the Japanese air force in 1937. Such devastation by modern weapons encouraged support for a policy of appeasement.

Joachim Fest, a German historian:

'There can be no question about who was to blame . . . Hitler's urge to bring things to a head so controlled events that any wish to compromise by the western powers was bound to come to nothing. His entire career was directed to war.'

World depression

At the end of the First World War President Wilson had hoped that all countries would get rid of import and export duties. Goods would then cost less and so people would buy more. This would help to create jobs for everyone and create prosperity. In a prosperous world the new democratic countries which had been created at Versailles would become successful. The world would have been made safe for democracy.

In 1929, however, the world was plunged into an economic depression. World trade declined and workers lost their jobs. Countries raised their import duties in an attempt to protect their own industries from foreign competition. This only succeeded in reducing world trade even further. The result was a vicious spiral. Unemployment meant that fewer people had the money to buy goods. This meant that there was even less work in the factories and so even more people became unemployed. In Japan it encouraged the officers in the army to seek a way out through capturing the land and resources of first Manchuria and later the whole of China. In Germany it helped to create the desperation which led many people to vote for the Nazis and put Adolf Hitler in power. In Britain it helped to make appeasement an even more attractive policy since the government could not afford new weapons.

Q

1 Long-term causes of an event are those that create situations where an event can occur. Short-term causes are those that trigger the event to happen in a particular year. Below are a list of some causes of the Second World War. Add any others that you can think of to this list. Then sort them into long and short term causes.
   - The Japanese invasion of Manchuria
   - The Nazi-Soviet Pact
   - The Anglo-German Naval Agreement 1935
   - The world economic depression
   - The Treaty of Versailles
   - The German invasion of Czechoslovakia

2 Which do you think is the most important long-term cause of the war? Explain your answer. The best way to work out your answer is to try and imagine what would have happened if a particular cause had not occurred. If you can find one that might have prevented another cause from happening, then this is the most important cause.

3 Do you agree with Joachim Fest's interpretation on the left, above? Was Hitler solely to blame for the outbreak of war? Use the evidence from this section to back up your answer.

7 The Second World War: 'The Last Time there was Cheering'

This chapter focuses on two key issues:

- *Why were the Germans so successful in the early stages of the war?*
- *Why were the Axis powers of Germany, Italy and Japan eventually defeated?*

In 1939 the Canadian poet, Milton Acorn, wearily wrote these lines on the outbreak of war:

> 'This is where we came in; this has happened before
> Only the last time there was cheering.'

The 'last time', of course, refers to the war in 1914. Even the enemy was the same. This weary reluctance to get involved in another war was understandable but the Second World War was a very different war to the First World War. The men and women who fought it certainly cheered in 1945 when it was all over. They believed that they had rid the world of a monstrous evil.

In September 1939 Hitler planned a short, local war with Poland (see pages 158–9). Germany was equipped to fight such a war. To his astonishment, the invasion of Poland provoked Britain and France into declaring war on Germany. He had not expected this and Germany was not ready for a war against the major powers of Britain and France. Nonetheless, Germany could have won the war in 1941 if Hitler had not made two crucial errors that year. His decision to invade the Soviet Union and the declaration of war against the United States became Hitler's downfall.

1939–41: YEARS OF AXIS VICTORY

Hitler had a plan for the political domination of Europe. He planned to create a German empire in which the east European states would provide *Lebensraum* (living space) for his German master race. This would mean, to begin with, the conquest of Poland and then the Soviet Union (although the Russians, of course, didn't know this). Poland was occupied without too much difficulty by the end of September, after the Germans launched their surprise invasion on 1 September. Poland's problems were made much worse by the Russian invasion from the east (17 September). This had been agreed between Russia and Germany in their non-aggression pact in August.

Britain and France both had a treaty with Poland and declared war on Germany. For the British and French, however, the first seven months of the war were rather dull because there was no fighting on land between them and the Germans. This period from September 1939 to April 1940 was called 'the phoney war' or *sitzkrieg* – a joke from the new type of *Blitzkrieg* (lightning war) the Germans were using so successfully.

Germany invades Poland; Britain and France declare war on Germany	1939
Germans invade France; Italy declares war on Britain and France; France surrenders	1940
German invasion of the Soviet Union; Pearl Harbor	1941
Soviet victory over the Germans	1942
Italy surrenders	1943
D-Day; US naval victories over Japan; final German offensive (Battle of the Bulge)	1944
Germany surrenders; the war in Europe is over; atom bombs dropped on Japan; the Second World War is over	1945

Invasion of Norway

The phoney war came to a dramatic end in April 1940 when Germany invaded and occupied Norway. Norway was important to Germany because Germany's supply of iron ore came from Sweden through the Norwegian port of Narvik. In 1939 Sweden provided nearly 30 per cent of Germany's iron ore. Norway's west coast would also provide useful air and naval bases for attacks on Britain. The British and French sent troops to oppose the Germans but they achieved very little and had to withdraw.

This setback led to new governments in France and Britain. Chamberlain, Britain's Prime Minister since 1937, was thought of as the man who had failed to stop Hitler. Parliament decided that a more aggressive leader was needed. They chose Winston Churchill. He had long been opposed to Chamberlain's appeasement policy before the war, and didn't think much of Chamberlain's half-hearted efforts against Germany. He became Prime Minister of a coalition government of Conservatives, Labour and Liberals on 10 May.

Germany's Blitzkrieg 1939–41. Its new mobile, mechanised tactics brought rapid defeat to one country after another.

The fall of France

The loss of Norway in April was a setback to the Allies but worse things were to come. On 10 May Germany invaded Belgium, Holland and then France. Once again, the Germans caught their enemies unprepared. The overwhelming defeat of France in just six weeks was Hitler's greatest military campaign in the war. He planned and executed it against the advice of his more cautious generals. But, as on other occasions, the victory was mostly due to the bungled plans and efforts of his enemies as well as the fine quality of his troops.

The French High Command was sure that their expensive line of underground forts, the Maginot Line (see page 4), would protect France from a German attack. It probably would have done if the Germans had decided to attack the Line, but they did not. A key feature of *Blitzkrieg* (the new mobile and mechanised war that the Germans were fighting) was that the attackers avoided the enemy's strongpoints. The Maginot Line ended at Sedan where France's border with Germany ended.

To the astonishment of the French, the Germans broke through at Sedan. The French had thought that the Ardennes Forest, to the north of Sedan, was too thick for tanks to pass through. French resistance crumbled as the German tanks raced to the Channel coast where the Germans planned to cut off the retreat of the 150 000-strong British Expeditionary Force (BEF). For once, caution got the better of Hitler and he ordered Guderian to slow his advance on Dunkirk. It was from Dunkirk that the remainder of the BEF and the French army would try to escape to Britain. In theory it was left to Goering's *Luftwaffe* (air force) to pound the beaches and wreck the evacuation.

The *Luftwaffe*, however, was unable to operate and over 330 000 British and French troops managed to escape from Dunkirk by boat in the first week of June 1940. It was a remarkable achievement to escape from right under the noses of the encircling Germans. The British press and radio hailed the evacuation – 'Operation Dynamo' – as the 'miracle of Dunkirk'. The BBC broadcaster and writer, JB Priestley, described Dunkirk at the time as 'an epic of gallantry' but it was also a shattering defeat for the British army.

Britain had clearly abandoned its only ally and huge amounts of vital equipment. France surrendered on 22 June and the Germans gained two years' worth of oil supplies. Hitler allowed a pro-German French government, led by Marshal Pétain, to rule the south of France from the town of Vichy. This area became known as 'Vichy France'. A similar development took place in Norway where a Norwegian Nazi, Quisling, headed the pro-German government there.

France surrendered to the Germans in June 1940. Britain was afraid that the powerful French navy would fall into German hands. In July the Royal Navy asked the commander of the French fleet docked at Mers-el-Kebir in Algeria to join the British or at least sail to a neutral port. The French admiral refused and the British opened fire. French sailors are shown here trying to put out a fire. 1380 were killed but Churchill's ruthlessness showed that Britain was determined to fight on – even at the cost of attacking a former ally.

Why was *Blitzkrieg* so effective?

Hitler had prepared for a short but vigorous war. Germany had a small number of well-trained and equipped mechanised tanks supported by motorised infantry (troops in trucks). German equipment was not really any better than that of the Allies and their armed forces weren't any bigger but they were put to better use. Both the British and French used their tanks in small numbers, spread thinly among their troops. The Germans grouped their tanks in highly effective armoured units.

Artillery and dive bombers began the process by 'softening up' the enemy. They shelled the enemy front and rear, increasing their panic and fear. Germany's *Blitzkrieg* strategy concentrated armoured columns of tanks and troops in lorries at key points against the enemy. They used their concentrated fire-power, speed and greater numbers to smash their way through the enemy's weak positions. The better-defended positions were bypassed and cut off from reinforcements. While this was happening paratroops were busy seizing enemy HQs, telephone exchanges or bridges. Then they would wait for the fast-moving armoured columns to reach them.

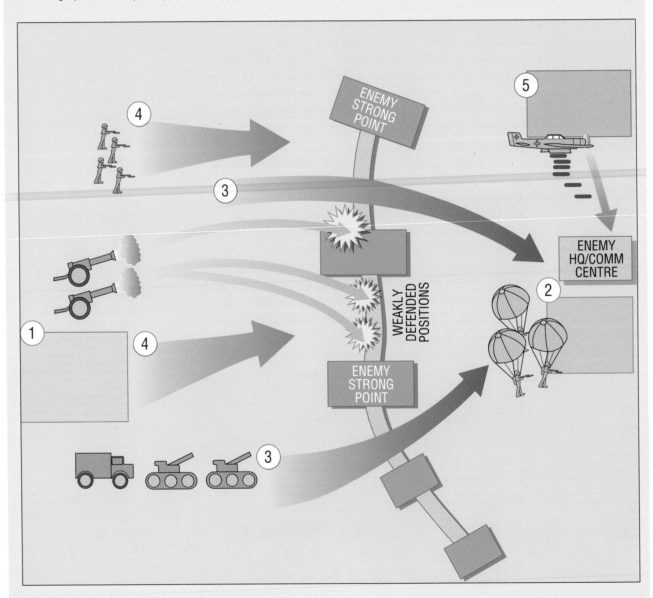

Look at the illustration of a typical German *Blitzkrieg* attack. Copy the illustration into your file and then fill in the blank spaces on the illustration using the correct labels from the following:

A: Parachutists dropped behind enemy lines to capture key positions such as bridges and HQs until relieved by armoured columns coming up in support.

B: Infantry on foot follow up to deal with enemy strongpoints.

C: Tanks and troops in lorries bypass enemy strongpoints.

D: Artillery shell enemy frontlines and rear positions.

E: Dive bombers attack enemy troop reinforcements.

The Battle of Britain

Britain expected a German invasion at any time but before it could take place, the Germans had to gain control of the skies by destroying the Royal Air Force (RAF). From July to September 1940 the Battle of Britain was fought between the RAF and the *Luftwaffe* to see who would control those skies and whether or not an invasion would take place. German troops could only be transported across the Channel if they were safe from attack by planes.

After France's defeat Hitler had offered peace terms to Britain. Some members of the British government, such as Lord Halifax, were keen to discuss these. It seemed that Britain's chances of resisting a German invasion were slight but Churchill, in public at least, was not interested in negotiating with Hitler. Britain would fight on and his stubborn defiance helped to inspire the British nation through the next six, dark months.

7 September 1940

Hermann Goering, in charge of the *Luftwaffe*, had devised a sensible strategy. He bombed radar stations, fighter bases, and in early September, he bombed aircraft factories. The RAF was finding it very difficult to make up its losses and the battle was in Germany's favour although the Germans did not know it. 7 September proved to be a watershed: Hitler, outraged by a British bombing raid on Berlin, ordered a switch in tactics. He told Goering to bomb London and other major cities in an effort to terrorise Britain into surrender.

For Dowding, the man in charge of Fighter Command, this brought welcome relief. The factories could turn out 500 Spitfires a week and the damaged airfields could be repaired as the *Luftwaffe* concentrated on targets like London that were not vital to war production.

A Hurricane, in the foreground, and a Spitfire in flight. The Spitfire was the best fighter plane of the war until the US Mustang appeared in 1942. The Hurricane made up two-thirds of the RAF's fighter planes in 1940 and its importance has been under-estimated.

The bombing of Britain's cities, called the 'Blitz', lasted until May 1941. Hitler had already given up on 'Operation Sealion' (in which he planned to invade Britain) as early as mid-October 1940 because his real ambitions were to the east, in Russia. The RAF was able to defeat the Germans because of the foolish change in tactics on 7 September. The Spitfire (the best fighter plane at the time) also helped, as did radar. Radar gave advance warning of air attack and allowed the enemy to be intercepted long before they reached their target. In this way Dowding was able to concentrate his limited number of fighter planes at the right point and time. Germany, at this time, did not have this vital weapon.

1 Why was Norway so important to Germany?

2 Why did the Maginot Line fail to defend France in 1940?

3 Why was it important for JB Priestley to refer to a defeat like Dunkirk as an 'epic of gallantry'?

4 Why was the Battle of Britain so important?

5 Why was Goering's switch in tactics on 7 September such a mistake?

6 Some historians have claimed that Hitler was never very interested in invading Britain. Does the evidence in the text support this? Explain your answer.

7 Why were the Germans so successful in the early stages of the war? The table below contains five reasons that explain the early successes of the German armed forces. These reasons, as they stand, are only general statements. Your task in the second column is to find evidence from the text that supports these statements. In the third column you should write a comment of your own assessing the importance of each of these reasons. One example has already been done for you.

Reason	Evidence	Importance
1 Germany's armed forces were better prepared and trained for their new *Blitzkrieg* style of warfare	The Allies used their tanks in small numbers, spread among their troops while the Germans grouped them together	The Allies were taken by surprise by this tactic and lost several key campaigns in Poland, Norway and France
2 Germany acquired vital supplies of raw materials from the countries that it conquered		
3 There were groups in the occupied countries who were willing to collaborate (cooperate) with the Germans		
4 The British and French were not ready for the new style of warfare and used out-of-date tactics		
5 Germany chose the place and moment for the attack and so always had surprise on its side		

1941–43: THE TIDE BEGINS TO TURN

Russian 'hailstorm'

Hitler invaded the Soviet Union on 22 June 1941 and ordered his troops to flatten Russia 'like a hailstorm'. The reasons for 'Operation Barbarossa', the codename for the invasion, were both military and political. Hitler needed Russia's vast raw materials of oil in the Caucasus and wheat in the Ukraine to support his army and population. But he was also obsessed by ideas about race. To Hitler the Russians were an 'inferior' Slav race, fit only to be the slaves of the new German empire that he was creating. Russia's fertile plains could provide even more *Lebensraum* than Poland. Russia was also at the heart of world Communism and Hitler detested Communists.

The Soviet army had done very badly during its brief war with Finland in the winter of 1939–40. This convinced Hitler that the Soviet Union could be beaten in six months. But the invasion of the USSR was his biggest mistake of the war so far, especially with Britain still undefeated in the west. Germany was now committed to a war on two fronts. Hitler's arrogance and contempt for his enemies was to prove his most serious failing.

Hitler massed a huge army of 153 divisions (three million men), 3700 tanks and 2800 aircraft. But the Russians had even more troops – far more than the Germans expected. The Russians fell back, trading men and territory for time. As they retreated they 'scorched the earth', destroying everything that might provide food or shelter for the Germans. The Germans captured tremendous numbers of Soviet troops – three million by the end of 1941. But Stalin, the Soviet dictator, ignored the losses in men and materials. He had ordered 1500 factories (80 per cent of industrial output) to be moved by rail to the east, away from the fighting. The Germans seemed to face a never-ending supply of both men and tanks despite the numbers that they captured or destroyed.

Hitler had three principal targets for each of his army groups: Army Group North (AGN) was ordered to capture Leningrad (an important centre for the armaments industry); Army Group Centre (AGC) headed for the capital, Moscow; Army Group South (AGS) set out for the Ukraine. Only AGS took its objective. Leningrad was beseiged for three years until January 1944 and was never taken. AGC came within 60 kms of the capital in December 1941 but was halted and then driven back.

(below) Stalin did not appeal to Russians to defend Communism from the Germans. Soviet posters of the period concentrated on basic human emotions to encourage resistance to the invaders. Nazi brutality made this a fairly easy task. This poster declares: 'Our hope is in you, Red Warrior' as helpless civilians caught behind German lines are executed.

Q **What emotions do you think this poster is designed to stir?**

ВСЯ НАДЕЖДА НА ТЕБЯ, КРАСНЫЙ ВОИН!

Stalingrad: 'Not a step back'

Hitler did not give up on the Caucasus oilfields. In the summer of 1942 he planned an offensive to capture Stalingrad. This would protect the flank or side of his army as it drove southwards towards the Caucasus. Stalin told the defenders of Stalingrad 'Not a step back.' For six months, from August 1942 to January 1943, every room within every floor within every building was fought over. Eventually the German VIth Army of 330 000 men, cut off and starving, was forced to surrender on 30 January. It was the biggest German defeat of the war so far. Soviet morale soared. The Germans could be beaten! The oilfields were saved. From now on the Germans were in retreat until, by August 1944, not a single German soldier was left on Russian soil and by December the Soviet Red Army was ready to invade Germany itself.

Two Russian snipers in winter camouflage uniforms. The Russians were much better prepared for the winter war than the Germans.

> **Q** Hitler hadn't bothered to issue winter clothing for his army. Why did he not think it would be necessary?

Why did Barbarossa fail?

Hitler believed that the Red Army would offer no serious resistance but he under-estimated the Soviet Union in three key areas. These were:

- the number of troops it could field;
- the courage and tenacity of these troops;
- the ability of the Russians to make up for losses of men and war materials.

Hitler's over-confidence also led him to invade without preparing for a winter campaign because he claimed that the war would be over before the winter. The Soviet forces were much better equipped for this while the Germans, exposed by the scorched-earth policy, simply starved and froze. The Red Army had taken on 75 per cent of Germany's military resources and could justly claim to have done the most to defeat Hitler. The Red Army eliminated no fewer than 607 German divisions (over 7.5 million men killed, captured or missing). The British and Americans accounted for just 176 divisions on the fronts where they fought the Germans.

Q

1 Why was the invasion of Russia such a serious error for Germany?
2 Why were the Germans making less progress than expected despite conquering such a vast area?
3 Why was Stalingrad such a decisive battle?
4 Which one of the reasons given under the heading 'Why did Barbarossa fail?' do you think was the most important? Explain your answer.

The defeat of Italy, September 1943

Mussolini, the fascist dictator of Italy, declared war on France and Britain on 10 June 1940. He was certain that France was beaten (which it was) and that Britain would soon follow (which it did not). The war proved to be a disaster for Italy and Mussolini. Mussolini was eventually overthrown and imprisoned, in July 1943, by a vote of his own Fascist Party and King Victor Emmanuel. The King simply ordered Mussolini's arrest. Fascism was fairly popular when Italy was at peace but it was quickly abandoned by the Italians after a series of humiliating failures against the British in North Africa. Italy surrendered to the British and Americans in September 1943, then changed sides and declared war on Germany in October.

Mussolini had been desperate to recreate the glories of the Ancient Roman Empire for Italy. This meant carving out a new Italian empire in the Mediterranean and North Africa at the expense of Britain. For this reason he invaded British-controlled Egypt from Italian Libya in September 1940. The Italian troops' equipment was inferior to that of the British. None of the Italian anti-tank guns, for example, could stop a British tank. They were poorly led and their morale was low. After initial successes the large Italian army was driven back and soon it was in rapid retreat. The Germans entered the war in North Africa in February 1941 to support Italy with a small force of four divisions (about 60 000 men).

Two Indian soldiers manning their machine gun in the Libyan desert in 1943. India contributed 2.5 million men to assist Britain in the war against Japan, Germany and Italy. 100 000 Indians became casualties in what was the largest volunteer army in history.

El Alamein: the beginning of the end

The Italian-German army was able to turn the situation around and in just four months they had recovered the ground that the Italians had lost earlier. Indeed, the German commander, Rommel, threatened to take the Suez Canal which formed a vital link in Britain's empire in the east. However, in November 1942 Montgomery and the British Eighth Army put an end to Rommel's string of victories at the Battle of El Alamein. It was Britain's first real victory over the Germans on land. The Suez Canal and the crucial oil fields beyond it were saved from capture.

In the same month the first American forces also landed in North Africa after Hitler's foolish declaration of war in December 1941. Six months later the remaining Italian-German armies surrendered in Tunisia. The war in North Africa was over and Hitler had lost an opportunity to find the oil that his forces so desperately needed.

(above) Mussolini reviewing the Italian Eighth Army in 1940. Its equipment and troops were Italy's finest but instead of being used against the British in North Africa it was sent to Russia and destroyed at Stalingrad.

The invasion of Italy, July 1943

The Anglo-American forces landed in Sicily in July and then quickly crossed over onto the Italian mainland. Italy surrendered immediately as expected, but the Germans poured over 400 000 troops into the south of the country to meet the Allied advance. The Germans chose the best defensive positions, making the most of the mountainous terrain. Slowly the Allied forces fought their way up the country. Churchill had expected a quick campaign but the Germans were not defeated in Italy until the very end of the war in April 1945.

These Italian soldiers are surrendering to the Allies in Sicily. Units of the Italian army soon found themselves fighting the Germans who were now occupying their country.

Why do you think these soldiers look so cheerful?

How effective was the bombing of Germany?

Arthur Harris became the commander of the RAF's Bomber Command in February 1942. He firmly believed that the war could be won by intensive bombing of Germany's cities. There was also some rivalry with the more 'glamorous' Fighter Command of the RAF that had saved the country during the Battle of Britain. He wanted to prove that the bomber was just as important.

'Bomber' Harris put his theories into practice and in May 1942 launched the first 1000 bomber raid over Germany with Cologne as the target. This one raid killed about 40 000 Germans and a week-long raid over Hamburg in July and August 1943 killed 45 000. About 750 000 German civilians perished as a result of British and US raids over Germany's cities. This is far more than the 60 000 Britons killed by German raids. Fifty thousand RAF bomber crew lost their lives and about the same number of Americans also died.

It has been a matter of some controversy whether these raids really did help defeat Germany. The British government ignored Harris in the 1946 honours list and it refused to issue a special Bomber Command campaign medal although medals were issued for the Battle of Britain fighter pilots. Harris was bitter about this treatment and resigned from the RAF in 1946.

SOURCE 1:

In 1942 Harris issued this statement to all the crews of the RAF's bomber squadrons:

'It has been decided that the main purpose of your bombing operations should now be focused on the morale of the enemy civilian population and, in particular, on the morale of the industrial workers . . . We are bombing Germany city by city and ever more terribly in order to make it impossible for her to go on with the war.'

Adapted from Arthur Harris, Commander in Chief, Bomber Command, 1942

SOURCE 2:

One modern historian has written this about the Allied bombing campaign over Germany:

'The bombing of cities remained Bomber Command's main way of proving the claim of air power to be a war-winner. The civilian population was the main target with factories, in the words of a Bomber Command directive, as a bonus . . . In Berlin the damage was severe enough to cause many to leave the city and to close all the schools. Despite this, less than half of the city's industries stopped work and many of the stoppages were brief . . . Yet morale did not break in either Berlin or Hamburg. Bomber Command failed to bring German industry to a halt.'

Adapted from P Calvocoressi: *Total War* 1972

SOURCE 3:

A different view on the effectiveness of the bombing campaign is offered by this historian:

'On October 14, 1943, 291 US Flying Fortresses set off to attack the greatest centre of German ball-bearing production. The fortresses did severe damage but 60 were shot down. The strategic bombing offensive brought the German war economy almost to the point of collapse.'

Adapted from Brigadier Peter Young: *World War 1939–1945* 1966

SOURCE 4:

A third view is provided by AN Frankland's comment:

'British Bomber Command and the Eighth USAAF [United States Army Air Force] did produce an oil famine in Germany, the collapse of its transport system and a fearful levelling [destruction] of its great cities. These results were too late to win the war on their own, but they did make a decisive contribution to the defeat of Germany.'

From *The Oxford Companion to the Second World War* 1995

SOURCE 5:

The statistics of German industrial and military output (below) from 1940–44 should give some clues as to how effective the bombing campaign was. Industrial output is in millions of tons.

	1940	1941	1942	1943	1944
Coal	268 m	315 m	318 m	340 m	348 m
Steel	21 m	28 m	29 m	31 m	26 m
Oil	4.8 m	5.7 m	6.6 m	7.6 m	5.5 m
Tanks	2200	5200	9200	17 300	22 100
Aircraft	10 200	11 800	15 400	24 800	39 800

Adapted from *The Oxford Companion to the Second World War* 1995

Answering a question like the one in this activity is not an easy task. You must go through several stages in order to work out how effective the bombing campaign over Germany was. The procedures are basically another version of what an historian would do. First you have to decide what it was Bomber Command set out to do.

1 Harris identified two basic aims for Bomber Command in Source 1. The first was to destroy the morale of the civilian population and especially its industrial workers. What was the second?

2 In what way does Source 2 support Source 1 as far as the aims of Bomber Command are concerned?

3 What does Calvocoressi in Source 2 say about whether these aims were achieved?

4 How does Brigadier Young in Source 3 disagree with Calvocoressi? Which of Bomber Command's aims does Young not comment on?

5 Frankland in Source 4 claims that the bombing produced an 'oil famine' in Germany. Does Source 5 support this in your view?

Once you know this, you can use the evidence provided to measure the achievements of the campaign against this test – did the bombing achieve what it set out to do? This is done by checking one piece of information from the sources against another to see if they support or contradict each other.

6 Go through each of Sources 2, 3 and 4 and point out where, if at all, the statistics support the views in the sources or where they contradict them.

7 People often have more than one reason for saying something. Harris believed that bombing could win the war but it is possible that he had another reason for supporting this policy. What might it have been? Does this other reason make the view in Source 1 any less useful?

8 Using Sources 1, 2, 3, 4 and 5 and your own knowledge, explain in an essay of 300 words or more whether you agree with the following interpretation: 'The bombing of Germany did not seriously damage Germany's ability to wage war.'

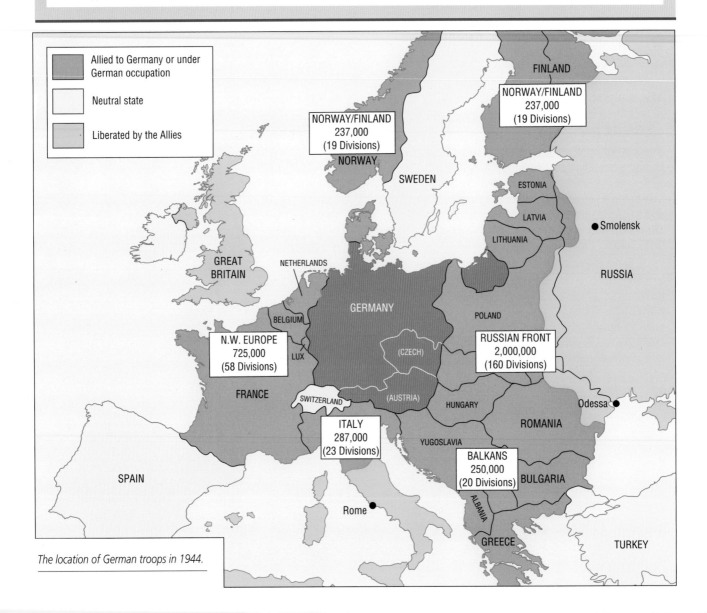

The location of German troops in 1944.

THE END OF THE WAR IN EUROPE

The Second Front, June 1944

After the German invasion of Russia in June 1941 Stalin had repeatedly asked Churchill and Roosevelt to open a 'Second Front'. This meant an Allied invasion of German-occupied France. This, he calculated, would force the Germans to withdraw troops from the war against Russia so that they could deal with the British and Americans in France. Stalin had to wait until June 1944 for this invasion to take place. Churchill told Stalin that an invasion of Italy had to come first. Stalin suspected that the British and Americans really wanted to do very little and leave the Russians to bear the human cost of the war against the Nazis.

Eventually the American General Eisenhower, commander of all the Allied forces, decided that the good weather expected for 6 June 1944 would last long enough for a seaborne invasion of France to take place. D-Day was set for 6 June. He gave the go-ahead for 'Operation Overlord' with the simple instruction: 'Let's go.' The choice of the Normandy beaches took the Germans completely by surprise. None of the ports on the Normandy coast were suitable for the Allies to unload the huge amount of supplies and equipment that they would need for an invasion. Therefore the Germans, including Rommel, expected an attack across the shortest sea route at Calais.

What the Germans did not know was that the Allies planned to bring their own 'ports' with them in the form of secret weapons called 'Mulberries'. These were artificial harbours that could be towed across the Channel so that tanks, trucks and supplies could be unloaded onto them. Even after the first landings had taken place Hitler was convinced that the invasion at Normandy was not real. He held back two nearby tank divisions (over 500 tanks) until it was too late. When he was eventually ready to use them the British, American and Canadian divisions had established a firm hold on French soil.

Sixty thousand troops landed on the first day of Operation Overlord and within a week over 300 000 troops were in France. After three months the number had grown to two million men pitched against the 600 000 troops

A part of a Mulberry harbour seen here carrying war provisions and trucks.

Casualties in the Second World War had a better chance of surviving than they did in the First World War. This was largely due to two new medical developments: penicillin and blood transfusions. Here a wounded American is receiving blood plasma. Plasma, unlike real blood, can be stored in dried form without being damaged and it saved thousands of lives as a result.

available to Hitler. The Germans were gradually driven back towards Germany. To add to this, more bad news arrived for Hitler from Romania in August 1944. The Romanians had changed sides and abandoned their German allies. The Romanians had previously provided Germany with 23 per cent of its oil supplies and now this was lost.

Arnhem and the Ardennes Offensive

There were only two setbacks to the Allies' progress: Arnhem (September 1944) and the Ardennes Offensive (December 1944). Montgomery planned to use airborne troops at Arnhem to seize vital bridges in Holland behind the German lines. These would be essential to the invasion of northern Germany later. But the reinforcements failed to fight their way through and the attack collapsed. The losses at one of the bridges at Arnhem were especially severe. Of the 10 000 troops sent there, 8000 were killed or captured.

Hitler launched one last desperate counter-attack at the Ardennes in December to prevent an invasion of Germany. He used his final reserves and fuel resources. Initially the Battle of the Bulge, as it is also known, was very successful and the Allies were taken completely by surprise. But successful air attacks and Allied superiority in numbers eventually broke the German offensive at the end of January 1945. By using his vital reserves in Europe and not against the Russians, Hitler lost more of Germany (including Berlin) to the Red Army.

Q

> 1 Why did the Italian army do so badly against the British in North Africa?
> 2 Why was El Alamein such an important victory for Britain?
> 3 Why was Stalin so keen to form a Second Front?
> 4 In what way did it cause friction between Russia and its western allies?
> 5 What crucial error did Hitler make after the Normandy landings had begun?

The end of Hitler's Germany

In March the Allies crossed the Rhine into Germany from the west. In the following month the Russians took Berlin, the capital of Nazi Germany. Hitler shot himself on 30 April. Two days earlier Mussolini, formerly Hitler's main ally, had been executed by Italian Communist **partisans**. His body was left hanging upside down from a garage in Milan. On 8 May Germany surrendered unconditionally. Hitler had boasted that Nazism would last 1000 years but twelve had proved more than enough.

The Holocaust

The end of the war came too late for approximately six million Jews who were the victims of Hitler's Holocaust. This was the deliberate extermination of Europe's Jews under the Nazi regime. It was the result of Hitler's obsession with creating a 'master race' (*Herrenvolk*) of Germanic peoples. He almost succeeded. From 1942 onwards Himmler, the chief of the SS, organised the 'Final Solution' by shooting or gassing those Jews who were not of immediate use to the Nazis as slave labour. This policy was so efficient that only 50 000 of Poland's 2 700 000 Jews survived the war.

The SS did not only rely on Germans to carry out this policy. Many Poles, French and Russians in areas under Nazi control assisted in identifying and capturing Jews for the occupying Germans. The British authorities in the German-occupied Channel Islands cooperated with German laws concerning Jews. Anti-Semitism (the hatred and persecution of Jews) was not something that only the Germans believed in.

This poster won the New York Museum of Modern Art competition in 1945. Propaganda was used by both sides to persuade people to think or behave in a certain way. Sometimes the appeal was an emotional one, such as in this poster of Adolf Hitler.

Q Why do you think that this poster proved so successful?

THE WAR IN THE PACIFIC

The Japanese attack on the American naval base at Pearl Harbor in the middle of the Pacific Ocean should not have come as a complete surprise to the Americans. The Japanese and the Americans were the two great Pacific powers who competed with each other to dominate the region. The USA was content with economic domination of the region but the Japanese wanted to control South East Asia by conquering it.

Japanese conflict with the USA seemed inevitable, especially after the Americans imposed a ban or boycott on the sale of oil to Japan in July 1941. The boycott was imposed because Japan had occupied China since 1937 and it came as a severe blow to the Japanese economy as it depended on the USA for two-thirds of its oil supplies. The military leaders realised that Japan could never dominate South East Asia unless it controlled its own supplies of vital raw materials like oil, rubber, iron ore and rice. These could only be acquired through war. If Japan was to stand any chance in a war against the USA it would have to strike first. So the Japanese planned a devastating blow against the USA's Pacific fleet at Pearl Harbor in Hawaii.

Pearl Harbor

The fact that the Japanese attack was carried out before a declaration of war united and enraged the American people. This poster was designed to remind Americans of what President Roosevelt called a 'day of infamy'.

American intelligence had cracked the Japanese secret code and knew that an attack against the USA was planned but they were not sure where. It was assumed that the target would be the Philippines and not Pearl Harbor. As a result, the Americans were looking elsewhere when the Japanese fleet sailed undetected 5500 kilometres across the Pacific to within 450 kilometres of Hawaii. Two waves of Japanese aircraft pounded the Pacific fleet of 70 ships in its harbour on Sunday morning, 7 December 1941.

Six battleships and ten other ships were sunk and 164 planes destroyed. 2400 servicemen and civilians also died. Although the damage inflicted was devastating, it was not as great as the Japanese had hoped. The American aircraft carriers which were a key target were out on manoeuvres that morning and the Japanese commander, Nagumo, had decided not to attack the ship repair facilities or the oil storage units. This meant that the damaged vessels could be repaired quickly and the US fleet still had the fuel to hit back when it was ready. But that would not be for another six months.

In the long term, Pearl Harbor was not a success for the Japanese. The attack enraged public opinion in America, especially as it came before an official declaration of war. Had Japan occupied Pearl Harbor and seized the vast oil supplies there, things may have been different. All that Admiral Yamamoto achieved was to delay the full impact of America's anger.

'Withering on the vine'

For the next six months, Japan had a free hand in the Pacific and in South East Asia. They launched simultaneous attacks against the British in Burma and Malaya where vital raw materials like oil and rubber were to be found. Japanese troops pushed back the British, Australians and Americans as Japanese victory followed victory. Britain lost Singapore, its key naval base in the Far East in February 1942. The loss of Singapore and the 62 000 British and Empire

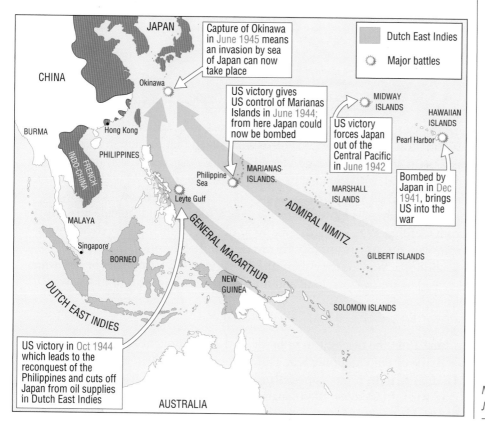

Nimitz and MacArthur's advance on Japan 1942–45.

troops taken prisoner were huge blows to morale. The fact that only 35 000 Japanese troops had achieved this made it even more humiliating.

The Americans took command of the Allied campaign in the Pacific. General MacArthur was to advance by land from the South West Pacific and Admiral Nimitz by sea across the Pacific Ocean. The Americans developed an 'island hopping' or 'leap-frogging' strategy. This was similar to Hitler's *Blitzkrieg*: strongly-defended enemy islands were isolated from support and reinforcements. They were, in MacArthur's words, 'left to wither on the vine'. This limited US casualties and sped up their progress across the vast distances and hundreds of islands held by the Japanese. In one spectacular push in 1944 MacArthur 'hopped' 930 kilometres to seize a Japanese base bypassing 40 000 enemy troops.

The turning-point

The spectacular run of Japanese victories came to an end with the Battle of Midway in June 1942. The Japanese planned to seize the US island of Midway but the US knew of the plan because they had deciphered Japan's secret code. The Americans ambushed the enemy's fleet and sank four aircraft carriers losing only one US carrier. It was a decisive blow and meant that the Japanese could no longer operate in the central Pacific.

These prisoners are about to set out on the 'March of Death' in April 1942. Over 2000 US prisoners and 8000 Filipinos died during the 100 km march to Bataan. Twenty-seven per cent of US prisoners died in Japanese hands. Statistics like these ensured that the Pacific War was even more ferocious than the one in Europe.

America's Pacific progress, however, proved to be costly. Japanese resistance was fanatical. The warrior code of *Bushido* stated that capture in battle was a dishonour. Japanese soldiers preferred to fight to the death. Iwo Jima, a tiny volcanic island, was defended by 23 000 Japanese troops. 22 000 fought to the death rather than surrender.

Other Japanese volunteered for *Kamikaze* (divine wind) suicide missions. From October 1944 onwards over 5000 pilots flew their planes packed with explosives into American ships. It was this kind of devotion to Emperor Hirohito that worried the Americans. What would US casualties be like when they had to attack Japan itself and not tiny islands hundreds of miles away?

From the Marianas to Okinawa

In June 1944 the biggest carrier battle of the war brought American victory in the Battle of the Philippine Sea. This victory allowed them to occupy the Marianas Islands. From Saipan island the US Army Air Force could now bomb Japan itself. In October 1944 Japan suffered another crucial defeat at the Battle of Leyte Gulf. Four months later this led to the reconquest of the Philippines

Japanese Kamikaze pilots pose before going on a suicide mission. The Kamikaze cult reflects the very deep contrast in culture between the Japanese and their American opponents. American servicemen were prepared for death but they didn't go out of their way to find it.

by MacArthur and Japan was cut off from its oil supplies in the Dutch East Indies. The loss of 60 million barrels of oil a year was a crushing blow to a country that could produce only two million barrels of its own oil. These barrels represented 80 per cent of Japan's total oil supply.

The capture of Okinawa took place in June after two months of vicious fighting. Thirteen thousand American soldiers and sailors had died to capture an island 550 kilometres from Japan itself. From here an invasion of mainland Japan could at last be launched. But at what cost to the USA?

The atomic bombing of Japan

On 6 August 1945 the Americans dropped the world's first atomic bomb on Hiroshima. Three days later they followed it with another bomb that they dropped on Nagasaki. Over 200 000 people were killed, and many died later from the effects of radiation.

On 10 August, the day after the bombing of Nagasaki, Japan agreed to surrender. It is generally assumed that the bombs forced Japan to make this decision but recent evidence suggests a different reason. The American fire-bombing of Tokyo in March had killed 85 000 civilians but the government of Japan had still fought on. Civilian casualties were probably not an issue. It is true that American lives were saved because a full-scale invasion of Japan was not needed, but this was not because of the dropping of the two atomic bombs. Japan agreed to surrender because President Truman had dropped the demand for unconditional surrender. Until then the Americans had insisted that the Japanese surrender and accept whatever terms the USA chose. The Japanese would surrender if Emperor Hirohito was allowed to stay on the throne. Truman agreed to this one condition and the war was over. He could have agreed to it before the bombing but then the awesome power of the weapon would not have been proved. By demonstrating the atomic bomb the USA warned the USSR not to confront the West after the war was over.

---

1 Why was the US boycott of oil sales to Japan such a blow to the Japanese economy?

2 Why could Pearl Harbor be described as a failure for Japan?

3 Why was 'island hopping' an appropriate strategy for the USA in the Pacific?

4 Why was the loss of the Philippines such a blow to Japan?

5 'The dropping of the atomic bombs on Japan was an unnecessary and brutal act.' What is your opinion of this view?

Q

▶ Why did the Axis powers lose the war?

Countries lose wars for a variety of reasons. Poor equipment, low morale, unsuccessful strategies and a lack of industrial resources can all play a part. The equipment of both the Italians and the Japanese was generally inferior to that of their opponents. But this was not the case for the Germans whose weapons matched and often out-performed those of their enemies. The morale of the Italian forces was generally much lower than that of the British but the Japanese and Germans fought stubbornly for their leaders until the very end.

However, some general reasons for the defeat of the Axis powers are put forward in the chart on page 183. Your task is to find evidence to support these reasons (from the text, the sources and the photograph and poster presented here) and then decide how important they were in causing the defeat of the Axis. There isn't a right or wrong answer for this final part. The strength of your answer depends on how well you argue your case and the quality of the evidence you have to support it. An example has been done for you but you are welcome to improve on it!

SOURCE 1:

German forces on various fronts in June 1944. Figures are calculated on the estimate that each division is roughly 12 500 troops (see map on page 174):

Italy: 287 500 (23 divisions)
France, Belgium, Holland: 725 000 (58 divisions)
Norway/Finland: 237 500 (19 divisions)
Balkans: 250 000 (20 divisions)
Russia: 2 000 000 (160 divisions)

SOURCE 2:

Japanese forces on various fronts in August 1943. Figures are calculated on the estimate that each division is roughly 18 000 troops:

Pacific: 270 000 (15 divisions)
Manchuria: 270 000 (15 divisions)
China: 468 000 (26 divisions)
Burma: 108 000 (6 divisions)
Korea: 36 000 (3 divisions)

SOURCE 3:

A comparison of Axis and Allied industrial and military production:

Oil supplies in metric tons, 1944
Axis forces: 11 m (Germany 9.5 m; Japan 1 m)
Allied forces: 263 m (USA 222 m; USSR 18 m; UK 21 m)

Coal production in metric tons, 1944
Axis forces: 486 m (Germany 433 m; Japan 52 m)
Allied forces: 890 m (USA 562 m; USSR 121 m; UK 192 m)

Aircraft production, 1944
Axis forces: 69 000 (Germany 40 000; Japan 29 000)
Allied forces: 163 000 (USA 96 000; USSR 40 000; UK 26 000)

Tank production, 1944
Axis forces: 19 400 (Germany 19 000; Japan 400)
Allied forces: 51 000 (USA 17 500; USSR 29 000; UK 4500)

Adapted from J Ellis: *The World War II Handbook* 1993

SOURCE 4:

At first the Germans were able to win the support of considerable numbers of men within the countries they occupied. About 800 000 volunteered for the Waffen SS – many of them from Holland, Belgium, Norway, France and later eastern Europe. As many as 25 per cent were killed. This poster is appealing to Belgians to enlist: 'You defend Belgium when you fight on the Eastern Front!' But as Nazi rule became more brutal fewer and fewer men volunteered to fight with the Germans.

SOURCE 5:

An impression of life under the Nazi occupation is reflected in this street hanging in Belgrade, Yugoslavia in 1941. Most forms of resistance led to the death penalty. When individuals could not be identified, the Nazis murdered entire populations of villages as punishment for partisan activities.

Reasons for defeat of Axis powers	Evidence in the text and sources	Importance of the reason in the Axis defeat
The Axis powers were unable to match the Allies' industrial production		
The Axis forces over-committed themselves by fighting on too many fronts		
The Axis forces depended on conquered territories for vital raw materials. As they retreated they lost these raw materials	The loss of the Dutch East Indies cut off Japan from 80 per cent of its oil supplies; Romania's decision to join the Allies in August cost Germany 23 per cent of its oil	The loss of raw materials such as oil was a crippling blow to the Axis since without adequate petrol supplies their armed forces were increasingly ineffective
The Axis had a lower output of military equipment		
The Axis failed to win support among the peoples they conquered		

Q

Extended writing

Write 300 words or more on the following question:

a Why were the Axis forces so successful in the early stages of the war?

b Why, however, did the Axis powers lose the war?

You will find it helpful to remember the following points, in addition to any of your own:

- the importance of surprise;
- Germany's *Blitzkrieg*;
- the economic and military strengths of both sides before America's entry;
- the military and economic impact of the USA's entry into the war;
- over-commitment of the Axis forces;
- ill-treatment of occupied peoples by the Axis powers.

8 The Cold War

1945	**Allied conferences, Yalta and Potsdam**
1948	**Communists in power in Czechoslovakia; Berlin blockade**
1949	**NATO established; Berlin blockade ended**
1953	**Death of Stalin**
1955	**Warsaw Pact established**
1956	**Khrushchev begins 'de-Stalinisation'; Hungarian Rising**
1959	**Castro takes power in Cuba**
1960	**US U-2 spy plane shot down over Soviet Union**
1961	**'Bay of Pigs'; Berlin Wall built**
1962	**Cuban Missile Crisis**
1963	**Nuclear Test Ban Treaty**
1968	**Soviet invasion of Czechoslovakia**
1972	**SALT 1**
1979	**Soviet invasion of Afghanistan**
1983	**American invasion of Grenada**
1989	**Berlin Wall comes down; Ceausescu executed in Romania**
1990	**Unification of East and West Germany**
1991	**End of Communism in USSR; end of the Cold War**

Part I: In the West

This section focuses on four key issues:

- How did the **Cold War** start?
- How effective were American efforts to halt the spread of Communism?
- How close were the **superpowers** to nuclear war during the Cold War?
- How did the Cold War come to an end?

THE ORIGINS OF THE COLD WAR

How did the Cold War start?

The Cold War was the state of tension between the Soviet Union (or Union of Soviet Socialist Republics – USSR) and its allies and the USA and its allies. This 'war' was one of words – the USSR and the USA never actually fought one another but several real wars did take place. The wars fought in Korea (1950–53), Vietnam (1965–75) and Afghanistan (1979–89) were all related to this state of tension.

The Russian Revolution in 1917 (see Chapter 2) and the efforts by the western governments of Britain, France and the USA (as well as a dozen others) to overthrow the new Communist government of Russia mark the beginning of the Cold War. But the real hostility did not develop until the closing stages of the Second World War.

Mutual suspicions

Each side was suspicious of the other. The Soviets believed that the West wanted to destroy Communism. At the same time, the West believed that the USSR was secretly trying to encourage Communist revolutions in the West. Josef Stalin, the Soviet leader from 1928 to 1953, was convinced that the British and Americans delayed the opening of the **Second Front** (see Chapter 7) during the Second World War. Their reason, Stalin believed, was so that the Soviets would suffer even greater casualties against the invading Germans. This would leave Russia too weak to threaten the West after the war.

However, it is quite likely that some degree of tension would have existed between the western powers and Russia, even if it had not been a Communist country. Whether Russia was Communist or Tsarist it was too big not to be a major world power. Its size made it a possible rival to the USA. The differences between the USSR's Communist system and the democratic **capitalism** of the USA are not the only reasons for this conflict.

Europe in 1945

The wartime alliance between Britain, the USA and the USSR only held together for the time that it took to defeat Hitler. Once it was clear that the war in Europe had been won, the tension within the alliance became severe. America's use of the atom bomb in Japan greatly raised the level of tension. The Americans had kept this weapon secret from the Russians. The USSR did not have the capability to make nuclear weapons at this time and so felt threatened.

There were three areas of dispute between the Big Three (Churchill, Stalin and Roosevelt):

- What should the Allies do with Germany?
- What should Europe's borders be after the war?
- What form of government should the countries of former Nazi Europe have?

What should the Allies do with Germany?

In February 1945, at a conference in Yalta in the Soviet Union, the three Allied leaders decided to divide Germany temporarily into four zones of occupation. France, on Churchill's insistence, was to be included as an occupying power. Berlin would also be divided into four. This represented a concession by Stalin as Berlin was deep in what would become the Soviet zone of occupation. Poland would be forced to give up some land to Russia but it would also get some German territory in compensation. The exact borders of the new Poland would be decided later.

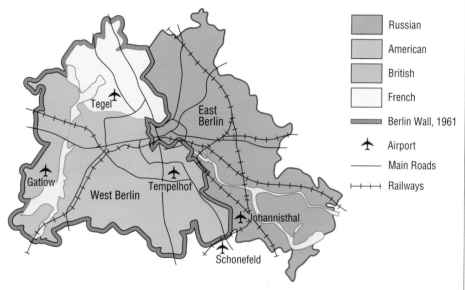

Divided Berlin.

Roosevelt was keen not to upset Stalin. He wanted the USSR to declare war on Japan so he brushed aside Churchill's protests against the treatment of Poland. The Americans feared that the war against Japan would be long and costly because the top secret atomic bomb was still not ready. They also wanted Soviet co-operation with the founding of the United Nations.

Churchill continually urged Roosevelt to take a tough line with Stalin by occupying more of Germany than agreed at Yalta. Churchill was already concerned that the USA might soon withdraw from European affairs as it had done after the First World War. This would leave Britain alone to face a mighty USSR in Europe. Roosevelt's death in April 1945 made Churchill's anxieties worse. Would his successor, the inexperienced Harry Truman, be fooled by Stalin into making yet more concessions?

Churchill made his concerns clear in a speech in the USA in March 1946. He warned Americans that an 'iron curtain' had descended across the continent of Europe from 'Stettin in the Baltic to Trieste in the Adriatic'. The curtain of iron referred to the barbed wire fences that, in Churchill's view, separated the free nations of Western Europe from the Russian-controlled dictatorships in the East.

What should Europe's borders be?

The borders of the new Poland and Germany were difficult issues for the 'Big Three'. Poland was under Soviet occupation so the Russians insisted that its western border move further westwards at the expense of Germany. Eventually it was agreed that the line marked by the rivers Oder and Neisse would form the new border between Poland and Germany. At the same time, Stalin took a large area of land on Poland's eastern border (a third of its pre-war territory) for the Soviet Union. Stalin justified this on the grounds that it had been Russian land before the Paris peace treaties that ended the First World War.

The three powers quickly reached an agreement on such issues as a trial for the Nazi war criminals, the disarmament of Germany and the need for free elections. But most of this was ignored. Some Nazi leaders were put on trial at Nuremberg. Ten were executed and 35 sentenced to life imprisonment. But the Russians and the Americans eagerly enlisted Nazi rocket scientists and military intelligence officers to work for them. They went unpunished. Their talents were too useful to be wasted in prisons, whatever their crimes.

Austria was divided up in the same way as Germany but here the division ended much sooner. All four powers withdrew in 1955, allowing Austria to become a neutral state, independent of the western powers and Russia. It was understood that Eastern Europe (including Poland, Czechoslovakia, Bulgaria, Romania, Hungary, Albania and Yugoslavia) would be under Soviet influence. The west of Europe (including Italy, Greece, France and Spain) would look to the USA for leadership.

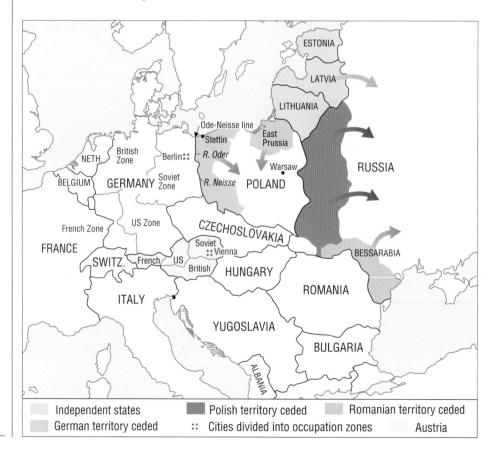

Territorial changes in Europe after the Second World War.

What form of government would the countries of former Nazi Europe have?

Stalin promised early free elections in Soviet-controlled Eastern Europe but these did not take place until 1947. They were not 'free' either because the results were controlled by the Communists. By the end of 1948 Stalin, with the Soviet army as back-up, had ensured that Communist parties, under the orders of Moscow, were in control of the whole of Eastern Europe. Non-Communist parties were not able to take part.

Only Yugoslavia managed to defy Soviet control. Here the Communist leader Josip Broz (better known as 'Tito') refused to follow Stalin's instructions. This was easier for Tito to do than the leaders of other Communist states because there were no Russian troops on Yugoslav soil – Tito's partisans had driven the Germans out on their own. Tito went on to develop a form of Communism that was less repressive and more popular than the Soviet version.

A US Zone
B French Zone
C British Zone
D Russian Zone

Europe in 1949.

Q

1 Copy the map outline above into your file or book and then follow the steps listed below:

- Devise a form of shading to represent all the East European states under Soviet control in 1949. Do not include Yugoslavia in this category.
- Use a different shade or colour to represent Yugoslavia as a Communist country not under the control of the USSR.
- Shade Austria as a neutral state because in 1949 it was still divided between Britain, France, the USA and the USSR.

2 Churchill described 'the Iron Curtain' as stretching from Stettin to Trieste. Why would Lubeck have been a better choice to mark the northern end of the Curtain? Mark a thick line from Lubeck to Trieste to show the course of the Iron Curtain by following the western borders of the Communist states.

3 Churchill also included Yugoslavia as being behind the Iron Curtain on the Soviet side. Why might this also be considered a mistake?

HOW EFFECTIVE WERE AMERICAN EFFORTS TO HALT THE SPREAD OF COMMUNIST INFLUENCE?

The stick and the carrot

America was as determined as Britain to make sure that Communist parties did not come to power in Western Europe but the USA's policy was more subtle. From 1947 onwards the Americans provided the huge sum of $13.5 billion in the **Marshall Plan** to rebuild the shattered economies of Europe. Communism thrived in poor, divided countries so by providing jobs and hope for the future a revolution would seem less attractive. As the historian JAS Grenville put it, 'Distress was the seedbed on which Communism flourished.' All the same, the USA did have plans to use troops in Italy if the powerful Italian Communist Party had won in the 1948 elections. The stick, it seems, could be a part of American foreign policy as well as the carrot.

Although both Italy and France had powerful Communist parties, they knew that they would not get assistance from Stalin if they attempted to seize power and establish Communist rule in their countries. Stalin recognised that Western Europe 'belonged' to the USA. Greek Communists ignored these arrangements and fought a bitter civil war against Greek royalists. Eventually, they were defeated because of British and American support for the anti-Communists and because Russia did little to help them, although some weapons did arrive from nearby Communist countries.

Britain and the USA were concerned that the countries of Eastern Europe all had Russian-dominated governments but they had to recognise that these now fell within the Soviet sphere of influence. They could do nothing about it. But when the USSR tried to force the western powers out of Berlin, the response by Britain, France and the USA was a firm one.

'Two halves of the same walnut'

In March 1947 President Truman made a key speech to the US Congress. He promised, in what became known as the **Truman Doctrine**, to assist 'any free and independent nations' struggling to maintain their freedom against 'armed minorities' or 'outside pressure'. The USSR was not mentioned by name but it was clear that Truman was referring to it. As Truman later said, the Truman Doctrine and Marshall Aid were 'two halves of the same walnut'. The 'walnut' proved to be a tough one as the Berlin crisis of 1948–49 was to show.

Q

1 How did tension between Communist Russia and the West first start?
2 How did the issue of the Second Front in the Second World War increase tension between Russia and the West?
3 Why could Roosevelt's request for Russia to enter the war against Japan later be seen as a mistake?
4 Why could both the Russians and the Americans be accused of being hypocrites in their attitude to Nazi leaders?
5 Explain the point of the reference to 'the stick and the carrot' on this page in describing American foreign policy after the war.
6 What do you think JAS Grenville meant by the phrase 'Distress was the seedbed on which Communism flourished' (on this page)?
7 Why did the Greek Communists get so little help from Stalin?

Q

Punch was a humorous British magazine that dealt with political matters. In 1947 it published this cartoon showing Stalin and Truman as rival hotel owners trying to tempt European customers (countries) to use their accommodation. 'Pension Russe' means 'Russian boarding house' which offered poorer accommodation than an hotel.

THE RIVAL BUSES

1 Name the other countries that would soon join Hungary in the 'Pension Russe'.
2 Whose bus – if any – did Austria choose in 1947?
3 What point was the cartoonist trying to make about Truman's political ideas by choosing that name for his hotel?
4 What point was the cartoonist trying to make about the economic conditions in the Soviet system by describing Stalin's accommodation as a 'pension'?
5 Why is this cartoon such a valuable source of evidence for an historian of the Cold War?

HOW CLOSE WERE THE SUPERPOWERS TO NUCLEAR WAR?

The tension increases

1948 was probably the worst year of the Cold War. The crisis caused by the Russian blockade of Berlin in June 1948 ranks alongside events in the Korean War and the Cuban Missile Crisis as critical moments when the Cold War might have become a 'hot' war.

In February 1948 Czech Communists had driven non-Communists out of the government and now had total control. The West's concerns were increased when a leading Czech liberal minister, Jan Masaryk, was supposed to have committed suicide by jumping from his apartment window. The general assumption was that he was pushed by the Communist secret police.

Stalin was angered in March by the decision made by Britain, France and the USA to unite their three sectors of Germany into a single state (later called West Germany) without his approval. This was a breach of the Yalta agreement that had stated that Germany was to be reunited as a single country. Russia had not received much of the $10 billion promised in reparations from Germany either. Some of this was supposed to come from the western sectors and the USA had stopped payments to Russia in 1946.

The Berlin Blockade 1948–49

The decision in June to go ahead with a separate currency for West Germany seemed to be the final straw. In the same month Stalin cut off all road and rail links from West Germany to Berlin which was 160 kilometres inside the Soviet sector of East Germany. The plan was to force the Allies to withdraw from their three sectors of Berlin. The city would be handed over entirely to the Russians. In the meantime, the West Berliners would be deprived of food and fuel.

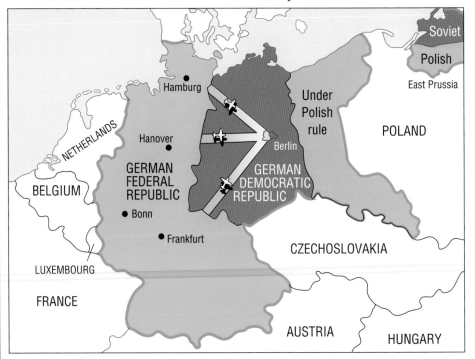

The divided Germany and the air routes into Berlin from the West.

Truman could hardly accept this development because it made a mockery of the Truman Doctrine. Over two million citizens in West Berlin had been handed over to Communist rule against their will. Any attempt to bring in supplies by land would risk war with the USSR. It is unlikely that public opinion in the West would have supported a war against a former ally (the USSR) in defence of a still hated former enemy (Germany). The only option was to provide food and supplies by air and trust that the Russians would have the good sense not to shoot down any of the western aircraft.

The Berlin Airlift

An aircraft left an airfield in West Germany every 30 seconds in the seemingly hopeless task of bringing the West Berliners the 4000 tons of supplies that they needed every day. Each plane could manage only 11 tons. Stalin clearly expected the West to give up and hand over the city. Eventually Stalin realised that this would not happen and he ended the blockade in May 1949.

The West Berliners' determination was remarkable. Only two per cent of the population fled to the east of the city where Communist rulers had filled the shops with food and goods.

The USSR and the West had realised that the crisis should not get out of hand. The Russians had made no effort to interfere with the airlift by shooting down the transport planes. The crisis of 1948–49 had passed without war but it rapidly led to a strengthening of the divisions between East and West. In 1949 the western powers created the North Atlantic Treaty Organisation (NATO) and then the Federal Republic of Germany (West Germany). NATO was a military alliance linking together 11 major western powers with the USSR as the obvious enemy. Its principal members were the USA, Britain, France, Italy and Canada. West Germany joined in 1955. Six years passed before the USSR responded in 1955 with its own military alliance of east European Communist states – the 'Warsaw Pact'. The Pact linked the USSR with East Germany, Czechoslovakia, Poland, Bulgaria, Albania, Romania and Hungary. The Cold War, it seemed, was here to stay.

Workers unloading supplies from a plane by the light of a jeep at Gatow airport during the Berlin Airlift. The airport's power came from the east of the city and the Russians had turned the electricity off.

> **Q What does this photograph tell you about the western powers' determination not be driven out of Berlin?**

The Khrushchev thaw

Stalin died in 1953 and with him went the worst period of tension between East and West. Stalin had taken risks in his confrontations with the West, especially over Berlin in 1948, and he did not always keep his word. He promised to hold free elections in Eastern Europe after the war but he did not. On the other hand, the USA promised to hold free elections in South Vietnam and these never took place either.

Stalin's death brought Nikita Khrushchev to power. Khrushchev was an earthy man of peasant origins. His behaviour was unpredictable and sometimes rough but he did genuinely believe in trying to ease the state of tension between the Soviet Union and the USA. In February 1956 he made a speech to the Twentieth Communist Party Congress in Moscow.

The speech has been noted for two things: anti-Stalinism and **peaceful co-existence**. This idea was that the rival political and economic systems should exist side by side without threatening to destroy each other. Khrushchev openly criticised Stalin's use of terror. No individual should ever have such power in Russia again and he called for a policy of 'de-Stalinisation'. This would allow the various Communist parties in Europe to rule less harshly and more in tune with the wishes of the people. He also wanted better relations with the West.

Nonetheless, there were confrontations between Khrushchev and the USA in the years up to Khrushchev's fall in 1964. Khrushchev, like the US President Kennedy, was sometimes forced into hostile positions by pressure at home.

Q

Incident	West's point of view	Soviet point of view
Events before 1945	Troops were sent to Russia to overthrow a government that had seized power by force. The Second Front was delayed until 1944 simply because the Germans were too strong in 1943.	
Military alliances: NATO and the Warsaw Pact		The USSR did not form its alliance of Communist states until six years after NATO was set up. This shows that the USA and its allies were planning war against the Communist states.
The Marshall Plan	This shows that the real concern of the USA was to help rebuild countries in Europe. This aid was also offered to the East European states but the Russians stopped them from taking it.	
The Truman Doctrine		The aggressive intentions of the USA were obvious from Truman's commitment to use military force against any country that wanted to be Communist.
Communist governments in Eastern Europe	Russia eliminated all the democratic parties in Eastern Europe and made sure that the 'elections' led to Communist parties taking over. In some cases opponents were brutally murdered.	
Berlin Blockade		The USSR's action in 'blockading' West Berlin was to stop the West from using the city as a spy centre against the Communist states of Europe.

1 The chart above refers to six crucial issues of the early Cold War in Europe. The West and the USSR had rather different views about these issues and some of these are outlined above. Your task is to copy this chart and fill in the missing points of view. So, your first point of view should explain what the Russians would have said about events before 1945. What would the Russians have thought about the West sending troops to overthrow the Communist government in 1918 and 1919, or about the delay in the opening of the Second Front in the Second World War?

2 Why did Truman view Stalin's action over Berlin in 1948 as an attack on the 'Truman Doctrine'?

3 What reasons did Stalin have to be angry with the West in the period immediately before the Berlin Blockade?

4 In what ways did the crisis over the Berlin Blockade also show the good sense of the Soviet and Western leaders?

5 In what ways did Stalin's death lead to a change in relations between the USSR and the West? In what ways did these relations not change?

The Hungarian Rising 1956

The events in Hungary in 1956 are a good example of how much (or how little) change Khrushchev would allow in the Communist system. Hungarians were encouraged by Khrushchev's speech in February and by Russia's willingness to allow the anti-Stalinist Communist, Gomulka, to take over the leadership of the Polish Communist Party in October 1956.

Hungary had been led by Matyas Rakosi since 1949. Rakosi was a Stalinist; he ruled through terror and fear by executing rivals and opponents. In July 1956 Khrushchev decided that he should be replaced. The people of Hungary wanted Imre Nagy (a popular, less repressive Communist) as their leader and Moscow agreed to this on 24 October. But the Hungarians hoped that Nagy would lead them away from the control of the USSR and this Khrushchev could not allow.

Nagy tried to control the popular nationalism which now swept across Hungary. His decision to allow free, multi-party elections alarmed Khrushchev, but it was Nagy's decision to leave the Warsaw Pact on 1 November which finally provoked the USSR into action. On 4 November Soviet tanks invaded Hungary. Some units of the Hungarian army joined armed civilians in resisting

A member of the hated Hungarian secret police lies dead in the street, killed by those Hungarians fighting to free their country from Soviet control.

the invaders. Members of Rakosi's secret police, the AVH, were hunted down and brutally executed in the streets. But it was a hopeless struggle. Some 20 000 Hungarians and 7000 Russians perished in the Rising. Nagy was secretly executed and replaced by Janos Kadar. Kadar was also a reformer (he wanted to change the system, like Nagy) but he also recognised the limits of what was possible.

The Hungarian Rising did not seriously affect East-West relations. The Hungarian rebels did appeal to the West for military support but were given only sympathy. The West accepted that the Russians had a free hand in the Warsaw Pact countries and this ensured that the Cold War 'game' was, for the time being, played out according to strict rules.

What was the Soviet view of the Hungarian Rising?

SOURCE 1:

The Russians claimed the Rising was planned by 'counter-revolutionary' elements against 'progressive' and 'patriotic' forces (supporters of the Communist system and the USSR). 'Counter-revolutionary bands' to the Russians meant Fascists and supporters of the USA. The following report appeared in *Pravda* (the official paper of the Soviet Communist Party) on 9 November 1956:

'Counter-revolutionary ringleaders organised an attack on the peaceful population, terrorised it, and murdered all progressive workers . . . The government was powerless to prevent these criminal excesses from continuing and spreading . . . Counter-revolutionary bands dragged Hungarian patriots through the streets, kicked and tortured them until these defenceless victims of terrorism died in horrible suffering. The Fascists prepared for slaughter. Everything which resembled **Socialism**, the Communist Party or friendship of the USSR was destroyed with fury.'

1 What do you think the Hungarian rebels would have said about the claim in *Pravda* that
   a they were 'Fascists';
   b they were murdering Hungarian 'patriots' in the streets?
2 'The government [of Imre Nagy] was powerless to prevent these criminal excesses from continuing and spreading'. Why do you think it was important for *Pravda* to mention this point?
3 Is there any sentence in this report with which the Hungarian rebels would have agreed? Explain your answer.
4 Bias occurs in history when the evidence is either deliberately distorted (by telling lies, for example) or by leaving important evidence out, even by accident, to produce an inaccurate account of an event. In what ways is this *Pravda* report an example of biased evidence?

The 'Prague Spring' 1968

The Soviet Union demanded two things of its 'allies' in Eastern Europe: they must remain members of the Warsaw Pact and the Communist Party must keep control. The Hungarian rebels broke both of these 'rules' and paid the penalty. Twelve years later, another group of reformers in Czechoslovakia tried to bring about less dramatic changes in the system.

Dubcek replaced Novotny as leader of Czechoslovakia's Communist Party in January 1968. Dubcek promised limited reforms in a policy that he described as 'Socialism with a human face.' Czechs would be able to travel freely to the West and workers would be given a bigger say in the running of their factories. These were acceptable policies to Brezhnev, the leader of the USSR after Khrushchev. Dubcek took care to make it clear that Czechoslovakia would remain a member of the Warsaw Pact.

The Soviet version of a no-entry sign: two tanks block off a Prague street in August 1968 after the invasion of Czechoslovakia.

During the early summer Dubcek, like Nagy before him, became carried away with the tide of popular enthusiasm for real change. He declared that free elections would be held and non-Communist parties allowed. Brezhnev was convinced that this would lead to the end of Communism and withdrawal from the Warsaw Pact. As in the case of Hungary, this would leave the USSR's border exposed to direct contact with the West.

In August 1968 Soviet and Warsaw Pact tanks rolled into Prague. The people offered no resistance. Dubcek was removed from office and sent into political retirement. Once again, the Soviet Union had made it clear to the West that nothing would be allowed that threatened its control over Eastern Europe. The West limited its response to nothing more than criticism of Russia's actions.

Q

There are interesting points of comparison between the Hungarian Rising and the Prague Spring. Comment on the similarities and differences under the following headings. One section has already been filled in.

	Hungary 1956	Czechoslovakia 1968
Policy towards free elections	Nagy promised free elections would be held.	Dubcek also promised to hold free elections.
Policy towards membership of Warsaw Pact		
Popular support for changes		
Soviet response to proposed changes		
Treatment of reform leaders (Nagy/Dubcek)		

Russia and China

Russia's relations with the other leading Communist power, China, began to worsen during the late 1950s. Mao Zedong had become China's first Communist ruler in 1949. But he criticised Khrushchev's policy of trying to ease tension with the West. This policy was called '**détente**'. The USSR refused to help China develop its own nuclear weapons, which was sensible because Mao believed that a nuclear war would be one way to destroy capitalism! He is said to have told an Italian Communist leader that after a nuclear war 'Three hundred million Chinese will be left, and that will be enough for the human race to continue.' China's criticism of Khrushchev (that he was going 'soft' on capitalism) placed the Soviet leader in a difficult position. He could not afford to be seen as giving in to the West.

U-2 over Russia

Despite China's criticism of Khrushchev he accepted President Eisenhower's invitation to visit the USA in 1959. The visit went well; Détente seemed to be securing better relations between East and West. The two men agreed to meet in May 1960 in Paris to discuss the matter of Berlin. However, only days before the summit an American high altitude U-2 spy plane was shot down by a missile over the USSR. The USA denied the existence of the plane or any spying missions because they thought that the pilot was dead and the plane destroyed.

Unfortunately for Eisenhower, the lie was soon exposed when the pilot, Gary Powers, was produced very much alive and admitted his spying role. Khrushchev broke off the summit and relations took a turn for the worse. Three months later they deteriorated even further.

The Berlin Wall

The two Germanys that were created after the war (the Communist East Germany and the capitalist West Germany) had started off in much the same terrible conditions. Just 15 years later, the difference between Communism and capitalism was obvious. East Germany had made little progress; there was little prosperity and its goods were of poor quality. West Germany on the other hand had become a wealthy, technologically advanced state. This had not been lost on East Berliners, especially the young ones. Half the 2.6 million East Germans who had made their way to West Germany through Berlin during the 1950s were under 24. They wanted a share in this prosperity.

Ulbricht, the Communist leader of East Germany, decided that the country could not afford to lose any more of its brightest prospects to the West. With Khrushchev's approval, during the night of 13 August 1961, work began on a 50 kilometre wall right around West Berlin, sealing it off from East Berlin and East Germany. East Berliners could no longer make their way across the city, even if they only wanted to visit friends or relatives.

Though this certainly harmed East-West relations, the Wall did not directly threaten West Berlin. As President Kennedy said, 'A wall is a hell of a lot better than a war.' The USSR could really do what it liked in its sphere of control but Kennedy visited West Berlin in June 1963 anyway. He wanted to reassure the people of West Berlin that the USA would stand by them. He made a rousing, inspiring speech in which he described West Berlin as the symbol of the free world against tyranny. He finished with the words, in German, 'Ich bin ein Berliner' (I am a Berliner). The crowd loved it, but perhaps someone should have told Kennedy that a 'Berliner' is also the name of local doughnut!

This photograph on the left shows how clearly the Berlin Wall cut through the heart of the city by dividing this street into two. Many people died trying to cross the wall.

Q Why do you think that the Berlin Wall became such an appropriate symbol of the Cold War before it was pulled down in 1989?

The Berlin Wall does not provide the most attractive backdrop to a family outing, but Berlin is a long way from the beach.

Kennedy and Khrushchev meet in Vienna, June 1961. The meeting did nothing to settle their differences but Khrushchev came away from the meeting thinking that Kennedy could be easily bullied.

Q

1 What do you suppose Mao meant by the sentence 'Three hundred million Chinese will be left, and that will be enough for the human race to continue' on page 196?
2 What was the impact of the U-2 spy plane incident in May 1960?
3 What was so worrying for the leaders of East Germany about those leaving to live in West Germany?

If relations between West and East in 1961 were bad, they were not nearly as bad as they were going to become a few months later. The Cuban Missile Crisis brought the world closer to nuclear war than at any time since 1945. Khrushchev was desperate to score a major success against Kennedy to show the hardliners in the Kremlin (the building where the Soviet Communist Party met) that he could be tough with the capitalist West.

SHOWDOWN OVER CUBA

The Bay of Pigs

Cuba was the focus of a major crisis in April 1961. Two years earlier in 1959, Fidel Castro, a Cuban nationalist leader, had taken power in Cuba. He overthrew a dictator, Battista, who was supported by the USA. The Americans were not pleased by the defeat of their ally and they did not like Castro's policies, especially the take-over of American-owned oil companies in Cuba.

The USA retaliated by refusing to buy any Cuban sugar – a disaster for the Cuban economy. Khrushchev stepped in smartly and offered to buy it instead. Relations between Castro and the USSR became friendly. The USA was convinced that Cuba was about to become a Soviet-style Communist state. That it was only 150 kilometres from the coast of Florida only increased American concerns.

The US Central Intelligence Agency (CIA) developed a plan to overthrow Castro using a small force of anti-Castro Cubans, trained by the CIA. Kennedy hesitated. He wanted to get rid of Castro but was not prepared to allow direct US military involvement. The CIA told him that the population of Cuba was anti-Castro and would join the revolt as soon as troops landed on Cuba. Kennedy gave in and the landing took place at the Bay of Pigs in April 1961.

It was a disaster from the start. The 1500 CIA-trained Cubans were trapped on the beaches; four US jets were shot down, revealing America's involvement to the world. Only direct US military support could save the operation but Kennedy refused. The ill-planned scheme collapsed with all of the CIA men captured or killed. Kennedy had wisely decided to cut his losses by not getting involved any further. On the other hand, he made an error of judgment by agreeing to the plot in the first place. Kennedy could not afford another failure like this.

The Cuban Missile Crisis

On Kennedy's orders the CIA continued to come up with daft schemes to get rid of Castro. One plan involved getting Castro to smoke an exploding cigar. Khrushchev offered Castro nuclear weapons as a defence and deterrent against a future US attack. Soon, in September 1962, 42 Soviet nuclear missiles had been installed on Cuban soil and now every major American city was within range of a nuclear missile.

(above) The canvas covers cannot conceal what this Soviet cargo vessel is carrying towards Cuba: six missile transporters packed along its sides.

On 15 October 1962 the Americans realised what was happening when photographs taken by high level aircraft proved the existence of these missiles. Forty-two Soviet missiles in Cuba may not have amounted to much when the Americans had 1685 missiles capable of reaching the USSR, but Kennedy could not let it pass.

Khrushchev, for his part, was bluffing. He knew that the USSR was incredibly weak in terms of nuclear weapons (only 80 or so of its missiles were capable of reaching the USA) and that his country would be obliterated in a war. But Kennedy did not know this and the Soviet leader thought that the inexperienced Kennedy could be bullied into accepting the Soviet missiles in Cuba. At the very least, Khrushchev thought he could use the missiles to bargain with. He would promise to remove the missiles from Cuba if Kennedy would remove US missiles from Turkey.

Kennedy's response

Kennedy had to act quickly because he believed the missiles were not yet operational and would not be ready to launch for another 14 days. Kennedy had three options:

- He could order a limited air strike against the missile sites alone.
- He could order a full scale invasion of Cuba.
- He could blockade Cuba by surrounding it with US warships and stop any further vital Soviet technical support reaching Cuba.

Kennedy's first two options could easily lead to war with Russia; the third option would still leave time for a peaceful solution. It was the Defence Secretary, Robert McNamara, who suggested blockading Cuba rather than bombing it. At first Kennedy had been ready to launch air strikes against the missile sites. Fortunately, he changed his mind and took up McNamara's suggestion instead.

Kennedy announced the third option on 22 October and demanded the withdrawal of the missiles as well. All Soviet vessels within 800 kilometres of Cuba would be searched.

'The postman only rings once . . .'

On 25 October Khrushchev wrote to Kennedy and offered to withdraw the missiles provided Kennedy promised not to invade Cuba ever. This was acceptable to the Americans but a further letter on 27 October upped the stakes when Khrushchev also demanded the withdrawal of US missiles in Turkey – right next to the Soviet Union. Kennedy could not agree to do this because it would look as if he was being bullied by the Russians. This was frustrating for Kennedy because the missiles in Turkey were out-dated and their withdrawal had already been planned.

On the same day that this second letter arrived, an American U-2 spy plane was shot down by a Soviet missile over Cuba and the pilot was killed. This led to a dangerous increase in tension even though the decision to shoot down the plane had not been authorised by Moscow. Khrushchev now seemed genuinely concerned that events were spiralling out of control and he decided to defuse the crisis.

Kennedy decided that he would simply ignore the second letter and replied only to the first letter. He offered to promise not to invade Cuba if the missiles were withdrawn. Unofficially there was also an offer to remove the missiles from Turkey at a later date. This proposal to remove the missiles from Turkey was not made public until 1969. On 28 October Kennedy's reply reached Khrushchev and he announced his acceptance of Kennedy's proposals. The crisis was over.

(below) Kennedy's tough line over Cuba was not supported by everyone in the West. Here British protesters show their opposition to his policy in London.

Q Such views were less popular in the USA. Can you suggest why?

▶ Reconstructing the Missile Crisis

SOURCE 1:

Fedor Burlatsky was a close adviser to Khrushchev between 1960 and 1964. In 1988 he published his account of life among the Soviet leadership:

'The idea of deploying the missiles came from Khrushchev himself. Khrushchev asked Malinovsky [the Soviet Defence Minister] why the Soviet Union should not have the right to do the same as America? . . . America had surrounded the USSR with bases . . . whereas the Soviet Union's missiles and atom bombs were based only on Soviet territory . . .

The placing of missiles in Cuba had at least two purposes. One of these – to defend Cuba – was justly stated by Khrushchev . . . In taking such a risk Khrushchev had, I believe, one further aim in mind . . . to secure new conditions for negotiations with the USA and bring about the possibility of compromise.'

Adapted from F Burlatsky: *Khrushchev and the First Russian Spring* 1988

SOURCE 2:

Khrushchev wrote two letters to Kennedy. The second contained the additional demand for the removal of US missiles from Turkey. (This was the letter that Kennedy ignored when he replied to the first which only demanded a promise not to invade Cuba again.)

'You say you are disturbed by Cuba, that it is 150 kms by sea from the shores of the USA, yet Turkey is right beside us . . . Do you believe that you can demand security for your country and the removal of weapons that you call offensive while not granting us the same right? . . . I therefore make this proposal: we agree to remove from Cuba those means [missiles] which you regard as offensive means . . . and make a pledge in the United Nations. Your representative will make a pledge to the effect that the USA . . . will remove its similar means from Turkey.'

SOURCE 3:

Khrushchev's memoirs were published after his death in 1971 in the West (but not the USSR). In them he spoke of his role in the crisis.

'I had the idea of installing missiles with nuclear warheads in Cuba without letting the USA find out they were there until it was too late to do anything about them . . . We had no desire to start a war. We sent the Americans a note that we agreed to remove our missiles and bombers on the condition that there would be no invasion of Cuba by the forces of the USA or anybody else. Finally Kennedy gave in and agreed to make a statement giving us such an assurance . . . It was a great victory for us, though, . . . a spectacular success.

N Khrushchev: *Khrushchev Remembers* 1971

SOURCE 4:

In 1992 the Russians finally released some of their documents on the crisis. These showed that the Americans had made one error of judgment. They had believed that none of the missiles in place in Cuba had nuclear warheads at the time. They were wrong as this source from an American historian makes clear.

'Soviet officials later revealed, however, that 36 intermediate range missiles with nuclear warheads were in place during the crisis . . . there were nine short-range nuclear missiles ready to be used against a US invasion . . . A shaken Robert McNamara [US Defence Secretary from 1961–68] declared in 1992 after he learned about this information, "This is horrifying. It meant that had a US invasion been carried out . . . there was a 99 per cent probability that nuclear war would have been initiated [started]." The actions of all three parties [the USA, the USSR and Cuba] were shaped by misjudgment, miscalculations, and misinformation.'

Walter Lafeber: *America, Russia and the Cold War* 1993

Historians write history by reconstructing the past. They do this from the evidence that is presented by primary sources such as 1–3 (above) and secondary ones such as 4. They check their sources for points where they agree and disagree and issues about which they have little to say. At the same time, historians bring in ideas of their own because it is their job to interpret the past and not just describe it.

The table on page 202 lists statements about the Cuban Missile Crisis. Some of these are supported by the evidence in the text or the four sources above and some are not. In some cases, the statements require judgments or comments on your part. Where there is evidence for your answers, you should quote the source or sources. An example has been done for you.

Statement	Your view	Evidence available
It was Khrushchev who came up with the idea of sending missiles to Cuba		
Khrushchev did not behave consistently during the crisis and nearly lost control	Khrushchev did seem to change his mind from day to day and the military in Cuba acted without orders	Source 2 is Khrushchev's second letter within 24 hours to Kennedy and it is much more demanding than the first. The text tells us how a US U-2 was shot down without Khrushchev being consulted
Kennedy handled the crisis well		
Khrushchev's aims were reasonable ones		
Kennedy was kept well informed by his advisers during the crisis		
There was never any real chance of a nuclear war breaking out		

Consequences

Surprisingly, the crisis led to an improvement in relations between the USA and the USSR. Both countries had come close to starting a nuclear war and had not liked what they saw. They agreed to set up a direct telephone link between the Kremlin and the White House so that they could discuss matters more urgently in a future crisis. In 1963 both countries signed the Nuclear Test Ban Treaty which outlawed nuclear tests in the atmosphere but not underground. At the time Kennedy came out of the affair very well. He gave the impression that he had handled the crisis cautiously by rejecting the military's demands for air strikes or an invasion of Cuba and by allowing Khrushchev to back down without humiliation. There was some criticism of Kennedy from both the right and left in the USA. Some, like the future President Richard Nixon, accused him of not seizing the chance to get rid of Castro as well as the missiles. Others claimed that the presence of a few dozen missiles in Cuba was no real threat to the USA and that Kennedy had brought the country close to a terrible war for nothing. But American public opinion showed its support by voting in large numbers for Kennedy's Democrat party in the November elections to Congress. They might have felt differently if they had known of the secret agreement to pull the US missiles out of Turkey.

Castro, the Cuban leader, felt humiliated because Khrushchev did not consult him before making his decisions. On the other hand, Castro now had a promise from America that his country would not be invaded. He also could rely on the economic and military support of the USSR – at least for as long as the USSR existed. In 1996, Castro was still in power and Cuba was still Communist.

(above) 'Thanks, pal!' This cartoon from the British magazine Punch was quick to see the connection between the Democrat success in the elections to Congress and the missile crisis. Kennedy is shown at the top of the ladder and Khrushchev at the bottom.

> **Q** Why do you think Khrushchev is shown holding the ladder in place for Kennedy with Kennedy saying 'Thanks, pal'?

(left) 'Over the Garden Wall.' This British cartoon from 17 October 1962 shows Kennedy on the left and Khrushchev seated on the right.

Q

Look at the cartoon above.

1 The tree on the left shows some of the countries where the Americans had military bases represented by branches. Which of these 'branches' was to prove a serious issue in the missile crisis? Explain your answer.
2 What do you think the cartoonist is suggesting by showing Khrushchev and Kennedy wanting to 'prune' the branches growing on their side of the garden?
3 What is the cartoonist suggesting by showing the Cuban branch as a rather small one? What is Kennedy's reaction to it?
4 How accurate a comment on the Cuban Missile Crisis is this cartoon? Give reasons for your answer.

For most Americans the crisis was a great success for Kennedy. His dramatic death at the hands of an assassin over 12 months later turned him into a hero. It began the process that converted an attractive president who had promised so much (but actually achieved little) into a world myth.

Khrushchev was luckier in that he was removed from power peacefully by the leadership of the Communist Party in 1964. They considered him to be too unpredictable. His manners were also considered too undignified by the conservatives who ran Russia. In one meeting at the UN he took off his shoe and banged the desk with it to make his point more forcefully.

Q

1 Why were the Americans so hostile to Cuba after 1959?
2 Why was the Bay of Pigs such a setback for Kennedy?
3 How do you think Kennedy handled the Cuban Missile Crisis? Support your answer with some evidence.
4 At what point, and why, do you think the missile crisis came closest to war?

Extended writing

1 In 1992 the historian Brian Dooley gave this interpretation of the Cuban Missile Crisis: 'In the end, the victory went to neither Khrushchev nor Kennedy, but to Castro.' Study the sources and information in this section and explain why you agree or disagree with this interpretation.
2 'Khrushchev and Kennedy were always in control during the "Cuban Missile Crisis" and so war was never likely.' Using the sources in this section and any other information explain in an essay of 300 words or more whether you agree or disagree with this interpretation of the crisis.

THE COLD WAR GOES GLOBAL

Non-Proliferation

The Nuclear Test Ban Treaty of 1963 had only limited success since France and China refused to sign it and continued to test nuclear weapons in the atmosphere. In 1968 the Non-Proliferation Treaty was signed by the USSR, the USA, Britain and 59 other countries. Its purpose was to stop the spread (or proliferation) of nuclear weapons to countries that did not have the necessary technology. Since then, however, Israel, India, Pakistan and South Africa have developed their own nuclear weapons and Iraq has tried to do the same.

During the 1970s both the superpowers looked for ways to limit the chances of a nuclear war. The USA had a commanding lead in its nuclear weaponry and Russia knew it could not afford to match it. The Soviet leader after Khrushchev, Leonid Brezhnev (1964–82), needed to cut back on military spending to try and improve the basic living standards of the Soviet population.

The result was the first Strategic Arms Limitation Talks Treaty (SALT 1) signed in 1972. Both powers had now accepted the logic of MAD (Mutually Assured Destruction) which meant that they realised that a nuclear war would inevitably lead to the destruction of both sides. SALT 1 limited the number of ICBMs (intercontinental ballistic missiles). These were the missiles that could reach each other's countries when fired from their own territory. SALT 2 was signed by Brezhnev and President Carter in June 1979 and called for further reductions in ICBMs. It wasn't carried out because of a sharp increase in tension between the superpowers following the Soviet invasion of Afghanistan in the same year. The US Senate refused to approve the treaty as a result of the invasion and SALT 2 was abandoned.

The Cold War in Africa

Brezhnev was prepared to confront the USA but not as directly as Khrushchev had done over Cuba. Civil war from the mid 1970s in the former Portuguese colonies of Angola and Mozambique provided the USSR with an opportunity to extend its influence into new regions of Africa. Angola, rather than Mozambique, became the focus of Cold War tensions because of its resources of oil.

The Russians provided weapons (and 50 000 Cuban troops) to the Marxist MPLA faction while South Africa and the USA backed UNITA (National Union for the Total Independence of Angola). South Africa sent troops to the area. The superpowers encouraged these conflicts by providing the weapons, troops and supplies that kept them going. In the early 1990s they lost interest as the Cold War came to an end but the conflicts continued nonetheless and so, in a sense, Mozambique and Angola remain victims of the Cold War.

The Soviet invasion of Afghanistan

In December 1979 Brezhnev ordered Soviet troops into neighbouring Afghanistan to set up a Communist government under Babrak Karmal. The presence of Soviet troops was supposed to be only temporary but the revolt by anti-Communist Moslem Mujaheddin fighters forced them to stay on. Soon the numbers of Soviet troops reached 100 000 as they struggled to keep Karmal in power and crush the Mujaheddin.

Gorbachev finally managed to withdraw Soviet troops from Afghanistan in 1989 but not before the USSR had sustained some 60 000 casualties. This ended a major point of friction between the two superpowers.

The invasion revived the Cold War tension of earlier decades. President Carter (1977–81) refused to sell the Russians American grain and the US boycotted the 1980 Olympics held in Moscow. President Reagan (1981–89) kept the Mujaheddin supplied with US weapons through Pakistan and in 1983 announced that America planned to develop a Strategic Defence Initiative (or Star Wars as it was popularly known). SDI would provide the USA with an anti-nuclear 'umbrella' in outer space. Here US weapons would destroy incoming Russian missiles.

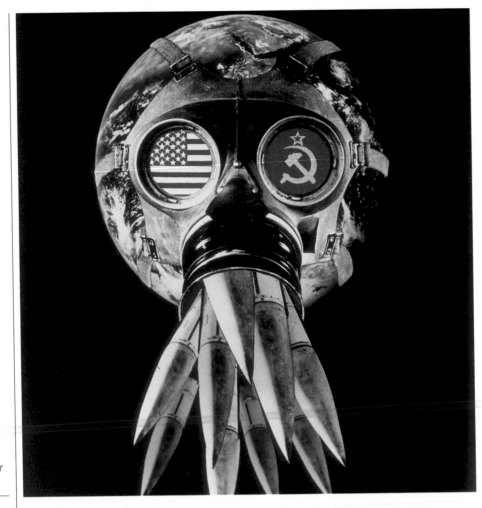

'Defended to Death.' This photomontage was made in 1983. It shows the Earth wearing a gas mask and the 'mouth' is stuffed with nuclear missiles.

Q

1 How can you tell that this photomontage is about the two superpowers?
2 How does the artist suggest that both superpowers are equally responsible for putting the world in this dangerous position?
3 What general point is he making about the state that the world is in and how does he get this across?
4 What events took place in 1983 that seemed to support the artist's rather gloomy thoughts about the Earth's prospects?

The Cold War in Central America

There was further tension in the early 1980s in what became known as the new Cold War. Events in Central America and the Caribbean were of special concern to Reagan. It seemed to him that the forces of 'the evil empire' (as Reagan described the USSR) were on the march there. American foreign policy in Central America since the 1930s had consisted of putting military dictators in power and getting them to follow policies in favour of the wealthy. This alliance between the army and the rich seemed the best way to secure American interests in the region against Communist take-overs.

By the early 1980s this policy was in tatters. Communists were already in control of Cuba. In Nicaragua the Communist **guerrilla** forces, the Sandinistas, had overthrown a US-backed dictator, Somoza, in 1978. There were anti-US guerrillas at work in El Salvador against another US-backed dictatorship. Communists had also taken power on the Caribbean island of Grenada in 1979.

Reagan decided it was time to get tough with the 'evil empire'. American weapons were supplied to anti-Communist forces in Nicaragua and El Salvador. He even launched an invasion in 1983 against the rulers of Grenada to get rid of its Cuban-backed Communist government. The island, he claimed, was being used by the Cubans to train Communist guerrilla fighters for use in Central America. The Cubans, in fact, were building an airport. But for Reagan Grenada represented another victory against the forces of world Communism.

SDI or MAD?

SDI was controversial because it suggested that the USA no longer accepted the principle of MAD and that the USA could wage a nuclear war and survive. This seemed to bring the possibility of such a war much nearer. But, in practice, SDI forced the Russians to accept that they had neither the technology nor the funds to match such a programme. They realised that they had better come to terms with the USA.

Fortunately, from 1985 the Russians had a new leader who was willing to face this fact head-on. Mikhail Gorbachev knew that the future of the Soviet Union depended on its ability to deliver a higher standard of living to its people. It could not afford to spend huge sums of money on the military. Gorbachev and Reagan quickly established a good relationship and the INF (intermediate-range nuclear forces) Treaty of 1987 was the result. All nuclear weapons of this type (some 2000 warheads, 75 per cent of which were Russian) would be scrapped. Although this sounded impressive, it represented a reduction of only four per cent in the nuclear weapons available to both sides.

HOW DID THE COLD WAR END?

The Cold War had dominated international politics for nearly 50 years. It had affected every major region of the globe. Conflicts in Europe, Asia, the Middle East, Africa, Central America and the Caribbean had all been points of tension in the rivalry between the USSR and the USA.

The initiative that had led to the end of the Cold War came from Gorbachev. This was an outcome Gorbachev wanted. It also led (as we now know) to the end of Communism in Europe. This was not part of Gorbachev's plan even though he recognised that the USSR could not retain control over the Communist countries of Eastern Europe and that there was little point in trying to do so.

The collapse of Communism

In the years immediately after the Second World War, the Communist states of Eastern Europe provided a vital territorial buffer against an invasion from the West. Nuclear weapons had long since meant that this buffer served no useful military purpose. By 1989, the peoples of Eastern Europe realised that they could go their own way and that Russia would not intervene. There would be no repetition of the invasions of Hungary in 1956 or Czechoslovakia in 1968 when the Russians had used force to crush attempts by these countries to follow their own policies.

The collapse of the Communist regimes in Eastern Europe followed swiftly one after the other. The pulling down of the Berlin Wall in November 1989 marked the beginning of the process. It had become the symbol of a divided Europe and now it was gone. Within 12 remarkable months, Germany was a united nation once again.

Czechoslovakia was the first to choose a non-Communist government at the end of 1989. Romania was next after a bloody revolution which ended first the 25-year-old personal dictatorship of Nicolae Ceausescu and then his life. Within the next two years not a single East European state still had a Communist government. Most astonishingly of all, neither did the USSR.

The end of the Soviet Union

By 1990 Gorbachev, President of the Soviet Union, had discovered that there is nothing quite so difficult to do as to try to control the process of change once it has started. To his critics his plans to introduce democracy and a free economy were either too drastic or too limited. The various republics of the USSR added to his problems by wanting to be free of Moscow's control. The Ukraine, Georgia, and Belarus were just three of the 15 former republics of the USSR who set themselves up as independent states.

The first to strike in August 1991 were the conservative Communist hardliners. They ordered units of the army to seize key buildings in Moscow and arrest Gorbachev and Yeltsin, the pro-reform President of the Russian Federation. It was a desperate last bid to hold together the Communist empire of the USSR but it was defeated by the courage of Boris Yeltsin. He appealed to the people of Moscow and the army to resist the coup and they responded. Within two days the plot had collapsed.

Gorbachev was also a victim of the coup. He had been arrested by the plotters and now owed his freedom to Yeltsin but Gorbachev had little cause to celebrate. By the end of 1991, the USSR, of which he was President, no longer existed and neither did its Communist system.

Gorbachev had believed that the Soviet people, once they were given their freedom, would try to make the Communist system work. But he was wrong. Seventy-four years of Communism had left the Russians with an average income that was just 10 per cent of an average American income and equal only to that of a Mexican. The 1990 grain harvest was one of the best ever but many faced starvation because transport problems meant that 40 per cent of the crop rotted or was eaten by worms and rats. The state paid its bills by printing more money and massive inflation was the result. In 1988 a small car cost 16 000 rubles; four years later it cost 16 times more at 250 000 rubles.

Russians felt that they had no reason to maintain a system that had done so little for their standard of living and so they turned their backs on Communism and Gorbachev.

Gorbachev had failed in his courageous bid to make the decaying Communist system both democratic and efficient but the world owes him a debt of gratitude. His vision of a world no longer threatened by the prospect of a nuclear war between the USA and the USSR has at least been realised.

Q

1 How successful do you think the Non-Proliferation Treaty of 1968 (page 204) has been?
2 Why was it so important that the superpowers accepted the principle of MAD?
3 How did the invasion of Afghanistan worsen relations between the USSR and the USA?
4 Why was it that America's anti-Communist policies in Central America and the Caribbean seemed to have failed by the early 1980s?
5 Which of Gorbachev's decisions led to the end of Communism in Eastern Europe?
6 Why do you think Gorbachev eventually found himself in an impossible position?

What were the most dangerous incidents in the Cold War?

Relations between the USSR and the USA varied a great deal between 1945 and 1992. They began on good terms during the Second World War, got worse after it, improved briefly and then deteriorated again. Eventually, with the end of the Soviet Union in 1991, the Cold War simply fizzled out. Below is a list of key incidents (all referred to in the text) that occurred during the five decades of relations between the USSR and the West:

- Nuclear Test Ban Treaty
- Berlin Blockade
- the dropping of the Atom Bomb on Japan
- SALT 1
- the INF Treaty
- the Bay of Pigs invasion
- the Soviet invasion of Afghanistan
- the Cuban Missile Crisis
- the appointment of Gorbachev as leader of the USSR
- the Hungarian Rising
- Khrushchev's speech to the Twentieth Congress of the Soviet Communist Party
- SALT 2
- the Berlin Wall
- Reagan's Strategic Defence Initiative (Star Wars)
- the end of Communism in the USSR
- the overthrow of Communist governments in Eastern Europe
- the US boycott of the Moscow Olympics.

Now complete the following tasks. (You can, if you wish, add any incidents mentioned in the text that are not given in this list.)

1 List them in chronological order, starting with America's use of the Atom Bomb in 1945 and ending with the end of the USSR in 1991.
2 Divide a piece of paper, with the title 'Superpower Relations 1945 – 91', into two columns: one headed 'Incidents leading to deteriorating relations' and the other headed 'Incidents leading to improved relations'.
3 Then decide which of the incidents listed above represent an improvement in Soviet-American relations. These go in the second column. The others represent a worsening in relations and therefore go in the first column. An example for each has already been done for you. You can, if you like, shade the first column in red to indicate the increased tension caused by these events and use another colour for the second column.

Superpower relations 1945–91

Incidents leading to deteriorating relations	Incidents leading to improved relations
The Hungarian Rising, 1956	The overthrow of Communist governments in Eastern Europe, 1989

4 Finally, choose the three most dangerous incidents from the first column and three from the second column that most helped to improve relations. Explain why you have chosen each of these six incidents.

Part II: The Cold War Goes East

1946	**Vietminh forces in conflict with French in Vietnam**
1949	**Communists come to power in China**
1950	**Outbreak of Korean War**
1953	**End of the Korean War**
1954	**Vietminh forces defeat French; Vietnam divided in two**
1955	**South Vietnam declared a republic**
1964	**Gulf of Tonkin incident**
1965	**US combat troops sent to South Vietnam**
1968	**Vietcong Tet Offensive penetrates Saigon**
1969	**Nixon begins US withdrawal from South Vietnam**
1973	**American troops withdraw from Vietnam**
1975	**Vietnam War ends as North Vietnam occupies Saigon**

This section focuses on two key issues of American policy in the Far East:

● *How and why did the US confront Communism in the Far East?*

● *How effective was American opposition to the spread of Communism?*

As you work through the section, try to remember these issues. You could make a note of any evidence and information that helps to answer these questions.

As you already know from your study of Part I of this chapter, the Cold War between the USSR and the West has its origin in the Russian Revolution which made Russia the first Communist state. The Second World War temporarily made Britain and the USA allies of the USSR, as they fought their common enemy: Nazi Germany. However, it was clear that, as the Second World War came to an end, relations between the Soviet Union and the western powers were changing for the worse.

These poor relations were not only limited to Europe. The USSR and the USA confronted each other in the Far East, first over China, Korea and then Vietnam. This chapter traces America's involvement in these countries as it tried to stop the spread of Communist influence.

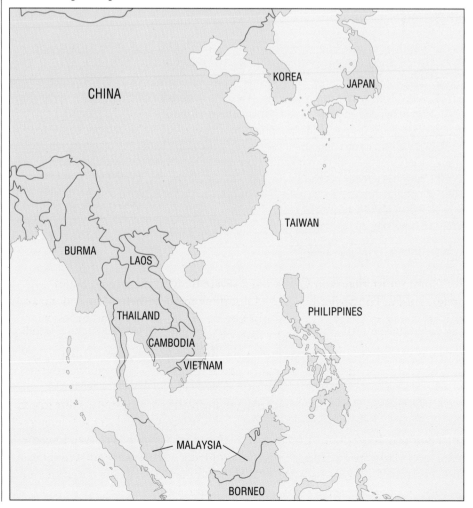

(right) South East Asia before the Second World War.

RED STAR RISING

Chinese Communists had been trying to overthrow the corrupt government of the Chinese Nationalist Party (*Guomindang* or *Kuomintang*) since the late 1920s. The civil war between the Communists and the Nationalists was halted while they both fought the invading Japanese after 1937. However, the uneasy truce between Communists and Nationalists quickly broke down once Japan had been beaten in 1945.

The USA decided that it wanted Chiang Kai-Shek, the leader of the *Guomindang*, to rule China and so gave military support to the anti-Communist forces. The Truman Doctrine (see page 188) committed the Americans to try to halt the spread of Communism wherever it appeared.

The Communist forces, led by Mao Zedong (Mao Tse-Tung), proved too well-organised and motivated for the **Nationalists** and the Communists defeated Chiang Kai-Shek in 1949. Chiang Kai-Shek's corruption was accurately reflected in the nickname 'Cash My Cheque'. He fled with what was left of his army to the island of Taiwan and claimed to be the rightful ruler of China. The Chinese Communists have never given up their claim to Taiwan and it remains a source of tension between the USA and China.

America supported Chiang Kai-Shek because he was anti-Communist but he was also a corrupt, brutal dictator whose policies favoured the rich minority.

Q **America found itself supporting a similar ruler in South Vietnam in the late 1950s and early 1960s with a similar lack of success. Can you think why?**

Chinese-Soviet treaty

The Communist victory in China was a severe blow to the United States' foreign policy. The Soviet Union had not done much to help Mao Zedong and relations between the two Communist powers were not very good to begin with. Stalin did not actually want a Communist victory in China as this could worsen his relations with the USA. But the Russians were quick to offer aid to their new fellow Communists in the Far East and a treaty was signed between the two countries in 1950.

This confirmed President Truman's suspicions that Communism threatened America's international interests. The Americans had planned to use China as a base from which to influence events in the Far East and to keep a watchful eye over Japan. This was no longer possible. Problems in Vietnam added to their fears. Here the Communist-backed Vietminh forces had set up a government in North Vietnam in defiance of the French **colonial** rulers.

Dean Acheson, the American Secretary of State for Foreign Affairs, suggested that the USA could prevent China from becoming a Soviet **satellite** by taking a less hostile line with 'Red' China. This was a subtle strategy but it was not tried until Nixon became American President in the early 1970s. Relations with China would remain strained as long as the USA continued to recognise Chiang Kai-Shek's state of Taiwan and not Mao's Communist state as the real government of China.

CRISIS IN KOREA

There was a chance that the USA might have established more friendly relations with China but the North Korean invasion of South Korea in June 1950 ended that possibility. Truman immediately declared that the US Seventh Fleet would defend Taiwan from any attack by Communist China. This promise had not been made by the USA before and relations between China and the USA remained frozen until Nixon became President.

Korea had belonged to Japan before the Second World War but Japan was forced to give it up once the war had ended. The north came under the control of the USSR and the south was controlled by the USA. Both countries withdrew their troops from Korea in 1949 but left a Communist government in North Korea under Kim Il Sung and a pro-American government in South Korea under Syngham Rhee. This division was acceptable to the USA and the USSR. Both governments in Korea were dictatorships so it was difficult for the USA to claim that it was defending democracy when the north invaded the south, but it was clear that the Communist north was the aggressor.

Q

1 Over which three countries in the Far East did the USA and the USSR confront each other?
2 Can you suggest why the uneasy truce between the *Guomindang* and the Communists was not likely to continue once Japan had been defeated?
3 What do you think was implied by Chiang's nickname 'Cash My Cheque'?
4 Why was Mao's victory in China a blow to America's Far Eastern policy?
5 What was the biggest obstacle to better relations between China and the USA (apart from China's Communism)?
6 Can you suggest any reason why US support for South Korea might have caused the American government some embarrassment? (Clue: what kind of government did South Korea have?)
7 The map on the next page shows South East Asia in June 1950 – just after the North Korean invasion of South Korea. Copy it into your file or exercise book and then carry out the following tasks:
   • Shade both the countries on the map which had Communist governments in control (red would be a good choice of colour!). In one of the boxes in the key shade the colour that you have chosen and write next to it: 'Countries with Communist governments'.
   • Shade North Vietnam in red stripes as it did not officially become Communist until the French surrendered in 1954. Shade Malaya in stripes as well because Communists here were involved in an unsuccessful war against the British. Describe these areas in the key as 'Areas where Communist revolutionaries are operating'.
   • Draw a large red arrow from the border of North Korea into South Korea to represent the North Korean invasion. Put the year '1950' in the arrow.
   • The Americans were convinced that Communism 'threatened' other parts of South East Asia, especially South Vietnam, Laos and Cambodia. So shade these in a colour of your choice and in the key label this colour as 'Areas seen by the USA as under threat of Communist revolution'.

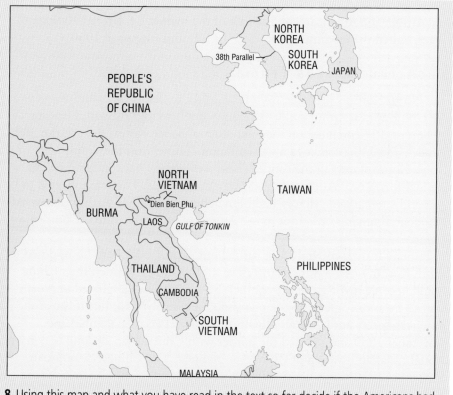

South East Asia in June 1950.

8 Using this map and what you have read in the text so far decide if the Americans had good cause to believe that South East Asia was close to Communist revolution.

The Korean War 1950–53

The Americans were able to get the United Nations to back the use of US force against the North Koreans. The Soviet representative in the United Nations Security Council would have vetoed (opposed) this had he been there, and the UN would not have become involved. Unfortunately for the USSR, they were boycotting the Security Council at the time in protest at the USA's refusal to allow Communist China into the UN. It was a huge blunder and one that they did not repeat.

At first the North Koreans swept easily across the 38th parallel that marked the border between the two Korean states in June 1950. The South Korean army crumbled and the North Koreans occupied the whole of South Korea

The bulk of the UN fighting in Korea was done by the US forces, but there were troops from 14 other countries including Britain present. This was a big contrast to the war in Vietnam that was to begin a decade later. America was not supported by its allies in Vietnam.

except for a small pocket of territory around the port of Pusan where General MacArthur, the American commander of the mainly US United Nations forces, halted the Communist advance in July and August of 1950.

MacArthur versus Truman

The North Koreans prepared for a final attack to defeat the South Koreans and the UN. But MacArthur suddenly launched a bold and successful landing at Inchon on 15 September on the west coast of South Korea, close to the 38th parallel, and 240 kilometres north of Pusan. This cut off the supply lines of the North Korean forces in the south. These were driven back in rapid retreat as the UN forces in Pusan fought their way northwards. The war appeared to be over and a remarkable victory had been achieved until MacArthur disobeyed President Truman's order not to use American troops close to the border with China.

Truman feared, correctly as it turned out, that if US troops (as opposed to South Korean ones) advanced too close to the Chinese border, then China would become involved in the conflict. Stalin, who had approved of North Korea's invasion, agreed that China should be involved for just this reason. American forces advanced rapidly northwards between September and November 1950 and reached the border with China. Mao Zedong may have thought that an invasion of China was planned. The Chinese response in November 1950 was to send 180 000 troops across the border to assist the North Koreans. This time it was the UN forces' turn to fall back in demoralised retreat.

MacArthur's dismissal

Truman and MacArthur. MacArthur was a very controversial American general. Truman dismissed him in 1951. This defused a very dangerous situation and calmed Soviet fears about America's intentions.

> **Q Why do you think Truman's decision was such a brave one?**

MacArthur had made no secret of his disagreement with President Truman's handling of the war. MacArthur wanted total victory, even if it was at the cost of a full-scale nuclear war with China. Truman was desperate to limit the scale of the war and so he dismissed MacArthur in April 1951. It was a brave and wise decision.

The Chinese were eventually halted at the end of May 1951. The two sides dug in almost where they had begun, along the 38th parallel, and this is where they stayed. An **armistice** in July 1953 finally brought the fighting to an end and a new border just to the north of the 38th parallel was agreed.

The Korean War in perspective

Forty thousand American troops died in Korea but many more would have perished if MacArthur had got his way and the American public soon came to understand that. MacArthur arrogantly dismissed the fighting abilities of the Chinese with almost racist contempt – they were only 'Asiatics'. The Americans should have learned their lesson here but they repeated their mistake when they underestimated the courage and commitment of the North Vietnamese 15 years later.

Truman had at least made an effective stand in defence of his own Truman Doctrine and he had prevented the spread of Communism into South Korea without a major war with China or the USSR. American policy now shifted to Vietnam where the spread of Communism was once again an issue.

The war in Korea brought about a rapid change in US policy elsewhere in South East Asia. The Americans promised to help the French colonial government in Vietnam in its campaign against the Vietminh who wanted to drive the French out of Vietnam. This anti-French campaign was led by Ho Chi Minh, a Communist whom the Americans had previously helped against the Japanese. The USA had supported the Vietnamese in their hopes of being freed from French rule but the success of Communist revolutions in the Far East since the war changed American minds. Now Ho Chi Minh was the enemy. The Americans' obsession with anti-Communism now led them to back a series of corrupt and unpopular rulers in South Vietnam just as they had in China with Chiang Kai-Shek.

Q

1 Do you think the USSR learned a lesson concerning its policy towards the UN as a result of the Korean War?
2 Do you think China's decision to become involved in the Korean War is understandable? Explain your answer.
3 Why should the USA have thought twice about getting involved in a war against the North Vietnamese?
4 How did the Korean War affect US policy elsewhere in the Far East?
5 'MacArthur was a great military commander but a poor statesman.' Discuss this view in a paragraph of 8–10 lines.

During the Second World War the Americans had widely supported the efforts of the Vietnamese to drive out both the Japanese and the French. America had made good friends of the Vietminh independence forces, including the Communist leader, Ho Chi Minh, shown here. This goodwill was soon recklessly thrown away as the USA gave their support to the French against the Vietminh.

◑ Why did US policy change?

Q

The different stages of the war in Korea.

This exercise will help you understand the five key stages of the war in Korea.

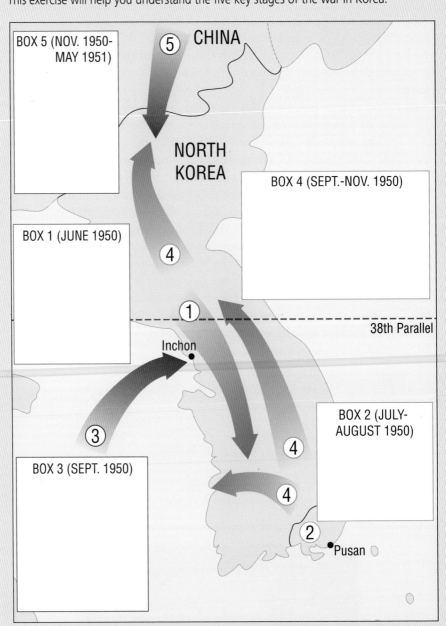

BOX 5 (NOV. 1950-
MAY 1951)

⑤ CHINA

NORTH
KOREA

BOX 4 (SEPT.-NOV. 1950)

BOX 1 (JUNE 1950)

④

①

38th Parallel

Inchon

BOX 2 (JULY-
AUGUST 1950)

③

④

BOX 3 (SEPT. 1950)

④

②

Pusan

- Copy the map above into your exercise book or file. It has to be a big map so that there is space on it for you to fill in the five marked boxes.
- Choose three different colours or shading to represent the forces of the UN, North Korea and China. Use these colours in the arrows marked on your map as follows: the North Korean arrow is numbered 1; the UN and South Korean arrows are 3 and 4; the Chinese arrow is 5.
- Now the boxes can be filled in with descriptions of the events that go with the dates already there. For example, you could fill in Box 2 with this information: 'During these months General MacArthur, the UN commander, halted the North Korean advance and stopped the South Korean forces from being driven into the sea.' Use the text to complete the other four boxes on the map.

Q

How did the Cold War change American policy in the Far East?

The chart below is designed to show how the Cold War affected America's position and policies in the Far East. Your task in this exercise is to copy the chart into your file or exercise book and fill in the remaining boxes. One of the boxes on Korea has already been done for you. Some hints as to what to write in each of the boxes are given below.

Box A: Civil war in China; Truman Doctrine; US support for Chiang against Communists; need for China's help in limiting Japanese influence.

Box B: Mao Zedong's victory and closer relations between the USSR and Communist China; USA no longer able to rely on China in the Far East; US fears over spread of Communism.

Box C: US attitude to divided Korea; willingness to withdraw troops.

Box E: US attitude to Ho Chi Minh during the Second World War; support for independence for Vietnam from France.

Box F: Impact of Communist victory in China and the Korean War on US policy in Vietnam.

	US policy before the crisis point	Change in US policy
China	A:	B:
Korea	C:	D: The USA was (and remains) committed to maintaining South Korea as a pro-Western country and separate from the Communist North.
Vietnam	E:	F:

Extended writing

'The Korean War brought the world closer to nuclear war than the Cuban Missile Crisis.' What is your opinion of this view? You will find it useful to comment on the following:
a whether there was any actual fighting in these crises;
b which countries were directly involved;
c the relations between the two superpowers at the time of these crises;
d events shortly before these crises in other parts of the world.

VIETNAM: 'A FINE HEROIC MOVEMENT'

American troops arriving in Vietnam were convinced that they were fighting a war in defence of freedom and decency against the evil of Communism. However, by the end of the war, US troops freely admitted to the sort of crimes committed in the massacre at My Lai (see page 223).

What had happened?

In the early 1950s the Americans provided money in support of the French against Ho Chi Minh's Vietminh forces. But after France's defeat in 1954 at Dien Bien Phu and the French withdrawal from Vietnam, the USA had to

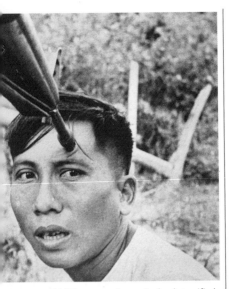

This Vietcong prisoner is clearly terrified as he waits to be interrogated at a US Special Forces Camp in January 1967. Perhaps he is aware that interrogation techniques included pushing prisoners out of airborne helicopters to encourage others to talk.

Q Can such methods be justified in a war against a guerrilla enemy?

become more directly involved. The 1954 Geneva Accords (or Agreement) divided Vietnam along the 17th parallel: Ho Chi Minh controlled the north and the American-backed Ngo Dinh Diem took over the south. The division was supposed to be a temporary one until elections for the whole of Vietnam could be held. They did not take place, largely because the Americans and Diem feared that Ho Chi Minh would win.

Kennedy versus 'godless tyranny'

Ho Chi Minh set up the National Liberation Front (NLF) in 1960 in the south to overthrow Diem and unite the country. The NLF's tactics were those of a **guerrilla** army. They attacked their enemy and then hid in the villages. They did not wear uniforms and so were hard to identify. Presidents Eisenhower and then Kennedy sent 'advisers' to help Diem's Army of the Republic of Vietnam (ARVN) deal with the NLF. Kennedy saw the confrontation in simple terms: the USA stood for 'freedom under God' whilst Communism stood for 'ruthless, godless tyranny'. Kennedy knew that a strong line against international Communism was a vote-winner at home and Kennedy needed votes.

Diem was corrupt and very unpopular. His pro-Catholic policies angered a mostly Buddhist population. He was supported by the wealthy landowners and so he did nothing to provide land for the mass of poor peasants. The NLF and its Communist **Vietcong** fighters grew rapidly and by 1963 they controlled the majority of the villages in the south. In areas under Communist control, the Vietcong distributed land to the peasants that Diem kept for his wealthy supporters. The USA decided that it had to get rid of Diem and gave its support to a plot by South Vietnamese generals to overthrow Diem. The overthrow (and assassination) of Diem in 1963 led to South Vietnam coming under the rule of the South Vietnamese Army. But this did not lessen the growing support for the NLF.

Gulf of Tonkin incident

President Johnson's advisers warned him about the 'domino theory'. They believed that South Vietnam's 'capture' by the forces of international Communism would send the other South East Asian countries of Laos, Cambodia, Malaya, Thailand and Indonesia tumbling towards Communism like dominoes in a line, one behind the other. Eisenhower first put forward the domino theory in 1954 and it has been a key element in American foreign policy ever since. Reagan also supported it and used the theory to justify American actions in Central America in the 1980s. But Johnson needed an excuse to convince the American public and Congress that the USA had to increase its involvement in Vietnam.

In August 1964 a clash between a US destroyer and North Vietnamese torpedo boats took place in the Gulf of Tonkin off the coast of North Vietnam. The Americans claimed that the North Vietnamese had launched an unprovoked attack against them but they did not produce any evidence to back this up. In fact, the USA had been in the area supporting a South Vietnamese special forces attack on a North Vietnamese island. Johnson asked Congress for the power to take all 'necessary steps, including the use of armed force' to assist any allied nation 'in defence of its freedom'. This meant that Johnson could now go to war without consulting Congress or the American people.

Neither Johnson nor Congress really expected that a major war would be needed to force the North Vietnamese to give up their claim to the south. This was the first and most serious of several errors of judgment made by the Americans in Vietnam.

The election for the presidency of the USA was due in November 1964. Johnson was a Democrat and he had been accused by his Republican opponent Goldwater of doing very little to fight Communism. In August 1964, after the Gulf of Tonkin incident, Johnson made this appeal to Congress for the power to use force against North Vietnam:

'The threat to the free nations of South East Asia has long been very clear. The North Vietnamese regime has constantly tried to take over South Vietnam and Laos. This Communist government has broken the Geneva Accords for Vietnam . . . The USA will continue in its basic policy of assisting the free nations of the area to defend their freedom . . . We must make it clear to all that the USA is united in its determination to bring about the end of Communist revolution and aggression in the area.'

Your task is to draw up a 15–20 line reply from Ho Chi Minh to Johnson's speech above. You should try to disprove what Johnson is saying and to make clear what North Vietnam's real aim is, according to Ho Chi Minh. The following issues are worth commenting on:

- Johnson's speech was sparked off by the Gulf of Tonkin incident but what proof does the US government have that the North started it?
- Does Johnson's speech have anything to do with the presidential election in November?
- How 'free' are the free nations of South East Asia e.g. South Vietnam under Diem or his military successors?
- Who really violated the Geneva Accords of 1954?
- What is North Korea's real aim?

Operation Rolling Thunder

Johnson thought that an intensive bombing campaign of military targets, 'Operation Rolling Thunder', would be enough to force Ho Chi Minh to back down. It did no such thing but it did force Johnson to send 23 000 troops to protect the air bases from which the planes flew. Soon they became actively involved in 'search and destroy' missions against the Vietcong (VC).

The Americans also tried other methods such as the 'strategic hamlet program' that proved to be a major political and military failure. The idea was

The NLF, unlike the Americans, attracted a lot of international support. This Cuban poster from 1969 reads 'NLF South Vietnam – nine years of example and victory.'

Q Can you think of any reasons why the Cubans would particularly want to support the Vietcong?

to uproot and move entire village populations away from areas controlled by the VC in order to deny them local support. This angered the South Vietnamese peasants and merely helped to spread Communist influence. By the end of 1965 Johnson had sent 165 000 troops to Vietnam and during 1969 the number reached a peak of 540 000.

The north kept the NLF and its own North Vietnamese Army (NVA) supplied with weapons through the Ho Chi Minh trail. This stretched from North Vietnam through neutral Laos and Cambodia to the south. The USSR and China provided much of the vital equipment, especially Soviet tanks and anti-aircraft guns. The Ho Chi Minh trail consisted of a network of over 15 000 kilometres of roads through jungles and mountains with as many as ten different routes between two points. If one route was bombed another could be used. Despite heavy American bombing, the Communists still probably managed to get at least two-thirds of their supplies through to the south.

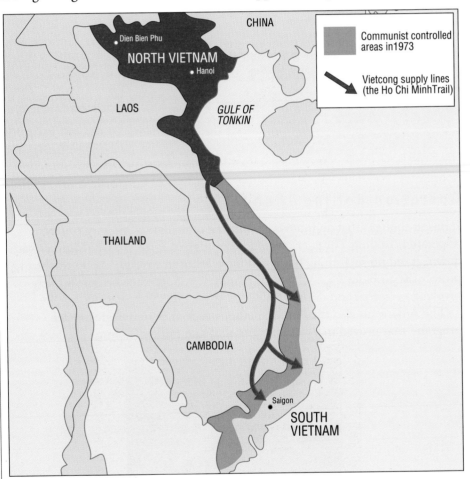

Map of Indo-China showing the Ho Chi Minh trail and 17th parallel.

The Tet Offensive: the light goes out

General Westmoreland, the US commander in Vietnam, claimed that he could see the light of victory at the end of the tunnel. This foolish belief was based on the principle of 'body count'. The US and ARVN forces were killing so many Vietcong that they believed they must be winning the war.

In January 1968 the supposedly defeated enemy launched their Tet or New Year offensive. Seventy thousand Vietcong fighters suddenly attacked a number of towns in the south. The Americans were taken totally by surprise since they had thought the towns were safe from an army that fought mostly in the countryside. Vietcong forces were even filmed fighting in the grounds of the American embassy in Saigon, the capital of South Vietnam.

The 1968 Tet Offensive by the Vietcong was a military disaster – the Vietcong lost 50 000 of the 70 000 men involved but it was a political success. It shocked the US public to see their troops fighting in their own embassy (right) against an enemy that was supposed to be at the point of defeat.

Q Why do you think the North Vietnamese would have regarded the Tet Offensive as a success?

The offensive was defeated within a month but it had a devastating effect on the American public. Americans saw, through television coverage, that the Communists were far from beaten and wondered how many more American lives would be lost. 9000 troops had been killed in 1967 and a further 14 500 were to die in 1968. The war was also costing $33 billion a year. It meant that Johnson's welfare programme (called the 'Great Society') designed to improve the lives of the poor had to be abandoned. The slums were left uncleared and hospitals and schools were not built. Because of this, Johnson knew that he had little chance of winning the election for president in 1968 and decided not to stand for re-election.

The Time Machine

This cartoon was published in the British magazine Punch *in 1967. It describes the effect of the war on President Johnson and his policies.*

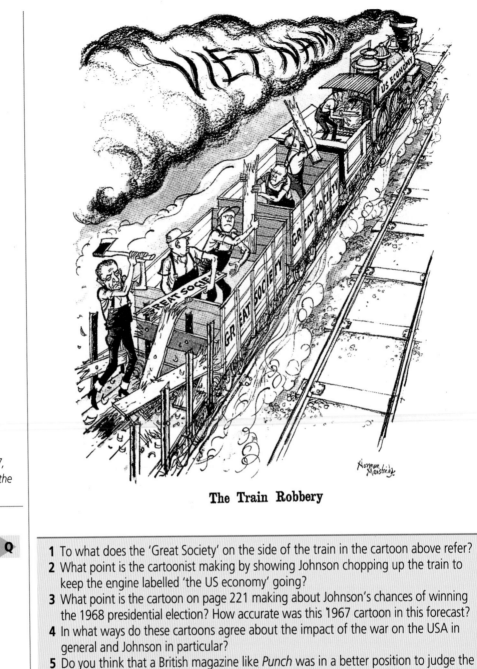

The Train Robbery

This Punch cartoon, also from 1967, features Lyndon Johnson wielding the axe at the rear of the train.

Q

1 To what does the 'Great Society' on the side of the train in the cartoon above refer?
2 What point is the cartoonist making by showing Johnson chopping up the train to keep the engine labelled 'the US economy' going?
3 What point is the cartoon on page 221 making about Johnson's chances of winning the 1968 presidential election? How accurate was this 1967 cartoon in this forecast?
4 In what ways do these cartoons agree about the impact of the war on the USA in general and Johnson in particular?
5 Do you think that a British magazine like *Punch* was in a better position to judge the impact of the war on the USA than an American publication would have been? Give reasons for your answer.

Low morale

Americans also wondered what kind of a war it was when a US major could tell a reporter that, after one South Vietnamese town had been reduced to rubble: 'It became necessary to destroy the town to save it.' The morale of the conscripts (men called up to fight by the government) was also very poor. Drug taking and desertion were serious problems. A report to Congress in 1971 stated that ten per cent were heroin addicts. Over 350 unpopular officers in 1971 alone were 'fragged' (killed or wounded) by their own men. This low morale was due to the strain of fighting a war against an enemy that was hard to find let alone kill. The VC hit-and-run tactics suited the dense forests of Vietnam where America's sophisticated military technology could play little part.

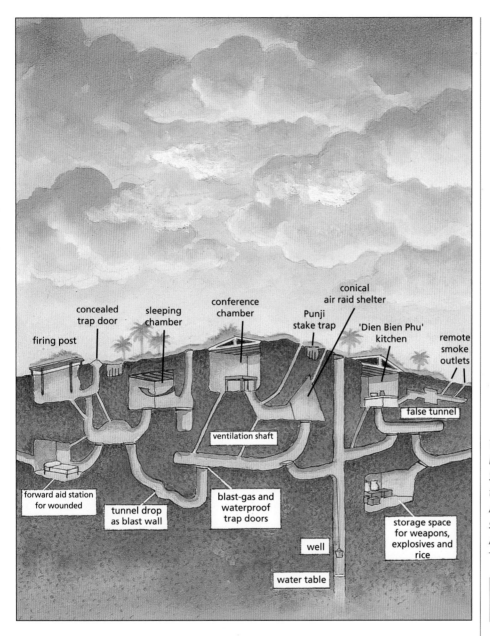

firing post

concealed trap door

sleeping chamber

conference chamber

Punji stake trap

conical air raid shelter

'Dien Bien Phu' kitchen

remote smoke outlets

false tunnel

forward aid station for wounded

ventilation shaft

tunnel drop as blast wall

blast-gas and waterproof trap doors

storage space for weapons, explosives and rice

well

water table

The resourceful Vietcong built 320 kilometres of tunnels like these around Saigon and in the forests. They enabled them to escape the worst effects of American bombing and to launch surprise attacks on unsuspecting American patrols.

Q Why do you think they made ambushes so effective?

The events of the My Lai Massacre (March 1968) confirmed the suspicions of many Americans: they were fighting the wrong war against the wrong people and in the wrong way. Over 300 Vietnamese women, children, babies and old men were gunned by American troops in the village of My Lai. Not all Americans were disgusted by these murders, though. The photographer who published pictures of the massacre and the journalists who wrote about it were accused of disloyalty to their country. One man complained: 'What do they give soldiers bullets for – to put in their pockets?'

Q

1 Why do you think that the Americans found it so difficult to fight a war against a guerrilla army?
2 Why do you think that the Americans were pleased to see the end of Diem?
3 Why did Johnson find it necessary to send combat troops to Vietnam during 'Operation Rolling Thunder'?
4 Both Kennedy and Johnson claimed that the Americans were fighting for the freedom of the South Vietnamese against tyranny. How accurate do you think this claim was?

How did the media affect the war in Vietnam?

The Vietnam War was the first war to be covered in depth by television. Opinions vary about the effect of this intense media coverage.

SOURCE 1:

Robin Day, a British television commentator, said that television coverage of the war made the Americans much more anti-war.

'One wonders if in future a democracy which has uninhibited [unrestricted] television coverage in every home will ever be able to fight a war, however just . . . The full brutality of the combat will be there in close up and colour, and blood looks very red on the colour television screen.'

From P Knightley: *The First Casualty* 1989

SOURCE 3:

On the other hand, there is evidence from an American magazine, *Newsweek*, that suggests that the effect of television pictures on the American public was rather different:

'A survey conducted for *Newsweek* in 1967 suggested a remarkably different conclusion: that television had encouraged a majority of viewers to support the war. When faced with deciding whether television coverage had made them feel more like 'backing up the boys in Vietnam' or like opposing the war, 64 per cent of viewers replied that they were moved to support the soldiers and 26 per cent to oppose the war.'

From P Knightley: *The First Casualty* 1989

SOURCE 2:

This photograph shows a Vietcong suspect being executed by an officer in the South Vietnamese Army during the 1968 Tet Offensive. The television coverage of the incident also showed the impact of the bullet on the man's head.

1 What reason does Robin Day give that will make the public react against wars?
2 What does the survey in Source 3 suggest was the reaction of most Americans to the war in Vietnam?
3 Given what you have read so far in these sources and in the rest of the chapter, is it possible to say how the US public would have reacted to the incident in Source 2?
4 The survey in Source 3 took place in 1967. Do you think that the results would have been any different for a survey carried out at the end of 1968? Explain your answer.
5 It is difficult to decide the usefulness of the survey in Source 3 since we don't know:

- how many people were interviewed;
- where the people interviewed lived;
- what sex they were;
- how old they were;
- what the precise questions were for the interview.

Explain why it is important for an historian to know the details for each of the issues above. For example, it is possible that men young enough to be conscripted might react differently to men too old to fight, or that the people interviewed might all live in a town whose main employment comes from making weapons.

NIXON: PEACE WITH 'HONOUR'

Richard Nixon narrowly won the 1968 presidential elections for the Republicans. He promised later to 'Vietnamise' the war. Vietnamisation meant increasing support for the ARVN forces while scaling down American combat troops. Negotiations began in Paris between Nixon's foreign affairs adviser Henry Kissinger and the North Vietnamese. Nixon stepped up the pressure on the north by resuming the bombing of North Vietnam. The USA dropped more bombs on North Vietnam during the war than all the bombs dropped by both sides in the Second World War. Nixon also ordered the bombing of neutral Cambodia in an unsuccessful attempt to cut the Ho Chi Minh trail. After five years of frustrating negotiations as the war continued, an agreement was finally signed in January 1973 in Paris. Henry Kissinger, Nixon's chief negotiator in Paris, and Le Duc Tho from North Vietnam were awarded the Nobel Peace Prize for their 'achievement'. Le Duc Tho rejected it. Perhaps he was too embarrassed to accept it.

US forces agreed to withdraw within 60 days and the North Vietnamese were not to extend the area under their control beyond the territory that they occupied at the time of the cease-fire. Nobody expected that the war would end when the last American forces left Vietnam in April 1973. Nixon had cleverly revealed that secret negotiations with North Vietnam were taking place in January 1972. Ten months later he won the 1972 election in November with a massive majority. The negotiations had served their purpose. The USA could retreat without losing too much face ('Peace with Honour', Nixon claimed) and the election had been won.

Hollywood 'discovered' the Vietnam War more than a decade after it ended. Born on the Fourth of July *tells of how a crippled Vietnam veteran, played by Tom Cruise, turns against the war. It was a successful film but not typical of most Vietnam veterans or 'vets', according to a* Time *magazine poll. In 1990 it asked 208 veterans if they were proud of the USA's role in Vietnam; 61 per cent said 'yes' and only 28 per cent said 'no'. The poll took place at the Vietnam War memorial in Washington.*

Q Does this make the poll more or less reliable, in your view?

The north quickly resumed the war and within two years the NVA had seized the capital of South Vietnam, Saigon. It was renamed Ho Chi Minh City in memory of the leader who had died in 1969. The Americans lost 58 000 people in what was their first ever defeat in a war. The NVA lost 900 000 (out of a population of 20 million) and the ARVN 250 000 killed. A further one million civilian deaths must be added to this.

A scene from the film Platoon. *Oliver Stone was a Vietnam veteran who was critical of the war. He wrote the script for* Platoon *in 1976 but no film studio would make the film. It was made ten years later by a small independent company and the US army refused to give any assistance with the making of the film.* Pravda, *the Soviet newspaper, said (in June 1987) it was because the generals realised that the film would not do anything to help ''the patriotic education of Americans for military actions in the future''.*

Q What do you think *Pravda* meant by this?

Détente with China

As you have seen from Part I of this chapter, the USSR and the USA were looking for ways to improve their relations in the process known as **détente** by the early 1970s. This allowed the USA to withdraw without fearing that the Soviet Union would try to push for further gains in South East Asia. Nixon had been keen to improve relations with both the USSR and China. The USA took a big step towards better relations with China in 1971. Nixon recognised Communist China as the legal government of China. Taiwan was expelled from the United Nations and Communist China took its place. In the following year, 1972, Nixon visited China.

All this was a dramatic switch in American foreign policy. Nixon continued his policy of détente with a visit to the USSR in May 1972 to sign a nuclear arms limitation agreement (see page 204). However, while relations with China have generally been friendly since the early 1970s there have been moments of tension. The Chinese Communist government's brutal massacre of 1000 or more pro-democracy students in Tiananmen Square in Beijing in 1989 was severely criticised in the West. In 1996 the Communists held military exercises around the island of Taiwan to remind Taiwan and the US government of its claim to the island. The Americans sent a fleet to the area to remind China that they would continue to defend Taiwan's independence.

Q

1 Why did the My Lai Massacre (page 223) help the cause of those who were against the war?
2 What do you suppose the man meant by the remark about My Lai: 'What do they give soldiers bullets for – to put in their pockets?'
3 Why do you think 'Vietnamisation' was such a popular policy amongst Americans?
4 Explain why the events of 1968 could be seen as a turning point in the war.
5 How true was Nixon's claim that the US withdrawal meant 'Peace with Honour' for America?

Why did the USA lose the war?

Countries lose wars for a mixture of military, economic and political reasons. The Axis powers in the Second World War lost because their economies were too weak to keep up their military efforts. Below is a list of reasons that explain why the USA lost in Vietnam. Your task in this activity is to provide some evidence from the text and sources to support each reason and to decide whether it is political, economic or military. One example has been done for you.

Once you have completed the chart below write 25 lines in response to this statement: 'The USA lost the war in Vietnam for mostly political reasons.' What is your opinion of this view?

Reasons for America's defeat	Military, economic or political	I have found the following evidence in the text and sources to support this
The South Vietnamese government's policies were unpopular		
The Vietcong had the support of the peasants in the south		
The war was costing the USA too much		
US troops had low morale and motivation		
Public opinion became hostile to the war and forced the USA to withdraw		
China and the USSR provided vital military and economic aid to North Vietnam	military and economic	The USSR provided tanks and anti-aircraft guns; North Vietnam's economy depended on Chinese and Soviet help
The USA failed to win the support of South Vietnam's peasants		
VC guerrilla tactics were more suited to fighting in the dense forests		
The USA failed to cut off the supply lines to the VC from the north		

Extended writing

'America failed in its attempt to stop the spread of Communism in the Far East because it did not use enough force.' What is your view of this interpretation of US policy in the Far East? You should refer to American policy towards China, Korea and Vietnam and write 300 words or more.

▶ What were American troops fighting for in Vietnam?

The following sources concern the soldiers' views of what they were fighting for in Vietnam. The American government claimed that the USA was in Vietnam to defend freedom, keep the south free from Communism and to prevent Communism spreading into other parts of South East Asia. The purpose of this investigation is to establish how far American troops shared their government's policies.

SOURCE 1:

Tim O'Brien served in Vietnam as a conscript – he didn't volunteer to fight. This extract is taken from his book and in it he describes a conversation he had with the Army Chaplain, Captain Edwards, while he was still in training in the USA. Diem, Khanh and Thieu referred to in this source were all American-backed rulers of South Vietnam between 1955 and 1973. Napalm is an explosive.

'Look, what do you know about Communism, O'Brien? Do you think they're a bunch of friendly, harmless politicians, all ready to be friends and buddies? . . . Do you think Ho Chi Minh will bring heaven to South Vietnam?'

'Well sir, there's little evidence that South Vietnam under the Communists will be a worse place than South Vietnam ruled by a Diem or a Khanh. I mean there's no . . . evidence . . . that all the lives being lost, the children napalmed and everything – there's no good evidence that all this horror is worth preventing a change from Thieu to Ho Chi Minh . . . I see evil in the history of Ho Chi Minh's rule in the North. I see evil . . . in the history of the string of rulers we've helped in the South. Evil on both sides . . .'

'O'Brien, I'm surprised to hear this, really. You seem like a nice fellow. But, listen, you're betraying your country when you say these things . . . I've been in Vietnam. I can tell you, this is a fine heroic movement for American soldiers.'

Adapted from Tim O'Brien: *If I die in a Combat Zone* 1972

SOURCE 2:

Doug Ramsey was taken prisoner by the Vietcong. His captors took him to a village that had just been burned to the ground by some South Vietnamese troops. The author, Neil Sheehan, was a journalist in Vietnam, and told his story:

'The rubble of the hamlet was still smoking, and it was obvious that these people had returned only a short time before to discover what had happened to their homes. Children were whimpering . . . Women were poking through the smouldering debris of the houses trying to salvage cooking utensils and any other small possessions that might have escaped the flames . . . The soldiers had also burned all of the rice that had not been buried or hidden elsewhere and had shot the buffalo and other livestock and thrown the carcasses down the wells to poison the water supply . . .

He felt sick and angry, betrayed and yet also responsible . . . Ramsey had had enough. If this was to be the price of preserving the American way of life, he did not want to be a part of it.'

Adapted from Neil Sheehan: *A Bright Shining Lie* 1988

SOURCE 3:

Sergeant Donald Duncan served in Vietnam as a volunteer and was in charge of a Special Forces team of highly-trained volunteers like himself. In his book, *The New Legions* he described a conversation between two of his team leaders, Bill Kane and Hunky Kovacs:

'Hunky, do you have any idea why we are here?' Kane asked.

Kovacs almost exploded. 'Of course I know why we're here – to fight the Vietcong' – he crashed his hand on the bar and made the glasses jump.

'Who are the Vietcong, Hunky?' The louder Kovacs shouted, the quieter Kane became.

'The Commies . . . the enemy . . . the people trying to overthrow the government . . .'

'Did you ever stop and think why', Kane interrupted, 'that the reason they fight the government [of South Vietnam] is that they know it's as rotten as we do?' . . .

Kovacs glared at us and shouted, 'You both talk like traitors . . .'

Kane, probably thinking of his eighteen years in uniform, almost choked. He recovered enough to ask, 'Why are we traitors, Hunky?'

'Because you're talking about such things. The president is the Commander-in-Chief – if he says "Go to Vietnam", we go to Vietnam. You should not ask why. You are a soldier. You obey orders . . . you fight . . . you are not paid to think . . .'

Adapted from D Duncan: *The New Legions* 1967

SOURCE 4:

David Donovan served as an officer in Vietnam during 1969. He summarised America's role as follows:

'We have seen the creation of a new empire by North Vietnam . . . We have seen Laos occupied by the Hanoi [North Vietnam] government. We have seen Cambodia robbed and starved by Cambodian Communists and then occupied by the North Vietnamese. South Vietnam has been occupied, colonized and finally absorbed by North Vietnam . . . We were right to resist terror and war being inflicted on a poor and backward people . . . The South Vietnamese government had many faults, but Ho Chi Minh and his Communist Party have . . . left a trail of cruelty, famine, and tyranny . . . I maintain in the face of all accusers that we who served in Vietnam did so when our only thought was duty and our only cause was freedom.'

Adapted from D Donovan: *Once a Warrior King* 1985

SOURCE 5:

This Vietnamese woman is weeping over the body of her dead child.

1 Your first task with these sources is to decide whether they support America's role in Vietnam or oppose it. You must also provide some evidence from the relevant source to back up your view because this is one of the most important rules in writing history well. Copy the source grid below and then fill it in. It has already been started to give you an idea of what to do.

2 Bill Kane (Source 3) was not forced to fight in Vietnam – he volunteered. Do you think this makes his view more valuable to an historian who wants to know about the morale of US troops in the war? Explain your answer.

3 Kovacs (Source 3) was also a volunteer. Does this make it easier or harder for an historian to draw any conclusions about the attitude of Special Forces volunteers to the war? Explain why.

4 Historians try to cross reference sources to see if the view of one source is supported by others. Generally, the more support there is for that view the more reliable the source is. Using this cross-referencing method and only these sources, would you say that the view of O'Brien or Kovacs is the more reliable? Give reasons for your answer.

5 Using Sources 1–5 and your own knowledge, explain whether you agree or disagree with this interpretation of the Vietnam War: 'The USA lost the war in Vietnam because American troops turned against the war.' Remember that there are two issues to consider here; whether these sources support the view that US troops did turn against the war and whether this explains why America lost the war.

Source	Character or description of source	For or against America's role in Vietnam	Evidence to support this view as follows:
1	O'Brien		
1	Army Chaplain		
2	Ramsey		
3	Kovacs	For America's role	Kovacs says that the US troops are there to fight the Vietcong, 'the Commies'; he claims their role is to stop 'the overthrow of the government'.
3	Kane		
4	Donovan		
5	Photograph		

Glossary

Abdicate	when a monarch gives up the throne
Anti-Semitism	the hatred and persecution of Jews
Appeasement	a policy of making concessions to avoid conflict; the policy used by Britain towards Germany in the 1930s
Armistice	an agreement to stop fighting in a war while peace terms are discussed
Blitzkrieg	German for 'lightning war'. *Blitzkrieg* involves the use of tanks and motorised troops to achieve speed and surprise
Capitalism	an economic system in which the government's role is very limited and businesses are owned privately
Census	an official population count
Chancellor	the prime ministers of Germany and Austria are called chancellors
Coalition	a government formed by two or more different political parties
Cold War	a state of tension – but not actual war – between the Soviet Union and the United States and their allies
Colony	a country under the control of another more powerful country (e.g. Vietnam was a colony of France until 1954)
Communism	a system of government which opposes democracy and individual freedom and favours government control of the economy
Conscription	the compulsory recruitment of men, and sometimes women, into the armed forces
Constitution	a set of laws and rules which control how a country is governed; e.g. it is part of the US Constitution that there must be an election for the presidency every four years
Consumer	someone who purchases goods, especially those which improve their standard of living, such as cars, furniture and household goods
Democracy	a system of government where the leaders are voted in to office by the people
Détente	the easing of tension between the Soviet Union and the United States
Dictatorship	government by a ruler with total power over a country and who does not tolerate opposition
Fascism	a system of government which opposes democracy and individual freedom and supports extreme nationalism
Great powers	those countries which led the world in economic and political terms in the period before the First World War

Guerrilla	a type of soldier who uses hit-and-run tactics and generally does not wear a uniform, making him hard to identify
Industrialisation	the rapid development of industry so that most of a country's wealth comes from its industry
Isolationism	the policy followed by the USA between the two world wars. America would concentrate on its own concerns and not get involved in the rest of the world's problems
Lebensraum	German for 'living space'. Hitler planned to use Eastern Europe as 'living space' for the German people
Mandate	a former colony (especially a German colony after the First World War) governed by another country on behalf of the League of Nations until it achieved independence
Marshall Plan	America's programme of economic aid to Europe after the Second World War
National minority (see also State control)	a group of people living in one country while belonging to the nationality of another country
Nationalisation	a policy which involves the government or state taking control of one or more industries
Nationalism	a feeling of patriotic support for one's country which can involve trying to free it from foreign control (e.g. Ho Chi Minh) or trying to dominate other countries (e.g. Hitler)
No Man's Land	the area between enemy trenches which neither side controls
Non-aggression pact	an agreement between two or more countries not to attack each other. Germany and the Soviet Union signed one in 1939
Partisans	resistance fighters, often civilians, operating behind enemy lines against foreign occupation
Peaceful co-existence	policy proposed by Khrushchev to allow the USA and the Soviet Union to live side by side without conflict
Plebiscite	a vote to decide an issue (also known as a referendum)
Prohibition	the ban on the manufacture and sale of alcohol in the USA 1920–33
Proportional representation	a system of voting where the seats awarded in a parliament are in direct proportion to the number of votes cast (e.g. ten per cent of the votes leads to ten per cent of the seats)
Protection	an economic policy designed to discourage foreign imports by using tariffs against them, so making them more expensive
Reichstag	the German parliament
Reparations	compensation for war damage paid by Germany after the First World War
Sanctions	economic or military penalties imposed on a state, often by the League of Nations or the United Nations

Satellite	a country largely under the control or influence of another powerful state (e.g. East Germany was a satellite of the Soviet Union until the late 1980s)
Second Front	the invasion of France by the Allies to free it from German control; the strategy supported by Stalin
Self-determination	the right of a people to choose the country to which they belong
Serfdom	slavery
Socialism	a system of government which supports democracy and a greater government involvement in economy and society
Soviet Union	the old name for the country which is now mostly Russia when it was a Communist state 1917–91
State control (see also Nationalism)	a policy which involves the government or state taking control of one or more industries
Suffragette	a campaigner for the right of women to vote and one who is willing to use direct action
Superpowers	a term used to describe the Soviet Union and the United States
Supreme Court	the highest court in the United States which decides whether laws or policies conflict with the US Constitution
Tariff	a tax on foreign goods which makes them more expensive and therefore less attractive to consumers
Truman Doctrine	policy named after President Truman which committed the US to oppose the spread of Communism
Vietcong	a term used to describe the Vietnamese Communists who fought the French and then the Americans

Index